SpringerWienNewYork

European Community Studies Association of Austria
(ECSA Austria) Publication Series

Volume 6

Schriftenreihe der
Österreichischen Gesellschaft für Europaforschung
(ECSA Austria)

SpringerWienNewYork

Fritz Breuss
Gerhard Fink
Stefan Griller (eds.)

Services Liberalisation
in the Internal Market

Springer Wien New York

Univ.-Prof. Dr. Fritz Breuss
Europainstitut, Wirtschaftsuniversität Wien

Univ.-Prof. Dr. Gerhard Fink
Europainstitut, Wirtschaftsuniversität Wien

Univ.-Prof. Dr. Stefan Griller
Europainstitut, Wirtschaftsuniversität Wien

Financial support was given by *Bundesministerium für
Wissenschaft und Forschung,* Wien,
and the
European Commission, DG Education and Culture, Brussels

© 2008 Springer-Verlag Wien
Printed in Austria

SpringerWienNewYork is a part of Springer Science + Business Media
springer.com

Typesetting: Camera ready by editor
Printing: Ferdinand Berger & Söhne Gesellschaft m.b.H., 3580 Horn, Austria

Printed on acid-free and chlorine-free bleached paper
SPIN: 11299110

CIP data applied for

ISSN 1610-384X

ISBN 978-3-211-22401-4 SpringerWienNewYork

Preface

The drafting and subsequent adoption of the European Union's "Services Directive" provoked a previously unknown public debate on a pan-European scale. This discussion predominantly concentrated on fundamental questions of European integration – sometimes under misleading buzzwords like "social dumping" – and thus largely moved away from the core concepts introduced by the Directive. In contrast, the book at hand follows a different focus:

On the one hand it provides for a comprehensive legal analysis of the Services Directive in the context of existing EC-law. In this regard, fundamental legal questions concerning trans-national services provision in the EU Internal Market under the new legal framework established by the Directive are raised and answered accordingly.

On the other hand, the present book features a transdisciplinary approach towards cross-border service-provision in the EU. Therefore, the legal analysis is complemented by contributions of economists: the first estimates the macroeconomic effects of the Services Directive and discusses concurring research, the second addresses the liberalisation results so far achieved within the financial market sector, one of the fore-runners of services liberalisation in the European Union. Here the main research focus lies on the potential competition-efficiency nexus in the banking sector.

Thus, this book is aimed to offer an analytical added value to the reader through its comprehensive assessment of the Services Directive.

Drafts of all contributions were the subject of an academic debate organised by the Europainstitut in 2005 and 2006 in the framework of a respective research project at the Vienna University of Economics and Business Administration. In particular, the international conference "Services Liberalisation in the Internal Market" on June 12 and 13, 2006 in Vienna, co-organised with ECSA Austria, has produced considerable input for this volume. The editors of this volume express their sincere thanks to the Vienna University of Economics and Business Administration for funding a real-time research-project on services liberalisation. Also we are indebted to the European Commission, DG Education and Culture, for its assistance, namely for generously supporting both the organisation of the international conference "Services Liberalisation in the Internal Market", and the publication of this book.

Fritz Breuss

Gerhard Fink

Stefan Griller   January 2008

Table of Contents

Armin Hatje

Services Directive – a Legal Analysis

I. Free Market *vs.* European Welfare Model

"Started as a tiger but ended as a bedside carpet" – this or something like this was the reaction of many commentators to the announcement that the Council of the European Union had agreed on an amended version of the Directive of Services in the single European market. It is certain: hardly any legislation project of the European Union has caused so controversial reactions as the Commission's proposal of February 25, 2004 on the Services Directive in the single European market.[1]

A. History

With this Directive the country of origin principle should be introduced to the realm of services interchange. It allows the providers of services to work under the rules and provisions of their country of origin. This has the obvious advantage not to be forced to deal with a foreign legal system, which alone for lack of knowledge of service modalities can be a barrier to trans-boundary activity. Most trade associations and companies greeted the project as a necessary step towards an efficient Single European Market for the provision of services.[2] Nevertheless criticism prevailed. Objections were not only limited to media statements and expert groups as in so many cases of European politics. In some Member States and even in Brussels people protested against the Commission's plan. At least for a short period of time something that political scientists and constitutional theorists had always demanded developed: An European public.[3] The precise matter of protest, however, should not belie that many critics are by no means only concerned about

---

1   COM/2004/2 final, February 25, 2004.

2   See *De Koster* (2006).

3   On the subject of a demand for a European public see for example *Grimm* (1995).

the freedom of services. The focusing of the European economic policy on the ideal of liberal trade and services interchange as a basic principle is subject to criticism. Against this especially the "European welfare model" is cited – without however specifying what has to be understood by this term.[4] In any case, a general uneasiness was perceptible with respect to politics that in all areas of economy follow liberal principles and trust more in the market than in the intervening state. The protest was quite successful. The European Parliament proposed numerous modifications that in the Council were met with approval by a couple of Member States. On April 4, 2006 the Commission submitted an amended directive proposal, which on May 29, 2006 was discussed in-depth and approved in all essential points by the Council.[5] The Directive was adopted on December 12, 2006 and published on December 27, 2006.[6] The Member States then would have 3 years time to take the required implementation measures.

B. Initial Question

The complexity of this subject and the limited space give reason to focus on one pivotal question: is the services Directive legally suitable to reach the aspired goals? This would only be the case, if compared to today's legal situation the Directive would promise a judicial surplus. A "surplus" in this context shall be understood as a "less" of legal barriers to the free exchange of services among Member States or in other words: a plus of freedom to provide services across national boundaries. In this respect, especially the existing case law of the European Court of Justice concerning the freedom of establishment and services serves as a benchmark. This case law has not only opened the door that lets providers and recipients of services step through the bushwhack of national legislation onto foreign territory. We also owe a relatively balanced concept

---

4   In its revised version the Commission refers explicitly to the European welfare model that for instance played a major role in the communication of the European Parliament.

5   Amended proposal for a Directive of the European Parliament and of the Council on services in the internal market, COM/2006/0160 final, April 4, 2006; Presidency compromise text, 9683/06, May 24, 2006 wherein the passages changed by the Council have been marked.

6   Directive 2006/123/EC of the European Parliament and of the Council of December 2006 on services in the internal market.

that combines the European law claim for liberalisation with the legitimate political demands of the Member States for control and participation to the European Court of Justice.

II. Aims and Conception of the Directive on Services

A. Aims

The political aims of the Directive are evident: it is a contribution to the so called Lisbon Agenda, according to which Europe shall become the most competitive knowledge-based economic area of the world by 2010.[7] As part of this agenda the Commission regards a better use of the economic potential of services, which amount to 70 % of the GDP of most Member States, but only to 20 % of the cross-national exchange of goods and services. In an accurate and very recommendable survey of 2002, the Commission has listed, where, according to its research, the barriers to a free exchange of services are to be found. The potential of a liberalised market of the provision of services is thereby estimated to mount up to several hundred thousands of jobs.

Judicially it concerns the completion of the internal Market with respect to the provision on services, i.e. an objective that is especially legitimised through European Community Law by Articles 2, 3 and 14 EC Treaty. Accordingly the first proposal of the Directive was formulated aggressively. Although the new draft is much more contained in many respects and especially highlights the social component of European integration, the utmost concern of the Directive remains unchanged: removing barriers to the establishment of service providers and the exchange of services, improvement of the quality of services with the additional aim of creating new jobs in the EU.[8]

Furthermore, the Commission regards the Directive as an instrument that shall *proactively* induce the Member States to sift

---

7   Report from the Commission to the Council and the European Parliament on the state of the internal market for services presented under the first stage of the Internal Market Strategy for Services, July 30, 2002; Communication from the Commission to the Council and the European Parliament – An Internal Market Strategy for Services, COM/2000/0888 final, December 29, 2000.

8   See in particular the 3. Explanatory consideration of the initial version (fn 1) and of the adopted directive (fn 6).

through their national legal order to find the remaining barriers to the free exchange of services. The Commission no longer wants to work towards the realisation of the provisions on the single market only *reactively* by way of protracted infringement procedures. Especially since the then imminent enlargement of the European Union to 25 (soon 27) Member States would further complicate each individual check of conformity of national law with European Community law.[9]

In addition, a horizontal regulation, that is a regulation that comprises several sectors and areas of trade in goods and services, could have the advantage of avoiding in the future the need for specific legal approximation measures that always entail the danger of different or even contradictive regulations. In other words: the Directive shall disburden the European legislator and therewith promote the clarity and coherence of Community Law.[10] Although further measures are not excluded.

Finally, the form of a framework directive was chosen in order to countervail the dangers of uniformity of the national legal systems and overregulation. In fact, the term "framework directive" is not a legal term that automatically leads to certain conclusions. However, by using this term, the Commission indicates that it does not aim at a detailed harmonisation, which would limit the scope of national freedom excessively.[11]

B. Conception

The Directive aims to achieve this goal by way of material guidelines for the Member States concerning the freedom of establishment and services. Procedural simplifications and reporting requirements for the benefit of consumers shall simplify the assertion of one's rights. The implementation and execution of the Directive is accompanied by an evaluation process that shall be the basis for further legislative efforts to further liberalise the services market. The Commission aims to establish a "substantial internal market for the provision of services" by 2010.[12]

---

9   See proposal of the Commission (fn 1), 11.
10 *Ibidem*, 9.
11 *Ibidem*.
12 *Ibidem*, 12.

III. Scope of Application and Legal Basis

A. Scope of Application

Already the nested definition of subject and the scope of application reveal the political explosiveness of the Directive. According to Article 2 it is applicable *"for the services offered by a provider of services who has his permanent establishment in one of the Member States"*. "Service" can be understood, according to Art. 4 no. 1 as *"any self-employed economic activity, normally provided for remuneration, as referred to in Article 50 of the Treaty"*. The Directive is only applicable to services that are provided or called across national boundaries. Therefore, the Directive is based on an understanding of the term services that complies with the services term of Article 50 of the EC Treaty and the case law of the European Court of Justice.[13]

However, the initially wide scope of application of the Directive was significantly limited during the process of debate. Already the "panic clause" in Article 1 of the Directive clarifies, which areas shall remain "untouched" by its content. This applies especially to public services and forms or organisations, such as services of general economic interest, as well as essential services that are provided by public entities, monopolies providing services, the protection of public law entities and the granting of state aid. Excluded are furthermore: criminal law, labour law and social law, as well as national fundamental rights, including the national provisions on tariff autonomy and industrial action. The provision is more political placebo than a judicial necessity since the Directive does not contain any provisions that aim at regulating the said entities or areas of law.

Article 2 of the Directive lists the general exceptions to the scope of application more substantially. According to this provision the directive does not apply to:
–   non-commercial services of general interest, such as the operation of educational and cultural institutions,
–   financial services,
–   electronic communication services and networks,
–   healthcare services,

---

13   See for instance ECJ C-205/84 *Commission/Germany*, Re (1986) ECR 3755; C-154/89, *Commission/France*, (1991) ECR I-659 para. 7.

- gambling activities,
- activities which are connected with the exercise of official authority,
- transport services, including harbour services,
- services of temporary work agencies,
- and (according to reports especially on German request) social services relating to childcare, social housing and support of families and persons in need,
- and private security services.
- Finally, the area of taxation is excluded.

Further exceptions are specifically laid down in the chapter on the freedom to provide services. All things considered, it can rightfully be asked whether there are any services of importance left to which the Directive is still applicable.

The Council of the European Union refers in its press release especially to three areas that hopefully will benefit from more liberalisation:
- business services: management consultancy, certification and testing, advertising, recruitment services;
- services provided both to businesses and to consumers, such as legal or fiscal advice, real estate services, construction, distributive trades, the organisation of trade fairs, car rental, travel agencies;
- consumer services, for example in the field of tourism, including tour guides, leisure services, sports centres and amusement parks.

Whether these sectors are indeed in a position to generate the hoped for jobs, cannot be subject of a legal analysis. Doubts are however apposite.

B. Legal Basis

The Directive is based on Article 47 para. 2 s. 1 and 3 as well as Article 55 EC Treaty. The said provisions permit the enactment of directives that shall facilitate the taking up and exertion of self-employed activities with or without a permanent establishment. The present draft of the Directive follows this competence framework. Also the principle of subsidiary (Article 5 para. 2 EC Treaty) and the principle of proportionality (Article 5 para. 3 EC Treaty) are in essence adhered to.

IV. Freedom of Establishment

The material substance of the Directive consists of the provisions of Articles 9 *et seq* concerning the prerequisites for permanent establishment of self-employed persons and enterprises offering services. These provisions allow for the fact that several services, as for instance construction work or legal and tax advice, can often only be provided in a reasonable way if a branch is established in the state of destination. The Directive thus aims at removing the associated administrative barriers. It follows in principle the case law of the European Court of Justice. However, there are fundamental problems concerning the scope of application, the preconditions and the legal consequences.

A. Fundamental Problems of the Scope of Application

The understanding of the term establishment in the Directive is based on the criteria used in the prevailing case law that focuses especially on the time element of permanent establishment and the quality criterion of an actual integration into the economy of the host county.[14] A fundamental problem however is that the Directive only applies to acts of permanent establishments that are connected with the provision of services. Therefore, permit regulations for establishments for the production of goods would be excluded. A division of establishment law into provisions on services and provisions on goods cannot be ruled out. However, this would not be an inevitable consequence of the Directive but a national decision.

B. Prerequisites of an Obligation to Obtain a Permit

The Directive takes up the prerequisites of an obligation to obtain a permit developed by the European Court of Justice. According to this, permissions for permanent establishment may – unless another European law harmonisation applies – only be demanded for if
– the permission requirements are non-discriminatory with respect to the service provider, and if[15]
– they are justified by compulsory reasons of general public interest and proportionate.[16]

---

14   See ECJ C-211/89, *Factortame*, (1991) ECR I-3905 para. 20.

15   See ECJ C-2/74, *Reyners*, (1974) ECR 631 para. 16/20.

16   See ECJ C-55/94, *Gebhard*, (1995) ECR I-4165 para. 37; C-250/95, *Futura Participations SA* (1997) I-2471 para. 26; C-212/97, *Centros*, (1999) I-1459.

Member States are obliged to make sure that their legal order is in conformity with these requirements and give account for it.[17]

C. Requirements for Permit Prerequisites

In a second step, Member States have to verify, whether the permit prerequisites come up to certain requirements based again on the case law of the European Court of Justice. The respective criteria – administrative law requirements – have to be non-discriminatory, justified by compulsory reasons of public interest and proportionate. In addition, the Directive demands of national permission requirements

– to be precise and unambiguous,
– to be drafted in an objective manner,
– to be transparent and accessible.[18]

Furthermore there is the prohibition of double control that prohibits the repeated application of tantamount prerequisites already checked in the country of origin or even in the country of destination.[19] For instance: the credibleness of a tradesman if already positively established by a ratification procedure in the country of origin. However, the right of Member States to independently assess the equality of the respective prerequisites remains untouched.

D. Legal Consequences

As far as the Member States tie the establishment of a service provider to a permission, they are obliged to grant this permission if the conditions are fulfilled. The freedom of decision thus is bound.[20] The decisions have to be made within a period stipulated by the Member State, otherwise they are – after the expiration of this time limit – automatically considered to be authorised.[21] The permissions may not be limited in time and must be effective for the entire sovereign territory of the respective Member State. Ex-

---

17 Article 15 para 5 and 39 of the Directive on services in the internal market.

18 Article 10, para. 2 of the Directive

19 Article 10 para. 3 of the Directive; constitutive ECJ C-71/76, *Thieffry*, (1977) ECR 765 para. 19.

20 Article 10 para 5 of the Directive.

21 On the topic of permission fictions as instrument for securing the practical efficiency of European Community Law see *Hatje* (1998), 233.

ceptions are only permissible if justified by imperative reason of public interest.[22] Therefore, in this area, a partly significant change of national permission regulation is to be expected. Reasons have to be given for the denial or revocation of a permission and a remedy must be admissible.[23]

V. Freedom to Provide Services

The core of the Directive and the bone of contention are Articles 16 *et seq* concerning the freedom to provide services across national boundaries.

A. The "Bone of Contention"

The first draft provoked a Europe-wide storm of protest. Its trigger was a conception that was discussed in the media and the scientific community under the catchword "country of origin principle". According to this with respect to trans-national services in general only the provisions of the country of origin should be applicable to allow especially small and medium-sized businesses to provide services in other Member States without substantial consulting and administration efforts. Economic and socio-political objections have already been outlined above. From a legal point of view the first draft of Article 16 and its current phrasing can only be evaluated if one recalls the initial primary law situation.

B. Initial Primary Law Situation

According to this the country of origin principle is not, a (legal) term of the EC Treaty. In fact, it is at best a heuristic category, which is used especially to concisely characterise the effects of certain regulations.

1. Country of Origin Principle

The country of origin principle has its seeds in the dawn of free traffic of goods, which has for a long time shaped the dogmatic of the fundamental freedoms. As is generally known, the European Court of Justice had – starting with the *Dassonville* decision of 1974[24] in its *Cassis de Dijon* ruling[25] – developed the principle of

---

22   Article 13 para. 4 of the Directive.

23   Article 10 para. 6 of the Directive.

24   ECJ C-8/74, *Dassonville*, (1974) ECR 837.

25   ECJ C-120/78, *Cassis de Dijon*, (1979) ECR 649.

free traffic of goods from a mere prohibition of discrimination to a prohibition of restriction. Only with respect to so-called sales modalities according to the *Keck* formula solely a prohibition of discrimination applies.[26] For the rest – negatively phrased – all governmental measures, which hinder, directly or indirectly, actually or potentially the free traffic of goods are prohibited. Positively phrased: any product, lawfully produced or marketed in the territory of one Member State is in principle marketable in the whole European Community.[27] In this respect, we can talk about a "country of origin principle". However, the experiences in the free traffic of goods sector have also shown how high the requirements for this principle are, since it is based on a mutual recognition of legal standards, which again is only possible if an extensive legal conformity, a respective trust and comparable economic circumstances already exist.

2. Limits to the Country of Origin Principle

Even under these ideal conditions the country of origin principle is not unlimited.[28] Member States are allowed to enact certain restrictions if they either satisfy the exceptions of the Treaty or serve other unwritten mandatory requirements in the general interest, in the latter case, however, only if the national regulations are applicable to domestic *and* foreign products without distinction.[29] The so-called "mandatory requirements in the general interest" are a creation of the European Court of Justice. They form an open catalogue of *non-commercial* subjects of protection accepted by European Community law. On the level of justification, they strike a balance between the extended scope of protection of the fundamental freedoms and the legitimate political configuration claims of the Member States.[30] As mandatory requirements in the general interest are for example accepted: the defence of the consumer, the fairness of commercial transactions, fraud abatement and socio- and cultural

---

26   Constitutive joint cases C-267/91 and C-268/91, *Keck and others*. (1993) ECR I-6097; also C-292/92, *Hünermund*, (1993) ECR I-6787.

27   See in particular ECJ C-120/78, *Cassis de Dijon* (REWE / Bundesmonopolverwaltung für Branntwein), (1979) ECR 649, para. 14.

28   So rightly *Becker* (2000), para 45.

29   ECJ C-120/78, *Cassis de Dijon*, (1979) ECR 649, para. 8.

30   *Nicolaysen* (1996), 49.

policy aims.[31] Therefore, the *Cassis* jurisdiction has – against certain expectations – not superseded the European harmonisation. Certainly, the focus has shifted from a vertical, the single product concerning harmonisation, to a more horizontal, product spanning European harmonisations, as for instance regulations on the labelling of food, prohibited additives and many others. Especially in the field of technical safety a vertical harmonisation is still indispensable even after the *Cassis* ruling.

3. Freedom to Provide Services and Country of Origin Principle

How does the country of origin principle work with respect to the freedom to provide services? In this regard, the European Court of Justice has meanwhile created a quite complex and "fine-spun" case law, constantly pointing out that the country of origin principle is an "elemental"[32] or "fundamental"[33] principle. Protected are both the active freedom to provide services, where the provider betakes himself to the Member State of the recipient,[34] and the passive freedom to provide services, where the recipient is present in the Member State of the provider.[35] In addition, also services fall within the scope of protection, which are rendered trans-boundary without the provider or the recipient leaving their respective Member State.[36] Examples are for instance telecommunication services and trans-boundary advertising and marketing services.[37] Only with respect to activities permanently connected with the exercise of official authority the provisions on the freedom to provide services (Article 55, Article 45 EC Treaty) do not apply in the respective Member State.

According to the wording of Article 50 para. 2 EC Treaty the principle of equal treatment of own and foreign citizens is applicable to the provision of services. The principle of equal treatment grants that providers are allowed to perform an activity in another Member State under the same conditions as set out for the nationals

---

31   In-depth: *Becker* (2000b), para. 35 ff.

32   ECJ C-158/96, *Kohll*, (1998) ECR I-1931, para. 41.

33   ECJ C-205/84, *Commission/France*, (1986) ECR 3755 para. 27.

34   ECJ C-33/74, *Van Binsbergen*, (1974) ECR 1299.

35   ECJ joint cases C-286/82 and C-26/83, *Luisi/Carbone*, (1984) ECR 377.

36   ECJ C-384/93, *Alpine Investments*, (1995) ECR I-1141.

37   For further examples see *Holoubek* (2000), para. 53 *et seq.*

of the respective Member State. According to Articles 55, 46 EC Treaty, exceptions are only permissible if they are justified on grounds of public policy, public security or public health.

The European Court of Justice has however derived from the freedom to provide services a concrete right to demand the elimination of any restriction on the freedom to provide services, even if it applies to national and foreign providers of services alike, if it is liable to prohibit or otherwise impede the activities of a provider of services established in another Member State where he lawfully provides similar services.[38] Thus, the *Cassis* formula applies in principle also in the field of services. This means that services that are lawfully provided in one Member State may in general also be offered in other Member States. In addition, the Court has also objected to provisions of the country of corporate domicile of a provider, because they indirectly hindered trans-boundary activities.[39] A more recent example is the *Carpenter*-case. It dealt with the expulsion of a non-EU national from Great Britain. In the opinion of the European Court of Justice, the freedom to provide services prohibits the expulsion even of a non-EU national, if the person in question as wife and mother enables her husband to offer his services abroad.[40] In conclusion, the freedom to provide services in principle offers a choice between the law of the country of origin and the law of the country of destination.

However the effective scope of the freedom to provide services is disputed. Still open remains especially the question, whether the *Keck* ruling can be conferred to the freedom to provide services, that is, whether in the case of sales and distribution modalities only the prohibition of discrimination applies?[41] According to the permanent jurisprudence of the European Court of Justice the free exchange of services *may be restricted only by provisions, which are justified by the general good and which are applied to all persons*

---

38   EJC C-429/02 *Bacardi France* (2004) ECR I-6613 para. 31.

39   ECJ C-384/93, *Alpine Investments*, (1995) ECR I-1141; C-70/95, *Sodemare*, (1997) ECR I-3395; C-60/00, *Carpenter* (2202) ECR I-6279.

40   See fn 39; although it has to be considered that the European Court of Justice in the Article 234 EC Treaty procedures does not decide the original case, but only gives directions to the national judge on the interpretation of European Community law.

41   For more details, see *Frenz* (2004), 961 *et seqq.*

*or undertakings operating within the territory of the state in which
the service is provided in so far as that interest is not safeguarded
by the provisions to which the provider of a service is subject in the
Member State of his establishment.*[42] In the last part of the sentence
the idea discussed under the catchword country of origin principle
emerges most clearly.[43] Admittedly, the provisions of the country of
destination remain decisive. Only with respect to their application
prior performances in the country of origin have to be taken into
consideration.[44]

In addition, all limiting requirements must be objectively
necessary and the same result may not be obtainable by less restrictive rules. That is, the principle of proportionality must be respected.[45] Member States may therefore not provide that services
may only be offered under the same conditions necessary for a permanent establishment. Since this would deprive the freedom to
provide services of its practical merit, consisting precisely in the
ability to develop cross-border activities without having to comply
with the requirements for permanent establishment. In this respect
especially residence, presence and registration obligation are highly
problematic and only permissible under very narrow conditions.[46]

C. Original Conception of the Directive

The original version of the Directive was – even measured by primary law standards – very ambitious.

1. Overview

According to Article 16 of the first proposal of the Directive –
headline: country of origin principle – the Member States should
ensure that providers are subject only to the national provisions of
their Member State of origin. In return, the Member State of origin
should be responsible for the control of the provider, even with

---

42   ECJ C-205/84, *Commission/Germany*, (1986) ECR 3755 para. 27.

43   See also ECJ C-110/78, *Van Wesemael*, (1979) ECR 35.

44   See also for instance ECJ C-58/98, *Corsten*, (2000) ECR I-7919 para.
     31.

45   See for instance ECJ C-154/89, *Commission/France*, (1991) ECR I-
     659 para. 15.

46   See for instance C-493/99, *Commission/Germany*, (2001) ECR I-
     8163 para. 18.

respect to services provided by him in another Member State.[47] In addition, the permissible derogations from the country of origin principle were reduced to indispensable grounds of public policy or public security or the protection of public health or the environment.[48] Thereby, the state access to non-resident providers and their activities was quite narrowly limited, while the Directive according to critics did not provide for an adequate balancing mechanism for the protection of other legitimate interest, as for example the integrity of the labour and welfare system.[49] To this legislative gap came the fear of cheap competition from foreign countries – and to put it bluntly: the fear of cheap competition from the new EU Member States.[50]

2. Criticism

The original concept of the so-called *Bolkenstein* Directive, named after its initiator, had several constructional flaws:

Firstly: the provisions of the country of destination should not be applicable even if they had no hindering effect. Thereby the Directive's approach transcended even the case law of the European Court of Justice.

Secondly: the standards in the 27 Member States for the taking up and carrying on of service activities are apparently so different that a mutual recognition by all parties concerned even in principle did not seem acceptable.

Thirdly, and in connection with this, the derogation possibilities for the Member States were restricted to concerns of public policy or public security or the protection of public health or the

---

47 Article 16 para. 2: Member States of origin shall be responsible for supervising the provider and the services provided by him, including services provided by him in another Member State.

48 Article 17 no.17 und Article 19 para 1 of the first proposal for a Service Directive.

49 Though Articles 34–38 provided under the headline "control" for obligations of the Member States for mutual assistance, experiences in other areas of European Community Law have however shown that by this means a national solely responsible administrative supervision can not be substituted.

50 This fear could also not be dissipated by Articles 24 and 25 of the draft on the posting of workers and the continued validity of the so called Posting Directive 96/71/EC.

environment. Also insofar the path of the case law of the ECJ was abandoned and the carefully balanced relation between market liberalisation on the one hand and the legitimate public interests in the regulation of an open market on the other hand was – at least in the view of several interest groups – put at risk.

Fourthly, there existed serious scepticism with respect to the ability and willingness of many Member States to apply their respective provisions with the necessary strictness to service providers acting in other Member States. It addition it was doubted with very good reasons that it would be possible to control in the countries of destination, whether foreign service providers adhered to their respective home legal order. An unlimited country of origin principle therefore would have in fact suspended the effectiveness of *all* legal orders concerned.

Fifthly and finally the changes in the general economic framework of the enlarged European Union were not sufficiently taken into account. The extremely unequal economic power of the Member States corresponds with a respective wage differential that especially in people-intensive industries cannot be easily compensated by technical innovation. Especially in the (health) care sector namely Germany and France feared an invasion of cheap providers, namely from the acceding countries. In other words: the basic economic decision of the EC Treaty in favour of a free market economy with an open competition (Article 4 para. 1 EC Treaty) is no longer unlimitedly accepted by all Member States since it became clear what socio-political and fiscal costs the open competition in an enlarged Union also for the developed industrial states may have.

D. The Adopted Version of the Directive

The adopted version of Article 16 of the Directive tries to eliminate these flaws. It is more closely based on the case law of the European Court of Justice. Primarily, however, it bears the traces of those fierce discussions. Especially striking: the country of origin principle has vanished from the headline of the respective chapter. In detail the following shall apply in the future:

1. Limitation to the Scope of Application

Firstly, the scope of application of Article 16 was in comparison to the first proposal of the Commission further limited. According to Article 17 of the Directive services of a general economic interest shall henceforth be excluded completely. Only exemplary the sectors of postal services, electricity, gas and water distribution and supply services, waste water services and the treatment of waste are listed. Considering that the EJC confers a large freedom of discretion to the Member States regarding the question, which activities shall fall within this category,[51] the importance of this decision becomes clear. Further exceptions affect socio-politically sensitive areas, such as the posting of workers to other Member States, the matters covered by Council Directive 77/249/ECC to facilitate the effective exercise by lawyers of freedom to provide services, the activity of judicial recovery of debts, the supervision and control of shipments of waste or the registration of vehicles leased in another Member State. With respect to these areas either the general legal principles of Articles 43 and 49 or special Community law rules apply.

2. Mitigation of the Country of Origin Principle

Article 16 was also mitigated: According to the new Version of Article 16 para. 1 *"Member States shall respect the right of service providers to provide services in a Member State other than that in which they are established. The Member States in which the service is provided shall ensure free access to and free exercise of a service activity within its territory."* The general exemption from the law of the country of destination has thus been omitted. From an administrative practical point of view service providers are therefore still under the control of the national authorities of the country of destination. However, Member States may not make access to or exercise of a service activity in their country subject to compliance with any requirements, which do not respect the following principles: National requirements

– shall be non-discriminatory,
– must be justified for reasons of public policy, public security, public health or the protection of the environment,
– and in addition have to be proportionate.

This power is further mitigated in Article 16 para. 2. According to this Member States may as a rule not impose any residence, presence or registration obligations on the provider, unless these restriction are in compliance with Article 16 para. 3 of the Directive, i.e. justified for reasons of public policy, public security, public

---

51 See ECJ C-159/94, *Commission/France*, (1997) ECR I-5815 para. 56; C-320/91 *Corbeau*, (1993) ECR I-2533; C-393/92, *Almelo*, (1994) ECR I-1477.

health or the protection of the environment. These prerequisites of the Directive codify the case law of the European Court of Justice – except for one important point: though Member States are entitled to apply their respective provisions concerning employment conditions, including these of collective agreements. Due to the remaining control competence of the countries of destination a factually possible social dumping, as feared on the occasion of the first directive proposal, is in principle no longer possible.

However, the canon of mandatory requirements still remains limited to material interests: public policy, public security, public health and the protection of the environment. In addition, Member States are obliged to present a written report to the Commission laying down the reasons for upholding certain legal obstacles.[52] Therein lies the real liberalisation potential of the Directive. The dogmatic legal question, whether the Community legislator is authorised to declare legitimate material interests of primary legislation irrelevant, can be answered by referring to the priority of secondary law harmonisations over the fundamental freedoms. Nevertheless arises apart from the limited scope of application a liberalisation surplus that should not be underestimated.

3. Codification of the Rights of Service Recipients

The claims of the service recipients are quasi the counter piece to the rights of the service providers. The provisions on the rights of the service recipients of the first draft Directive were almost unmodified accepted. According to Article 20 no requirements may be imposed on a service recipient that restrict the use of a service supplied by a provider established in another Member State. Also in this respect the Directive basically follows the case law of the European Court of Justice concerning the "service reception freedom".[53]

VI. Additional Provisions

The material requirements of the Directive on the liberalisation of the trade in services are complemented by requests to the Member States to simplify the administrative procedures and enhance their

---

52   Article 39 para 5 of the Directive.

53   ECJ joint cases C-286/82 and C-26/83, *Luisi and Carbone*, (1984) ECR 377 para. 10; C-186/87, *Cowan*, (1989) ECR 195, para. 15; C-158/96, of April 28, 1998; see in particular *Kluth* (2002), para. 27.

transparency and efficiency. Especially the obligation of the Member States to establish unitary information centres that shall lead service providers like beacons through the shelves of national administrative law and its procedures should facilitate the transnational exchange of services and the establishment.[54] Detailed provisions on administrative assistance intensify the cooperation between national administrations and thus create more trust.[55] The obligation of the Commission to present a summary report at the latest five years after the coming into force of the Directive[56] finally shows that with the European Directive on Services we are dealing with an example of experimental legislation which final design is still in the process of development.

VII. Conclusion

All in all the estimations that regard the Service Directive as an expression of Europe's incompetence to generate economic growth and employment by way of a doughty liberalisation of markets are overstated. Admittedly, it is not the great leap forward, that was initially intended, but at the most a little hop. However, with respect to several services the Directive will facilitate trans-national activity. Regarding the activities and economic sectors not covered to this day, not all has been said and done yet. Against the background of the experiences with the Directive and its Transformation they might either be included in the scope of application or become subject of a separate regularisation. Moreover, the Directive also represents a change of paradigm in the European economic policy. The Services Directive is the result – whether one cherishes it or not – of a comparably wide discussion in Europe, scarcely known before. Therefore, the Directive also generates a democratic surplus for Europe.

---

54   Article 33 of the Directive.
55   Articles 33–38 of the Directive.
56   Article 41 of the Directive.

References

Ulrich Becker (2000), Artikel 28, in: *Jürgen Schwarze* (ed.), EU-Kommentar, Baden Baden (Nomos) 2000.

Ulrich Becker (2000b), Artikel 30, in: *Jürgen Schwarze* (ed.), EU-Kommentar, Baden Baden (Nomos) 2000.

Arnout De Koster (2006), The point of view of the federation of Belgian enterprises on services directive, in: *Roger Blanpain* (ed.), Freedom of Services in the European Union, The Hague (Kluwer Law) 2006, 127.

Walter Frenz (2004), Handbuch Europarecht, Vol. 1, Europäische Grundfreiheiten, Berlin (Springer) 2004

Dieter Grimm (1995), Braucht Europa eine Verfassung?, in: Juristenzeitung 50 (1995), 581.

Armin Hatje (1998), Die gemeinschaftsrechtliche Steuerung der Wirtschaftsverwaltung, Baden-Baden (Nomos) 1998.

Michael Holoubek (2000), Artikel 49, in: *Jürgen Schwarze* (ed.), EU-Kommentar, Baden Baden (Nomos) 2000.

Winfried Kluth (2002), Artikel 50, in: *Christian Calliess / Matthias Ruffert* (eds.), EUV/EGV, Munich (Beck) [2]2002.

Gert Nicolaysen (1996), Europarecht, Vol 2, Baden-Baden (Nomos) 1996.

Niklas Maydell

The Services Directive and Existing Community Law

I. Introduction

There have been few examples of European Community (EC)-internal market legislation which have been discussed as widely and emotionally as the Services Directive (SD)[1]. This broad participation far beyond stake holders gave the impression that this legislative act might equally be able to and aiming at changing the fundamentals of the European Union. Although arguments brought forward in that public discussion had regularly only little to do with the actual proposal, the consideration as an exceptional piece of legislation was right. Indeed, the SD's aim and purpose is to change the legal framework of EU's service industry, accounting for about 75% of average employment in EU- national economies.[2] To this respect, today's EC-internal market legal framework is considered insufficient for the full realisation of the economic potential. It is thus the main objective of the Directive to develop a new, improved EC regulatory approach in order to overcome today's legal shortcomings. The evaluation of that objective, in other words an analysis of change, is also the main purpose of the present study. As a consequence the first chapter focuses on today's legal status-quo, hereby presenting relevant EC primary as well as secondary legislation in the field of cross-border service provision (II. Cross-Border Service provision in the Internal Market under the Current Legal Framework). The subsequent chapter goes into the structure and the details of the SD (III. The Service Directive (SD) – A Legal Analysis). This presentation is carried out under a threefold perspective: Firstly, the SD's provisions are interpreted in the Directive's context. Secondly, they are set into relation with the corresponding stipulations of the current legal framework, thus resorting

---

1   When referring to the "Services Directive (SD)" or the "Directive", this paper means the version of the directive as published in the Official Journal of the European Union L 376/36, 27.12.2006: Directive 2006/123/EC of the European Parliament and of the Council of 12 December 2006 on services in the internal market. Draft Services Directive 2004 ("DSD 2004") means the proposal for a Directive of the European Parliament and of the Council on services in the internal market, COM(2004) 2final/3 of 5 March 2004. Draft Services Directive 2006 ("DSD 2006") means the amended proposal for a Directive of the European Parliament and of the Council on services in the internal market, COM(2006) 160 final of 4 April 2006.

2   *Kox et al.* (2004/2005), 3.

to the previous chapter. And thirdly, the new legal framework resulting from today's legal status-quo and the Directive is analysed.
The last chapter (IV. Conclusion – Evaluating the Directive's Main
Innovations in the Light of Its Overall Aim and Purpose) completing the present study wraps up the most important findings by
evaluating the legal innovations caused by the Directive in the
framework of today's internal market law for services. It assesses at
the same time to what extend the primary aims of the SD – enhancing legal certainty for service providers and abolishing concrete national restrictions – are successfully met.

II. Cross-Border Service Provision in the Internal Market under the Current Legal Framework

A. Introduction

From an economic point of view, cross border service provision in
the EC-internal market can be carried out in three possible forms:
Under the first, the service provider moves to another Member State
in order to found an establishment there, either through a legally
independent undertaking (regularly a subsidiary) or a dependent
branch. He intends to deliver its services through the establishment
for an indefinite period of time. Under the second, the service provider or recipients crosses the Member States borders for the purpose of the service provision or reception. He envisages to return to
his country of origin (home country)[3] as soon as the service provision or reception has been accomplished. In this case no subsidiary
or branch is founded. Under the third, neither the service provider
nor the receiver crosses borders while only the service itself is doing so.[4]

---

3   Also referred to as "home state" in the following text, designating the
     Member State left by one of its nationals in order to provide or re-
     ceive services in another Member State. Conversely, the Member
     State to which territory access is sought by a national of another
     Member State in order to provide services there, is called "host
     state".

4   A forth possibility is of subordinate importance, namely that the pro-
     vider and the recipient move both to a third State (in the sense of not
     being neither the home nor the host State) and the service provision
     is carried out and received there. This will be briefly discussed below
     under II.B.2.d.

The first economic possibility corresponds to the freedom of establishment (Art 43 *et seq*) whereas the second and third fall under the free movement of services (Art 49 *et seq*) within the structure of the Treaty of the European Community[5]. Accordingly, when analyzing the regulative framework for the provision of services in the internal market both freedoms have to be taken into account. That is what the following two sections will focus at.

From a methodological point of view the following two sections use a legal analysis for the presentation of today's legal framework. Hereby the European Court of Justice's (ECJ) case law and academic literature's state of the art will be pictured without though going into details of controversial aspects. The section's primary purpose namely is to provide for a basis of comparison and reference point for the subsequent in-depth analysis of the Services Directive (SD).

B. The Free Movement of Services (Art 49 et seq *EC)*

1. Personal Scope of Application

a. Beneficiaries

Art 49 EC enshrines that the provisions of the Treaty concerning the free movement of services are to be applied *"in respect of nationals of Member States who are established in a State of the Community other than that of the person for whom the services are intended"*. It follows that under Art 49 EC only natural persons are entitled to make use of the free movement of services as service *providers* who have the citizenship of one of the Member States and who additionally are resident in one of the Member States. It is furthermore commonly acknowledged that also service *recipients* fulfilling these requirements are protected under Art 49 *et seq* EC.[6]

Apart from natural persons, also legal persons are potential beneficiaries of the free movement of services. Art 55 states that *"the provisions of Articles 45 to 48 shall apply to the matters covered by this chapter" (id est: "Services")*. To this regard Art 48 establishes that *"companies or firms formed in accordance with the law of a Member State and having their registered office, central*

---

5   Henceforth "EC-Treaty" or "EC" in connection with a certain Article (Art) of that Treaty.

6   *Randelzhofer / Forsthoff* (2004), para 15; *Müller-Graff* (2003), para 71.

administration or principle place of business within the Community shall (…) be treated in the same way as natural persons who are nationals of Member States".[7]

b. Subjects of Obligation

The rights under the free movement of services which are to be exercised by the group of natural and legal persons defined above have to be primarily granted by the Member States. This obligation is not confined to the Member State receiving the service or the service provider (host state) but also relate to the Member State of origin of the service or service provider (home state).[8] To this regard the Member States are responsible for every action or non-action of all bodies under direct or indirect control exercising official authoritative power. Member States are also bound by the obligations under the free movement of services when acting under private law capacity without exercising official authority.[9]

Furthermore Community organs are obliged to respect the provisions of the free movement of services.[10] Besides, under specific circumstances, also private natural or legal persons[11] can become obliged to guarantee the specific rights resulting from the free movement of services.[12] This special constellation shall not be deepened further here.[13]

---

7   Art 48 (2) defines "companies or firms" as being *"constituted under civil or commercial law, including cooperative societies, and other legal persons governed by public or private law, save for those which are non-profit-making"*.

8   Joined Cases 286/82 and 26/83, *Luisi and Carbone*, ECR 1984, 377, para 16, 37. Joined Cases C-34/96, C-35/96 and C-36/96, *de Agostini*, ECR 1997, I-3843, para 50.

9   Case 249/81, *Commission v Irland*, ECR 1982, 4005, paras 6 *et seq*. See *v. Wilmoswsky* (2003), para 23.

10 *Müller-Graff* (2003), para 63.

11 Defined under private law, in contrast to Member States and Community organs which are constituted under public law.

12 Joined Cases C-51/96 and 191/97, *Deliège*, ECR 2000, I-2549, para 47.

13 For a general introduction see: *Streinz* (2003), 302; *Randelzhofer / Forsthoff*, (2001), para 53 *et seq*, Fn 2.

2. Subject Matter Related Scope of Application

a. The System

The subject matter of Art 49 *et seq* EC depends on the definition of
"services" which is laid down under Art 50 EC. It states that *"services shall be considered to be "services" within the meaning of
this Treaty where they are normally provided for remuneration, in
so far as they are not governed by the provisions relating to freedom of movement of goods, capital and persons"*. Apart from the
element of "remuneration", Art 50 EC apparently defines "services"
by outlining *"what they are not"*.[14] A preliminary definition of the
free movement of services with five constitutive elements includes,
first, non-physical output, second self-employed activity, third
cross-border element, fourth non (economic) mergence with the
host State economy and fifth remuneration.

b. Non-Physical Output

The first element – non-physical output – results from the delimitation to the free movement of goods of Art 23 *et seq* EC. Services in
the sense of Art 49 *et seq* can thus only be those economic activities
which consist of a non-physical output.[15] In this sense goods are
synonymous with physical output. A distinction between physical
and non-physical output can reveal uncertainties in practice. The
Court, for instance, consistently held that electricity is considered to
be physical and thus protected by the free movement of goods.[16]

   In the event the circumstances of the case include both, physical and non-physical outputs, two possible constellations are conceivable: First, if the physical and non-physical parts of the economic operation can be separated, each of them will be protected
under its respective freedom, ie the free movement of goods and
services. This has been ruled by the Court, for instance, in connection with cross-border television services. The Court subsumed the
broadcasting of programmes under the free movement of services
whereas it regarded the connected trading with films and other de-
vices necessary for broadcasting as falling under the free movement

---

14   *Woods* (2004), 160.

15   *Randelzhofer / Forsthoff* (2004), para 25.

16   For instance Case C-158/94, *Commission v Italy*, ECR 1997, I-5789,
     paras 14 *et seq*.

of goods.[17] Second, if such a separation in physical and non-physical parts of the output cannot be carried out due to the circumstances of the case, the Court defines the core content of the economic activity. It then subsumes it either under the free movement of services or under that of goods. Under this constellation, the part of the activity not belonging to that core content represents a subordinate part of the activity. For example the printing of a book constitutes a non-physical output, it however results in a printed book, constituting a physical output and the activity's core content, thus falling under the free movement of goods.[18] Also the other way round, namely that trade in goods as a subordinate activity falls under and is protected by the free movement of services has been accepted by the Court.[19]

c. Self-Employed Activity

The element of self-employed activity results from the delimitation to the free movement of workers.[20]

Whether a (natural) or legal person[21] is carrying out an activity in an employed or self-employed capacity has to be assessed from a substantive, not formal, case-to-case related point of view. The Court has ruled to this respect that it *"must be answered in each case on the basis of all the factors and circumstances characterising the arrangements between the parties, such as, for example, the sharing of the commercial risks of the business, the freedom for a person to choose his own working hours and to engage his own assistants. In any event, the sole fact that a person is paid a "share" and that his remuneration may be calculated on a collective basis is not of such a nature as to deprive that person of his status of worker."*[22] A formally self-employed conception of the individual

---

17 Case 155/73, *Sacchi*, ECR 1974, 409, para 7; Case C-390/99, *Canal Satélite*, ECR 2002, I-607, paras 32 *et seq.*

18 Case 14/84, *Commission v France*, ECR 1985, 1339, 1347, para 12.

19 Case C-275/92, *Schindler*, ECR 1994, I-1039, paras 22–25; Case C-55/93, *Van Schaik*, ECR 1994, I-4837, para 14.

20 For a general overview on that delimitation see: *Craig / de Burca* (2003), 766.

21 Legal persons cannot fall under the free movement of workers, *arg*: Art 39 (2) EC.

22 Case 3/87, *Agegate*, ECR 1989, 4459, 4505, para 36.

working contract could become irrelevant in case such an analysis of the actual situation reveals an employed relationship.[23]

d. Cross-Border Element[24]

Equally to all other fundamental freedoms of the internal market, only those services which affect at least two Member States' markets are protected by the free movement of services. This results from the general aim and purpose of the fundamental freedoms aiming at establishing *"an area without internal frontiers"*[25], thus regulating only those economic activities crossing these frontiers. This is confirmed in Art 49 (1) EC.[26] Accordingly, the ECJ held that *"the provisions of the Treaty on the freedom to provide services cannot be applied to activities whose relevant elements are confined within a single Member State"*.[27]

As to the understanding of the *"relevant elements"*, four different, basic constellations fulfilling the cross-border element have to be distinguished: Firstly, those constellations are covered by the free movement of services in which the service provider is moving for the purpose of the service provision into another Member State. This follows from the wording of Art 49 (1) and 50 (3) EC.[28] Secondly, those constellations where the recipient instead of the provider of the service is shifting from one Member State to another for the reception of the service are equally protected by the freedom

---

23 Case 2/74, *Reyners v Belgium*, ECR 1974, 631, paras 15–16. Most recently: Case C-268/99, *Jany*, ECR 2001, I-8615, paras 68–70.

24 The cross-border element is also referred to in literature as "interstate element". See for instance *Craig / de Burca* (2003), 804. Arg: *"who are established in a State of the Community other than that of the person for whom the services are intended"*.

25 Art 14 (2) EC.

26 Arg: *"Who are established in a State of the Community other than that of the person for whom the services are intended"*.

27 Case 52/79, *Procureur du Roi v. Debauve*, ECR 1980, 833; Other examples: Case C-41/90, *Höfner und Elser*, ECR 1991, I-1979; Joint Cases C-225–227/95, *Kapasakalis*, ECR 1998, I-3239.

28 This has been named in German speaking literature "active free movement of services" or "Aktive Dienstleistungsfreiheit". See for instance: *Herdegen*, (2004), para 324. An equivalent terminology in English speaking literature is missing. Instead it is circumscribed as the *"freedom to provide services"*; See for instance *Barnard* (2004), 331; *Lenaerts / van Nuffel (2005)*, 227.

at hand. This has been confirmed by the ECJ's established case law since 1984.[29] The third constellation regards the situation where neither the provider nor the recipient of the service but only the substance of the service itself crosses the Member States' borders. The applicability of the free movement of services to such constellations has been confirmed by the ECJ – for instance – in connection with the provision of (cable) television broadcast services[30] or advertisement activities for financial services via telephone[31]. Under the fourth possibility the provider moves together with the recipient of the service provision to a third country (neither that of the provider nor that of the recipient) in order to carry out the service provision there. Also under such circumstances the free movement of services fully applies.[32]

e. Non (Economic) Mergence –
Principal Point of Delimitation to the Freedom of Establishment

The constitutive element of non (economic) mergence with the host Member State's economy is derived from the delimitation *vis-à-vis* the freedom of establishment. According to Art 50 (3) EC the free movement of services is defined through its temporary pursuit[33], in contrast to the freedom of establishment aiming at establishing lasting economic links with the host Member State. Especially in Case *Gebhard*, the Court has clarified the factors distinguishing the temporary provision of services from the exercise of the right of establishment.[34] The central *dictum* defines that the free movement of services always applies when a Community national moves to another Member State hereby only intending to deliver a certain predefined economic activity there while planning to return after its accomplishment. This implies a temporary nature of the provider's

---

29   Case 52/79, *Debauve*, ECR 1980, 883, para 9; Case C-198/89, *Commission v Greece*, ECR 1991, I-727, para 9.

30   Case 62/79, *Coditel v SA Ciné Vog Films*, ECR 1980, 881; Case 352/85, *Bond van Adverteerders v. Netherlands*, ECR 1988, 2085; Case 52/79, *Procureur du Roi v. Debauve*, ECR 1980, 833.

31   Case C-384/93, *Alpine Investments*, ECR 1995, I-1141, paras 20–22.

32   Case C398/95, *Elladi Touristikon*, ECR 1997, I-3091. paras 6 *et seq.*

33   Art 50 EC: "(…) *the person providing a service may* (…) *temporarily pursue his activity in the State* (…)".

34   Case C-55/94, *Gebhard v Consiglio dell'Ordine degli Avvocati e Procuratori di Milano*, ECR 1995, I-4165.

stay abroad which has to be *"determined in the light, not only of the duration of the provision of the service, but also of its regularity, periodicity or continuity"*. Moreover, *"the fact that the provision of services is temporary does not mean that the provider of services within the meaning of the Treaty may not equip himself with some form of infrastructure in the host Member State (including an office, chambers or consulting rooms) in so far as such infrastructure is necessary for the purpose of performing the services in question"*.[35] The concept of establishment, in contrast, allows and equally obliges a Community national to participate on a *"stable and continuous"* basis in the economic and social life, aiming to fully integrate into the host Member State's society.[36] This is regularly done by setting up a (legally independent) subsidiary or a (dependent) branch in that Member State.

In its most recent case law, however, the Court seems to replace the central criterion of "temporality" by a more economically orientated approach, treating *"economic activities which qualify as services under Art 49 EC irrespective of their duration"*,[37] thus bringing in line the legal and economic definition of services.[38] In *Schnitzer* and in *Commission v Portugal, Private Security Firms*, the Court stated that *"services within the meaning of the Treaty may likewise be constituted by services which a business established in a Member State supplies with a greater or lesser degree of frequency or regularity, even over an extended period, to persons established in one or more other Member States"*.[39] This makes it clear that it is the economic nature and not the duration of the activity that constitutes the decisive element of definition in legal terms and abandons the idea of subsidiarity of Art 49 *et seq.*

f. Remuneration

By covering only those services by the free movement of services which are *"normally provided for remuneration"*, Art 50 (1) EC relates to the Treaty's Art 2. This article introduces the Treaty's

---

35   *Ibidem*, para 27.

36   *Ibidem*, para 25.

37   *Hatzopoulos / Do* (2006), 927 *et seq.*

38   To this extend the Court seems to adopt the WTO's GATS approach.

39   Case C-215/01, *Schnitzer*, ECR 2003, I-14847, para 3; Case C-171/02, *Commission v Portugal, Private Security Firms*, ECR 2004, I-5645, para 25.

principal and limited applicability to "*economic activities*". Decisive for determining "remuneration" is that the economic activity is being performed in order to receive an economic value in return. It is essential that the remuneration constitutes an economic equivalent for the service rendered and does not just represent a negligible contribution to the costs as well as it is generally and regularly obtained for the service provision at stake.[40] Consequently, those services delivered without the intention of receiving an equivalent return or those which are provided for remuneration in a specific case only, normally not being part of the economic life, are not covered.[41] In this context it is not required that the remuneration is rendered by the recipient of the services himself, so long as remuneration is granted from some party with a specific relationship to the recipient, for example a medical insurance company.[42] Payments primarily funded from the public purse, which means tax-financed, do not result from such a specific relationship and thus do not constitute remuneration in the before established sense.[43] This is regularly the case with social, cultural and educational engagement of the Member States.[44]

Art 50 (2) EC names as examples for services constituting an economic activity delivered for remuneration those with "*an industrial and commercial character, activities of craftsmen and activities of the professions*".

g. The Free Movement of Services
and the Free Movement of Capital[45]

The free movement of services on the one hand and the free movement of goods, workers, and the freedom of establishment on the

---

40   Case 263/86, *Belgium v. Humbel*, ECR 1988, 5365.

41   Case C-159/90, *Unborn Children*, ECR 1991, I-4685, 4740 paras 25 *et seq. Randelzhofer / Forsthoff* (2004), para 37.

42   Case 352/85, *Bond van Adverteerders v. Netherlands*, ECR 1988, 2085; Case C-157/99, *Smits and Peerbooms*, ECR 2001, I-5473, paras 50, 52.

43   Case 352/85, *Bond van Adverteerders v. Netherlands*, ECR 1988, 2085, paras 17–19.

44   *Ibidem*, para 18.

45   The notion of the free movement of capital is to be understood in the present context as to include the free movement of payments (Art 56 (1) and (2)) as well.

other hand exclude each other's applicability. As regards the relationship with the free movement of capital, in contrast, an economic
activity can simultaneously fall under the scope of both, the free
movement of services and capital. This is described as "parallel
applicability" in literature.[46] From a substantial point of view, a
parallel applicability of the free movement of services and that of
capital is only conceivable as far as services are concerned which
include the transfer of capital or payments in the sense of Art 56 *et
seq* EC. This is basically the case with financial services such as
banking, insurance or investment activities. By means of two basic
arguments – the first being the Treaty itself, the second being based
on the ECJ's jurisprudence – the notion pf parallel applicability
shall be outlined. As regards the Treaty-based evidence for a parallel applicability of the two freedoms, Art 51 (2) EC shall be considered first. It underlines the parallelism by laying down that "*the
liberalisation of banking and insurance services connected with
movements of capital shall be effected in step with the liberalisation
of movement of capital*". As the free movement of capital has been
fully liberalised in 1994, this treaty provision could have been deleted in the following treaty revisions of Amsterdam and Nice.
Since this has not been the case, Art 51 (2) EC – as to avoid its
redundancy – has to be interpreted as aiming at enshrining the parallel applicability of the two freedoms at stake. Secondly, Art 57 (2)
EC explicitly includes "*financial services*" and "*the admission of
securities to capital markets*" under the scope of the free movement
of capital.

The relevant case law approves the thesis of parallel
applicability. The ECJ repeatedly applied – when assessing Member States' restrictions affecting different types of cross border financial services – the standards of the free movement of services as
well as those of capital for one economic activity.[47]

Summing up, services under Art 49 *et seq* EC which are related to the transfer of capital or payments in the sense of Art 56 EC

---

46   *Barnard* (2004) 481; *Ohler* (1996), 1802; *Schön* (1997), 743 ff; *Ress
      / Ukrow* (2005), para 23; *Kiemel* (2003), para 7f.

47   Starting with Case 267/86, *Van Eycke,* 21.9.1988, ECR (1988), 4769,
      25; C-484/93 *Svensson and Gustavsson,* ECR (1995), I-3955; C-
      118/96 *Safir,* ECR (1998), I-1897; C-279/00 *Commission / Italy,*
      ECR (2002), I-1425, 37.

are regularly protected under both freedoms, the free movement of services and capital.

h. Summary – Contrasting the Economic Perspective

A definition of "services" under the Treaty's free movement of services is particularly important not just because it determines its subject matter related scope of application but it also contrasts an economic definition of services. In economic terms, services are those business activities not belonging to initial production (eg mining, agricultural production) or manufacturing (eg steal fabrication), thus constituting the tertiary sector.[48] The economic definition hence relates to services as a downstream phase of economic activity *post* initial production and manufacturing. In contrast the EC-law understanding of services under Art 49 *et seq* EC focuses on the appearance of the economic activity at the point of border-crossing between two Member States. It therefore considers services as those economic activities which – at the point of border crossing (section II.B.2.d. – Cross-Border Element) – are aiming at non-physical output (section II.B.2.b.), to be created in a self-employed capacity (section II.B.2.c.), against remuneration (section II.B.2.f.) and without aiming at establishing in the host Member State's economic environment (section II.B.2.e. – Non-economic Mergence). This difference between the economic and legal definition approach has practical implications insofar as a service in the economic sense, such as the operation of a hotel in another Member State, is not necessarily regarded as a service under the Treaty's free movement of services (the operation of a hotel potentially falls under the freedom of establishment).[49]

---

48 Regulation 29/2002 EC amending Council Regulation (EEC) No 3037/90 on the statistical classification of economic activities in the European Community.

49 The differentiation between an economic and a legal definition of services is of major importance for the understanding of the delimitation between Chapter III and IV of the services directive. See below under section III.

3. Substantive Content of the Free Movement
of Services under Art 49 *et seq* EC

a. Introduction

Under the chapter on the free movement of services, Art 49 (1) EC
stipulates that *"restrictions on freedom to provide services within
the Community shall be prohibited "*. In its established case law the
Court there from deduced on the one hand a prohibition of all discriminatory Member States' requirements.[50] This follows the fundamental concept behind the free movement of services as well as that
behind the other Treaty freedoms, namely the obligation of equal
treatment between nationals of different Member States in their
pursuit of economic activity in another Member State than that of
their origin.[51] Art 50 (3) EC confirms to this regard that persons
from Member State X providing services in Member State Y may
do so under the same conditions as are imposed by Member State Y
on its own nationals. Insofar the provisions under the free movement of services represent a specification of the non-discrimination
principle of Art 12 EC.[52]

On the other hand, the Court there from developed a general
prohibition of requirements *"liable to prohibit or otherwise impede
the activities of a provider of services established in another Member State"*.[53] This means that it also prohibits non-discriminatory
requirements, which, together with the prohibition of discriminatory
requirements, has become known as the system of "general prohibition of/on restrictions" in the Court's practice.[54] Following this

---

50 "Requirement" thereinafter means any obligation, prohibition, condi-
    tion or limit provided for in the laws, regulations or administrative
    provisions of the Member States or in consequence of case-law, ad-
    ministrative practice, the rules or professional bodies, or the collec-
    tive rules of professional associations or other professional organisa-
    tions, adopted in the exercise of ther legal autonomy.

51 Case 33/74, *Van Binsbergen v Bestuur*, ECR 1974, 1299. General
    literature on the convergence of the freedoms: *Hatzopoulos / Do*
    (2006), 948 (2.3. Relations to the other freedoms).

52 Art 12 (1) EC reads: *"Within the scope of application of this Treaty,
    and without prejudice to any special provisions contained therein,
    any discrimination on grounds of nationality shall be prohibited "*.

53 Case C-76/90, *Säger v Dennemeyer*, ECR 1991, I-4221, para 12.

54 Most recently for instance in Case C-452/04, *Fidium Finanz AG*,
    Opinion of Advocate General *Stix-Hackl*, para 109.

classification, the prohibition of discriminatory requirements and that of non-discriminatory requirements shall be discussed in detail in the sections to come.

b. Discriminatory Requirements

Discriminatory requirements are those limitations on the exercise of the free movement of services which are imposed on the ground of nationality and / or the place of establishment.[55] It is required that discriminatory requirements, for instance in a national law, explicitly nominate a nationality and / or place of establishment element.[56] Standard of comparison for evaluating potential discrimination is an equally situated natural or legal person under the legal system of the Member State where the service provision takes place or where the recipient is located. It is not admissible for this evaluation to draw a comparison between the two legal systems, that of the host and the home Member State of the service provider. Consequently, this concept does not aim at harmonising the different legal systems of the Member States.

In the area of discriminatory requirements some authors have introduced the notion of "indirect discriminatory" requirements, thus labeling the category described before "direct discriminatory requirements".[57] It is argued that indirect discriminatory requirements do not relate to the provider's nationality or principal place of business but lay upon it a greater economic burden than compared with providers of the host State. For example the requirement to have an establishment in the host State additionally to that in the home State is said to be indirectly discriminatory. In other words, the host State's regulation formally treats all providers in the same way, substantially though it discriminates against foreign providers. Three arguments shall be brought forward against such a distinction: Firstly, the Court has never explicitly referred to the term "indirect discriminatory requirements" in its case law.[58] Secondly,

---

55 Case C-288/89, *Gouda*, ECR 1991, I-4007, para 10.

56 For example: A national legislative act allowing tourist guide services for nationals of Country X only. Compare Case C-375/92, *Commission v Spain*, ECR 1994, I-923, para 10.

57 *Craig / de Burca* (2003), 715. Also other terms are used in literature, such as "distinctly and indistinctly applicable measures" – see *Barnard* (2004), 346.

58 For instance *Barnard* (2004), 348, cites the insurance cases (eg Case 205/84, *Commission v. Germany*, ECR 1986, 3755). The Court

there are no commonly agreed criteria to differ between indirectly discriminatory requirements and non-discriminatory requirements. The greater economic burden which is believed to affect only foreign providers under this flawed category – and which is thus the principal argument of differentiation – is regularly carried by a host State provider to the same extend.[59] For that reason most of the examples above mentioned authors would consider as indirect discriminatory requirements are in fact non-discriminatory requirements in the present paper's sense (see immediately below section II.B.3.c.). And thirdly, the consequences these authors attach to their distinction do not differ from non-discriminatory restrictions, meaning that indirect discriminatory requirements can in contrast to direct discriminatory ones also be justified through overriding requirements and are not limited to one of the express (Treaty-based) justifications (as direct discriminatory requirements are).[60] Considering this reasoning, the present paper only differentiates between discriminatory and non-discriminatory measures.[61]

c. Non-Discriminatory Requirements –
The System of General Prohibition on Restrictions

ca. Introduction

As already introduced before, Art 49 (1) EC prohibits – besides direct discriminatory requirements – also those requirements *"liable to prohibit or otherwise impede the activities of a provider of services established in another Member State"*.[62] Art 49 thus demands

---

therein does not use the expression of "indirect discriminatory restrictions" but distinguishes between *"discriminatory requirements"* and *"requirements constituting restrictions on the freedom to provide services"* only (Case 205/84, paras 25–29).

59   Sticking to the example of the establishment requirement, it represents also for the host State provider a greater economic burden since its abolition or, more realistically, its limitation in scope and content would impact less on the provider in economic terms, especially in terms of compliance costs.

60   For the system of justifications, see below section II.B.3.d.

61   Compare (ie equally not acknowledging indirect discriminatory requirements) eg *Lenaerts / van Nuffel (2005)*, 197.

62   Case C-76/90, *Säger v Dennemeyer*, ECR 1991, I-4221, para 12. This formula has more than once been repeated in recent judgments, such as Case C-398/95, *SETTG*, ECR I-3091, 3119, para 16 or in the AG *Tizzano*'s Opinion to Case C-429/02, *Bacardi France*, ECR 2003, I-

not only the elimination of all discriminatory requirements applied on a person providing services on the grounds of his nationality but also the abolition of any restriction. This has been the Court's approach since – at least outspokenly – the before cited Case *Säger v Dennemeyer* in 1991. The most up-to-date affirmation of this principle by the Court was delivered in 2005.[63] A restriction in this sense is already existent due to the application of a different legal order.[64] It follows that Art 49 enshrines *a general prohibition on restrictions*[65].

To this regard, it is essential to clarify the scope of the general prohibition of restriction, which is disputed in literature. To put it differently, it has to be worked out to what extend Member States can not apply non-discriminatory requirements upon foreign service providers. Some authors tend to be indifferent *vis-à-vis* this question[66], others restrict its applicability to market access questions only[67], others in turn do not limit its scope, thus applying it to all Member States legislation affecting the foreign service provider at any point of time[68].

Randelzhofer / Forsthoff[69] follow a different approach. On the one hand they apply the general prohibition on restrictions test to all national measures regulating market access conditions for foreign service providers. Additionally, they apply the general prohibition on restrictions standard to those measures which intentionally and formally legislate for the conditions of exercise of the service but

---

6613, para 65: "*It must be borne in mind that Article 49 EC prohibits not only discrimination based on nationality but also more generally any restriction on the freedom to provide services by persons established in another Member State.*"

63   Case C-264/03, *Commission v France,* ECR 2005, I-8831, para 66.

64   For evidence from the most recent case law, see: *Hatzopoulos,* (2000), 961. Similarly: *Roth* (2002), 13. A minority of authors argues to treat double regulation through different legal orders as discrimination: *Kingreen / Strömer* (1998), 263, 120.

65   Different terminology with the same meaning can be found in literature, eg "*general prohibition on obstacles*", in *Lenaerts / van Nuffel* (2005), 187.

66   *Barnard* (2004), 350, 351.

67   *Eilmansberger* (1999), 440–442.

68   *Laenarts / van Nuffel* (2005) implicitly argue in this direction, 233.

69   *Randelzhofer / Forsthoff* (2004), para 98.

substantially affect market access conditions for the foreign services provider.[70] All other national regulation[71] has to be assessed under the prohibition of discrimination standards only.[72] A similar approach is taken by *Roth*, limiting the prohibition of restrictions to *"cases in which market access for the provider (and the recipient) of the services is impeded by a regulation"*.[73] He introduces four different kinds of regulation to be measured against the prohibition of restrictions, namely *"(1) regulations which impose certain conditions that have to be fulfilled before the provision of services may be taken up, (2) regulations as to the organisational structure of the provider of the service, (3) regulations concerning the service as a product, and (4) regulations concerning the distribution of the service"*. Although the distinction between market access and non-market access related regulation used by *Randelzhofer / Forsthoff* and *Roth* includes some unsolved questions, such as the meaning of *"substantially affecting"*[74], it shall be adopted in the present study as the Court has adopted this distinction in his most recent case law, too.[75] Following these considerations, a systematic overview of the

---

70   With an equal solution, though different line of argumentation: *Tietje / Troberg* (2003), para 108.

71   When referring to "regulation", every kind of legislative, administrative or judicative Member State's measure shall be meant.

72   This signifies a takeover of the *"Keck*-jurisprudence" from the free movement of goods to the free movement of services. Also favoring this takeover, see eg *da Cruz Vilaca* (2002), 33 *et seq.*

73   *Roth* (2002), 16.

74   *Randelzhofer / Forsthoff* (2004), para 99, try to draw the line between "irrelevanten und spezifischen Zugangsbehinderungen" without though establishing criteria for the actual distinction.

75   Opinion AG *Tizzano*, Case C-429/02 *Bacardi France*, para 62: *"It would be difficult to deny that the legislation in question constitutes an obstacle to access to the abovementioned services"*. The AG continues by assessing whether the prohibition of alcoholic advertisement substantially affects markets access, with the result that *"in either case, the conduct that the Code imposes on those negotiating television rights prevents several parties from offering or benefiting from one or more services "across Community frontiers""*." Furthermore he states that the general prohibition on restrictions *"also precludes national provisions which, even if they apply without distinction, are capable of directly affecting access to the market in services*

relevant case law shall be given.[76] This case law includes three groups of restrictions, those relating to the general and complete prohibition of a service, those regarding the phase of entrance of a service and those concerning the phase of exercise of a service.

cb. Prohibition of the Service or Limitation to a Certain Group of Providers

The ECJ declares those Member States' measures an interference with the general prohibition of restrictions which completely prohibit a certain service provision in their territory. This is equally true for those measures which limit the exercise of a certain service to a specific group of natural or legal persons. As examples from the case law serve prohibitions of lottery services or monopoly regulations in the same field.[77] From a dogmatic point of view, national prohibitions of services or limitations to certain groups of providers belong to the *admittance* of the service provision, ie the market access provisions. Also the next point to be analysed regards market access provisions.

cc. National Regulation on the Admittance of the Service Provision

The second group of Member States' measures prohibited under the general prohibition of restrictions concerns the different set of national rules establishing certain criteria for the lawful taking up of the exercise of the service provision. These rules differ very much in their extend and nature allowing to mention only some of them. The general *requirement* of an *establishment* for service providers is the most prominent example of the relevant ECJ case law. The Court ruled to this respect that a Member State demanding from a foreign service provider to found an establishment (another place of business) in the host Member State in order to be admitted to provide services on a purely temporary basis in that Member State

---

in the other Member State." This viewpoint has been confirmed by the ECJ's judgment: ECR 2004, I-6613, paras 30 *et seq.*

76 This classification is carried out on the basis of the analysis established by *Randelzhofer / Forsthoff* (2004), para 99 ff; by *Böhert et al.* (2005), 2; and by the *European Commission* in its Amended Proposal for a Services Directive COM (2006) 160 under Art 16 (= DSD 2006).

77 Case C-275/92, *Schindler*, ECR 1994, I-1039.

breaches the general prohibition of restrictions.[78] The Court clarified that this requirement would deprive the free movement of services under Art 49 *et seq* EC from its practical importance, no
longer differing between it and the freedom of establishment of Art
43 *et seq* EC. Even though a *residence requirement* does not automatically deprive the free movement of services from its practical
applicability, it is comparable with an establishment requirement as
far as its implications for the service providers are concerned. It is
therefore also principally prohibited under Art 49 EC.[79] Further
prohibited national measures concern obligations on the provider to
obtain an *authorisation* for the service provision from national authorities or *registration requirements*, such as within professional
bodies. Such authorisation requirements appear in different forms,
regularly relating to professional qualifications, for instance certain
diplomas. This prohibition does not merely embrace the content of
an authorisation requirement but also its formal appearance, such as
original documents or certified translations.[80] As far as registration
requirements are concerned the Court declared illegal the duty for
patent agents to register in specific books[81], the duty for certain
services providers to be entered into professional registers kept by
the Chamber of Commerce[82] and the duty for craftsmen to be listed
in a specific professional index ("Handwerksrolle")[83]. Similar to
registration requirements, the Court declared *compulsory membership requirements in professional associations* serving as precondition for the lawful service provision violating the general prohibition of restrictions.[84]

cd. National Regulation on the Exercise of a Service Provision

In addition to the previously discussed market access regulation,
Art 49 EC's general prohibition of restrictions also covers those
Member States' measures relating to the exercise of services but

---

78 Case C-131/01, *Commission v Italy*, ECR 2003, I-1659, para 42.

79 Case C-355/98, *Commission v Belgium*, ECR 2000, I-1221, para 23.

80 Case C-298/99, *Commission v Italy*, ECR 2002, I-3129, para 71.

81 Case C-131/01, *Commission v Italy*, ECR 2003, I-1659, para 27.

82 Case C-264/99, *Commission v Italy*, ECR 2000, I-4417, para 14.

83 Case C-58/98, *Corsten*, ECR 2000, I-7919, para 34.

84 Case 5/83, *Rienks*, ECR 1983, 4233, para 11.

substantially affecting admittance to the national market.[85] Here the Court recognised, for example, that national *legislation limiting the transmission time* allocated to TV-advertising breaches the general prohibition on restrictions of Art 49 EC.[86] In *de Agostini* the Court applied the general prohibition on restrictions to national *legislation on specific contextual aspects of television advertisement*.[87] Last but not least national *legislation concerning the protection of workers* has also been reviewed by the Court on the criteria of the general prohibition of restrictions system.[88]

d. The System of Justifications

National legislators have to take into account whether their envisaged measures constitute a breach of the non-discrimination and non-restriction impositions worked out above. Even though a national measure discriminates against a foreign service provider or provision or constitutes a restriction of it, the system of justification may be evoked. It is principally divided in those justifications being expressly enshrined in the Treaty and those being developed by the Court's jurisprudence only. Which one of the two has to be applied depends on the character of the national measure in breach.

da. Express Justifications (Art 55, Art 46 EC)

Art 55 in connection with Art 46 EC grants *"the applicability of provisions laid down by law, regulation or administrative action providing for special treatment for foreign nationals on grounds of public policy, public security or public health."* It follows that all Member States' measures – be they of discriminatory or non-discriminatory nature – can be justified by reasons of public policy, security or health. As to the interpretation of these three reasons of justification, the Court pointed out in its established case law that they have to be interpreted narrowly. Otherwise the free movement of services could be deprived of its efficiency.[89]

---

85   The herein mentioned case law reflects the author's view on the scope of the general prohibition on restrictions.

86   Case C-6/98, *ARD*, ECR 1999, I-7599.

87   Joined Cases C-34, C-35 and C-36/96, *de Agostini et al*, ECR 1999, I-3843.

88   Joined Cases C-369 and 376/96, *Arblade*, ECR 1999, I-8453.

89   Case C-260/89, *ERT*, ECR 1991, I-2925; Case C-355/98, *Commission v Belgium*, ECR 2000, I-1221.

With regard to public policy and security justifications, Member States are conceded a certain discretionary power of definition, resulting from the need of taking national differences into account.[90] As a bottom line the EC-law however justifications for only those measures which are *"directed against a genuine and sufficiently serious threat affecting one of the fundamental interests of society"*.[91] Pure economic reasons can thus never be justified under Art 46 (1) EC.[92] The "public health" justification can be evoked to limit the free movement of services in order to preserve the functionality and the specific design of the national health care system. The Court ruled that *"Article 56 of the Treaty permits Member States to restrict the freedom to provide medical and hospital services in so far as the maintenance of a treatment facility or medical service on national territory is essential for the public health and even the survival of the population."*[93]

All three reasons of justification under Art 46 (1) EC additionally have to fulfil the principle of proportionality. Although not expressly mentioned in the Treaty, this has been repeatedly affirmed by the ECJ's case law.[94] It requires that the national measure is suitable for securing the attainment of the objective which it pursues and that it does not go beyond what is necessary to attain it.[95]

---

90   Case 41/74, *Van Duyn*, ECR 1974, 1337, para 18, 19.

91   Case C-114/97, *Commission v Spain*, ECR 1998, I-6717; Case 30/77, *Bouchereau*, ECR 1977, 1999, para 35.

92   *"It must be recalled that aims of a purely economic nature cannot justify a barrier to the fundamental principle of freedom to provide services"*: Case C-398/95, *SETTG v Ypourgos Ergasias*, ECR 1997, I-3091, para 23)

93   Case C-158/96, *Kohll*, ECR 1998, I-1931, para 31.

94   Initially in the context of Art 30 EC only: Case C-367/89, *Richardt*, ECR 1991, I-4621, para 25. Since Case C-157/99, *Smits and Peerbooms*, ECR 2001, I-5473, para 75 and Case C-385/99, *Müller-Fauré*, para 68 also in the context of the free movement of services.

95   *Barnard* (2004), 241.

db. Justification through an
Overriding Requirement of the General Interest

A measure can also be justified by overriding requirements of the general interest.[96] This legal construction – which is not expressly enshrined in the Treaty – has been established by the ECJ in close dogmatic orientation to the system of express justifications.[97] A national measure can be justified under this system in case a) the measure is *not discriminatory*, b) the host Member State can prove the existence of an *overriding requirement of the general interest*, c) the measure corresponds with the principle of *proportionality*, and d) the overriding requirement is not already protected by *a measure (regulation) of the* service provider's *home Member State*.

First, the measure to be justified may not be discriminatory, signifying that only non-discriminatory measures can be justified.

Second, there does not exist an exhaustive list of the overriding requirements. The Court has recognised more than twenty overriding requirements so far[98], but consistently held that the list of requirements is in principle open. Member States can thus argue for new types of overriding requirements in proceedings in front of the Court without being capable of prejudicing in advance whether they will be honored. Some of those justifications of overriding requirements of the general interest already acknowledged by the Court within the free movement of services have been summarised in the case *Collective Anteenvoorziening Gouda*[99] some of them in subsequent judgments. In *Collective Anteenvoorziening Gouda* the Court recognised professional rules intended to protect recipients of the service, the protection of intellectual property, the protection of workers, consumer protection, the conservation of the national historic and artistic heritage and the widest possible dissemination of

---

96 Most recently acknowledged by the Court in Case C-243/01, *Gambelli*, ECR 2003, I-1303.

97 Acknowledged for the free movement of services in eg Case C-222/95, *Parodi*, ECR 1997, I-3899, 3922, para 19. The term "*imperative reasons relating to the public interest*" is synonymously used in the Court's case law, see eg Case C-272/94, *Guiot*, ECR 1996, I-1920, para 11.

98 The number of recognised requirements strongly depends on the systematisation approach concerning the relevant case law.

99 Case C-288/89, ECR 1991, I-4007, para 14.

knowledge of the artistic and cultural heritage of a country. Additional requirements of the general interest acknowledged by the Court in other cases are the integrity of the legal system[100], the independency of accountant services[101], the independency of lawyers concerning professional secrecy obligations[102], maintaining the good reputation of the financial sector[103], protection of the stability of the securities market[104], protection of the quality of manufacturing and processing services[105], the integrity of the trade flow[106], the protection of the social system[107], road traffic safety[108], safety of maritime transports in ports[109], environmental protection[110], the imposition of public service obligations for the granting of a license[111] and most recently respecting fundamental rights[112].

Thirdly, in case a Member State can evoke one of those overriding requirements or in case it can successfully introduce a new requirement, the principle of proportionality must be taken into

---

100 Case C-3/95, *Reisebüro Broede*, ECR 1996, I-6511.

101 Case C-106/91, *Ramrath*, ECR 1992, I-3351.

102 Case C-309/99, *Wouters*, ECR 2002, I-1577.

103 Case C-384/93, *Alpine Investment*, ECR 1995, I-1141.

104 Case C-101/94, *Commission v Italy*, ECR 1996, I-2691.

105 Case C-58/98, *Corsten*, ECR 1999, I-7919.

106 Case C-34/95, C 35/95, C-36/95, ECR 1997, I-3843.

107 Case C-275/92, *Schindler*, ECR 1994, I-1039; C-124/97, *Läärä*, ECR 1999, I-6067; C-67/98, *Zenatti*, ECR 1999, I-7289; C-159/90, *Grogan*, ECR 1991, I-4685.

108 Case C-249/00, *Commission v Netherlands*, ECR 2003, I-7485, para 67.

109 Case C-266/96, *Corsica Ferries*, ECR 1998, I-3949.

110 Case C-451/99, *Cura Anlagen*, ECR 2002, I-3193.

111 Case C-205/99, *Analir*, ECR 2001, I-1271, Case C-430/99, *Sea-Land Service* and Case c-431/99, *Nedlloyd Lijnen*, ECR 2002, I-5235.

112 Case C-112/00, *Schmidberger*, ECR 2003, I-5659, paras 71–74. This case concerns the free movement of goods, the Court however leaves its application open for the other fundamental freedoms: "*Thus, since both the Community and its Member States are required to respect fundamental rights, the protection of those rights is a legitimate interest which, in principle, justifies a restriction of the obligations imposed by Community law, even under a fundamental freedom guaranteed by the Treaty such as the free movement of goods.*"

consideration. It enshrines that the measure must be suitable for securing the attainment of the objective which it pursues and must not go beyond what is necessary in order to attain it (proportionality *strictu senso*).[113] In other words, it must not be possible to obtain the same result by less restrictive rules.[114] The fact that one Member State imposes less strict rules than another does not automatically mean that the latter's rules are disproportionate, since proportionality has to be measured against the underlying legitimate regulatory objective.[115] The Court has for example prohibited the following, already above introduced, measures because of their disproportionate nature: The obligation to have an establishment in the territory of the host Member State[116] or the obligation on the provider to obtain an authorisation or registration with a professional body or association[117].

Finally, the host Member States' regulatory objective underlying the restrictive measure may not already be met through the home Member State's legislation of the service provider. This signifies that host Member State authorities – before applying their national restrictive regulation upon the foreign service provider – must screen the service provider's host country legal order for the regulation of their envisaged restriction.[118] As a justification

---

113 See – alongside the cases cited – Case C-106/91, *Ramrath*, ECR 1992, I-3351, paras 29–31.

114 Case C-198/89, *Commission v Greece*, ECR 1991, I-727, paras 18 and 19.

115 *Lenaerts / van Nuffel (2005)*, 198.

116 Case C-493/99, *Commission v Germany*, ECR 2001, I-8163, para 22.

117 For example the obligation to obtain an extraordinary permission to be inscribed into the "Handwerksrolle", a German professional register: Case C-215/01, *Schnitzer*, ECR 2003, I-14847, EuZW 2004, 94, para 36 and 40. Also: Case C-198/89, *Commission v Greece*, ECR 1991, I-727, para 21.

118 This has been established by the Court *inter alia* in Case C-76/90, *Säger*, ECR 1991, I-4221, 4244, para 15: "*However, as a fundamental principle of the Treaty, the freedom to provide services may be limited only by rules which are justified by imperative reasons relating to the public interest and which apply to all persons or undertakings pursuing an activity in the State of destination, in so far as that interest is not protected by the rules to which the person providing the services is subject in the Member State in which he is established* and in Case C-288/89, Gouda, ECR 1991, I-04007, para 13:

through an overriding requirement of the general interest can only be evoked for non-discriminatory requirements and non-discriminatory requirements are only forbidden in the context of "*all national measures regulating market access conditions for foreign service providers*"[119], thus not relating to *post*-market access exercise regulation not substantially affecting market access, the present criteria of compulsory host-home-State-regulatory-comparison has to be met only with regard to market access regulation in the above established sense. This has been continuously proved by the Court's jurisprudence since apparently all existing case law establishing the present home-host-State-comparison relates to market access regulation only.[120] The Court has for instance declared a Member State's measure requiring the payment of employer's contribution – although already paid in its home State – violating the free movement of services.[121] This however does not deprive the host Member State, under the conditions established before, to define the level of protection of the overriding requirement, for example for consumers, according to its own considerations. It will thus principally only be obligatory for the host Member State to overtake the service provider's home Member State's regulation in case the underlying level of protection is identical.

C. The Freedom of Establishment

As mentioned above, the SD aims at facilitating cross-border services activity in the EC-Internal Market on a temporary basis as well as through the foundation of an establishment. Therefore the SD includes – besides the free movement of services – provisions relating to the Treaty's freedom of establishment (Art 43–48 EC). This fundamental freedom shall thus be briefly analysed in the present study, too. This shall be primarily done with respect to those

---

"*if the requirements embodied in that legislation are already satisfied by the rules imposed on those persons in the Member State in which they are established*". See also *Roth* (2002), 3.

119 See above, section II.B.3.c.

120 Case 71/76, *Thieffry*, ECR 1977, 765, 779 para 24/26; joined Cases 110 and 111/78, *van Wesemael*, ECR 1979, 35, 53 para 30; Case 220/83, *Commission v France*, ECR 1986, 3663, 3708 para 17; Case C-340/89, *Vlassopoulou*, ECR 1991, I-2357, 2383 para 15; Case C-101/94, *Commission v Italy*, ECR 1996, I-2691, 2725 para 17.

121 Joined Cases C-369/96 and C-376/96, *Arblade and Leloup*, ECR 1999, I-8453, para 80.

elements of the freedom differing from the free movement of services.[122]

1. Personal Scope of Application

a. Beneficiaries

Both, natural and legal persons, are protected under the freedom of establishment. While natural persons must possess the nationality of one of the Member States[123] in order to be recognised as beneficiaries, legal persons – companies or firms[124] – must be *"formed in accordance with the law of a Member State"* and must have *"their registered office, central administration or principal place of business within the Community"*.[125]

b. Subjects of Obligation

The subjects of obligation under Art 43 *et seq* correspond with those under the free movement of services above under section II.B.[126]

2. Subject Matter Related Scope of Application

Similar to the free movement of services, several constitutive elements define the scope of application of the freedom of establishment. These elements are (1) self-employed activity, (2) cross-border activity, (3) envisaged economic mergence, and (4) economic activity. Elements (1), (2) and (4) are similar as in the context of the free movement of services whereas element (3) is different and thus decisive for distinguishing between the two freedoms. Also the free movement of services' element of non-physical output is not relevant under the current freedom. Consequently only element (3) has to be elaborated in detail in the present section.

---

122 For the general question of convergence of the fundamental freedoms, see eg: *Jarass* (2002), 141 *et seq.*

123 Art 43 EC second sentence: *"by nationals of any Member State"*.

124 According to Art 48 EC "companies or firms" *"means companies or firms constituted under civil or commercial law"* or *"public or private law, save for those which are non-profit making"*.

125 Art 48 EC first sentence.

126 *Müller-Graff* (2003), para 33 ff.

a. Self-Employed Activity

Similar to the free movement of services, the freedom of establishment only covers activities exercised in a self-employed capacity. This represents the criterion of delimitation towards the free movement of workers, two freedoms which exclude each other.[127] For further details on the self-employed element, see above section II.B.2.c.

b. Cross-Border Activity

Similar to the free movement of services, the freedom of establishment only applies to cases involving at least two Member States' economies.[128] For further details thus see above section II.B.2.d.

c. Economic Mergence

While under the free movement of services the service provider or recipient only temporarily – for the duration of the service provision – operates in another Member State's market, the freedom of establishment requires a lasting economic mergence with the host Member State's economy, completely detached and independent from a single economic operation. The term "establishment" signifies that a Community national participates, on a stable and continuous basis, in the economic life of a Member State other than his or her State of origin, so contributing to economic and social interpenetration within the Community.[129] The participation is regularly but not necessarily carried out by the setting-up of an independent subsidiary or a dependent branch. This follows from the Treaty[130] as well as from past ECJ's case law[131] and has thus been the decisive criterion of delimitation between the free movement of services and that of establishment. As already elaborated above[132] the Court switched in its most recent case law to a more economically orien-

---

127 For instance Case C-106/91, *Ramrath*, ECR 1992, I-3351, 3381 para 16.

128 *Tietje* (2003), 253 *et seq.*

129 *Lenaerts / van Nuffel* (2005), 188.

130 According to Art 43 EC, freedom of establishment includes *"the right to take up and pursue activities as self-employed persons and to set up and manage undertakings, in particular companies and firms"*.

131 Case C-55/94, *Gebhard*, ECR 1995, I-4165, para 25.

132 See above section II.B.2.e.

tated classification, abandoning the subsidiarity of the free movement of services *vis-à-vis* that of establishment.[133] This makes the criterion of temporality a still valid, but less attractive point of reference.

d. Economic Activity

In contrast to the regulation of the free movement of services under Art 50 EC, the freedom of establishment's Art 43 *et seq* EC do not speak of *"remuneration"*.[134] Nonetheless, the Court has consistently held that the freedom of establishment only applies to "economic activities" in the sense of Art 2 EC. According to Art 2 EC "economic activities" potentially embraces all spheres, including cultural[135], educational[136], religious[137], social[138] and sportive[139] activities. This makes clear that also those activities not primarily exercised for market purposes are protected under the freedom of establishment. Essential though is that these activities are pursued in order to receive some form of remuneration, thus contributing to one's living.[140] Those activities for which no remuneration is envisaged are no economic activities in the sense of Art 2 EC and are excluded from the present freedom. As a result it can be noted that the delimitation between economic and non-economic activities within the free movement of services and the freedom of establishment – under Art 43 *et seq* through cross-reference to Art 2 EC and under Art 49 *et seq* through the notion of remuneration[141] – has to be drawn identically.

To sum up the freedom of establishment's subject matter related scope with the Court's words, is *"the actual pursuit of an eco-*

---

133 *Hatzopoulos / Do* (2006), 930.

134 In the German version of the Treaty the connection is however more obvious than in the English one: Art 49 (2) EC speaks of *"Erwerbstätigkeiten"*.

135 Case C-45/93, *Commission v Spain*, ECR 1994, I-911, 920 para 10.

136 Case 293/83, *Gravier*, ECR 1985, 593, 612 para 19.

137 Case 41/4, *Van Duyn*, ECR 1974, 1337.

138 Case C-70/95, *Sodemare*, ECR 1997, I-3395, 3433 paras 27–33.

139 Joint Cases C-51/96 and C-191/97, *Deliège*, EWS 2000, 405 para 41.

140 *Tietje / Troberg* (2003), para 59.

141 See above section II.B.2.f.

nomic activity through a fixed establishment in another Member State for an indefinite period" of time.[142]

3. Substantive Content of the Freedom of Establishment under Art 43 *et seq* EC

a. Introduction

As regards the substantive content, the present paper's author considers that of the freedom of establishment to be similar to that of the free movement of services. This is insofar true as the freedom of establishment also prohibits to the same extend directly and non-discriminatory national requirements and equally distinguishes between express justifications and those through an overriding requirement of the general interest.[143] The following will thus be limited to introduce the dogmatic foundations and examples from the case law under the freedom of establishment.

b. Discriminatory Measures

The Court repeatedly referred to Section III.A. of the "General Programme for the Abolition of Restrictions on Freedom of Establishment" from 18/12/1961[144] for a listing of forbidden discriminations.[145] Accordingly, Member States' measures only applied to non-nationals are discriminatory, such as the prohibition of certain activities, authorisation requirements, probationary periods, financial requisites, restrictions concerning the access to education, the possibility of equity participation in national companies, nationality considerations as regards the ownership structure or the openness of social security systems. For example national legislation demanding the respective Member State's nationality for the establishment and exercise of the business of private security firms has been declared

---

142 Case C-221/89, *Factortame I*, ECR 1991, I-3905, para 20.

143 For details see above section II.C. Substantive Content of the Free Movement of Services under Art 49 *et seq* EC. Following this uniform approach: *Randelzhofer / Forsthoff* (2004), para 70 *et seq*; *Tietje / Troberg* (2003), para 66 *et seq*. Identifying major differences between the freedom of establishment and that of services: *Jarass* (2002), 141 *et seq*.

144 OJ 1962, 2/36.

145 The Court did so for instance in Case 197/84, *Steinhauser*, ECR 1985, 1819 para 15; Case C-337/97, *Meeusen*, ECR 1999, I-3289 para 27.

violating the freedom of establishment as a discriminatory measure.[146]

c. Non-Discriminatory Measures

The application of the system of general prohibition on restrictions in the context of the freedom of establishment by the Court is a relatively new phenomenon.[147] The non-appliance was most probably motivated through the wording of Art 43, characterising the freedom of establishment as conferring the right to take up and pursue activities *"under the conditions laid down for its own nationals by the law of the country where such establishment is effected"*. Since *Gebhard*[148], however, it is commonly recognised in literature[149] and constantly ruled by the ECJ (see below) that the freedom of establishment also prohibits non-discriminatory measures, thus applying the system of general prohibition on restrictions as defined above under the free movement of services. The following provides for the most common examples of the relevant case law in which the Court qualified a Member State's measure as a non-discriminatory restriction[150]: Ban of certain economic activities (Case C-340/89, *Vlassopoulou*, ECR 1991, I-2357), national monopolies (Case T-266/97, *Vlaamse Televisie*, ZUM 2000, 1077, para 87), residential requirements (Case 33/74, *van Binsbergen*, ECR 1974, 1299, 1309 *et seq*; Case 39/75, *Coenen*, ECR 1975, 1547, 1555) and certain admission related qualification requirements (Case 71/76, *Thieffry*, ECR 1977, 765). As regards the scope of the general prohibition it has to be equally understood as under

---

146 Case C-114/97, *Commission v Spain*, ECR 1998, I-6717.

147 For instance in Case 147/86, *Commission v Greece*, ECR 1988, 1637, the Court found no violation of the freedom of establishment, since the prohibition of certain types of private schools indistinctly applied to Greek and other nationals.

148 Case C-55/94, *Gebhard*, ECR 1995, I-4165.

149 *Randelzhofer / Forsthoff* (2004), para 83 *et seq*; *Barnard* (2004), 231 *et seq*; *Tietje / Troberg* (2003), para 87 *et seq* ; *Kingreen* (2003), 658 *et seq*. With a contrary notion: *Hansen* (2002), 197 *et seq*.

150 Qualifying a Member State's measure as a non-discriminatory restriction signified for the *post-Gebhard* case law only that it was – if not justifiable – violating the freedom of establishment.

the free movement of services, thus affecting only those national measures which *"substantially hinder access to the market"*.[151]

d. The System of Justification

As regards the system of justification the above said under the free movement of services (section B.II.3.d. – The System of Justification) is equally true for the freedom of establishment. Also under the present freedom, only non-discriminatory measures can be justified by an overriding requirement of the general interest (case law based), thus potentially justifying discriminatory measures by Art 46 EC only (Treaty based).[152]

D. State of the Realisation of the EU-Internal Market for Services

1. Introduction

The present section has two principal aims: In the first place it shall give an overview of the fields in which service activities have been regulated by the European Community. To this respect only the legislative act and its scope of application will be presented. In the second place three specific sector-related directives, namely the E-Commerce, Television Broadcasting and the Credit Institutions Directive, shall be analysed in depth hereby identifying the main regulatory instruments used. This shall facilitate the understanding of the SD's envisaged regulatory framework and enable to develop possible regulatory alternatives for those parts of the SD considered inadequate. These three directives have been chosen since they contain the most advanced, in the sense of integrating provisions of all services related secondary legislation.[153]

---

151 *Barnard* (2004), 240.

152 *Randelzhofer / Forsthoff*, (2004), para 108 *et seq*; *Barnard* (2004), 240 *et seq*; *Tietje / Troberg* (2003), para 104 *et seq*.

153 Equally advanced in the field of professional services is Directive 2005/36/EC on the recognition of professional qualifications. It thus does not cover all aspects of professional services but is limited to the question of qualifications necessary for their exercise.

2. EC-Secondary Legislation concerning
the Free Movement of Services

Following the broad understanding of services under the SD[154], the present section considers all secondary legislation âs services related which is, legally speaking, based on the free movement of services only or concerning that freedom and the freedom of establishment as well.[155] To this regard only those legislative acts based on Art 47 (1) and (2), 52, 70–80, 94 and 95 EC shall be taken into consideration.

To start with, legislation on the *mutual recognition of professional qualifications* is one of the most topical centres of gravity of internal market legislation. In the field of recognition of qualifications the originally applicable law distinguished between general legislation – affecting a wide variety of different professional activities – and legislation being applicable to certain specific professions only. This is no longer true since the adoption of Directive 2005/36/EC.[156] Once implemented by the Member States[157] it will replace three general and twelve sectoral directives[158] on the recognition of professional qualifications and will apply to all Member State nationals wishing to exercise a regulated profession[159] in a

---

154 See below section III.E. on the SD's subject matter and scope.

155 Furthermore the presentation is limited to those legislative acts which directly relate to and regulate the exercise of the freedoms mentioned and does not take into account those acts which indirectly facilitate their exercise, such as for instance secondary law in the field of competition, indirect taxation or public procurement.

156 It entered into force on 20th October 2005.

157 The expiry date for transposition is the 20th October 2007.

158 Repealing Directives 77/452/EEC, 77/453/EEC, 78/686/EEC, 78/687/ EEC, 78/1026/EEC, 78/1027/EEC, 80/154/EEC, 80/155/EEC, 85/384/ EEC, 85/432/EEC, 85/433/EEC, 89/48/EEC, 92/51/EEC, 93/16/EEC and 1999/42/EC. They concerned the professions of doctor, nurse, dental practitioner, veterinary surgeon, midwife, pharmacist and architect.

159 Art 3 (1) (a) of Dir 2005/36/EC: "*A regulated profession comprises a professional activity or group of professional activities, access to which, the pursuit of which, or one of the modes of pursuit of which is subject, directly or indirectly, by virtue of legislative, regulatory or administrative provisions to the possession of specific professional qualifications; in particular, the use of a professional title limited by*

Member State other than that in which they obtained their professional qualifications, on either a self-employed or employed basis.

As regards other EC-legislation aiming at realising the free movement of services, a sectoral structure is still in widespread use.[160] In the *energy sector*, two directives primarily establish common rules relating to the organisation and functioning of the internal market for electricity and gas.[161]

Several legislative acts aim at deepening the internal market for *transportation services*. As regards *road transportation*, Council Regulation 684/92/EEC establishes common rules for the international carriage of passengers by coach and bus and is supplemented by Regulation 11/98/EC concerning own-account transport operators who are entitled, in their State of establishment, to carry passengers by coach and bus and who meet the conditions for admission to the occupation and the road safety criteria. As regards *railway transportation*, Directives 91/440/EC, 2001/12/EC, 2001/13/EC and 2001/14/EC facilitate the adoption of the Community railway services to the needs of the Single Market. *Maritime transportation services* are primarily regulated through Council Regulation 4055/86/EEC applying the principle of freedom to provide services to maritime transport between Member States and between Member States and third countries[162], Council Regulation 3577/92/EEC applying the freedom to provide services to maritime transport within Member States only, Council Regulation 3921/91/EEC laying down the conditions under which non-resident carriers may transport goods or passengers by inland waterway within a Member State and Council Regulation 1356/96/EC on common rules applicable to the transport of goods or passengers by inland waterway between Member States. Also a proposal on the further integration of port services has been released by the European Commission in 2004.[163] Relevant legislation in the field of *air*

---

   legislative, regulatory or administrative provisions to holders of a given professional qualification shall constitute a mode of pursuit."

160 This is of course not true for the envisaged SD, explicitly aiming at an horizontal scope.

161 Directives 96/92/EC on electricity and 98/30/EC on gas.

162 Such as for instance the right to carry passengers or goods by sea between any port of a Member State and any port or off-shore installation of another Member State or of a non-Community country.

163 COM(2004)654 final.

transportation services are Council Regulation 2407/92/EC which aims to lay down transparent, non-discriminatory rules on the criteria for economic and technical competency which must be met before air carriers can be granted licences to operate in the Community and Council Regulation 2408/92/EEC on access for Community air carriers to intra-Community air routes. Several other Council Regulations set out to liberalise price formation for Community air services.

In the field of the *information society, electronic communication services* have been at the centre of extensive regulation. These are services and/or networks which are concerned with the conveyance of signals by wire, radio, optical or other electromagnetic means, including therefore, the broadcasting of radio and television programmes. Most prominently in this context are Directive 2002/21/EC on a common regulatory framework for electronic communications networks and services (Framework Directive), Directive 2002/20/EC on the authorisation of electronic communications networks and services (Authorisation Directive), Directive 2002/22/EC on universal service and users' rights relating to electronic communications networks and services (Universal Service Directive), Directive 2002/19/EC on access to, and interconnection of, electronic communications networks and associated facilities (Access Directive) and Decision 676/2002/EC of the European Parliament and of the Council on a regulatory framework for radio spectrum policy in the European Community (Radio Spectrum Decision). Furthermore, a legislative act within the information society relevant to the free movement of services is Directive 2000/31/EC on *electronic commerce (e-commerce)* in the Internal Market. It sets up a legal framework to improve the legal security of such commerce in order to increase the confidence of Internet users by making information society services subject to the principles of the internal market and by introducing a limited number of harmonised measures.

In the field of *postal services* especially Directive 97/67/EC amended by Directive 2002/39/EC and Regulation (EC) 1882/2003 eestablish common rules concerning the provision of a universal postal service and the criteria defining the services which may be reserved for universal service providers and the conditions governing the provision of non-reserved services.

Legislative acts concerning *financial services* are comparably comprehensive, if not the most comprehensive ones, including banking, insurance and securities legislation.[164] In the field of banking, Directive 2006/48/EC legislates for the taking-up and pursuit of the business of *credit institutions*[165], Directive 2002/92/EC provides for insurance mediation to improve the working of the single market in *insurance* by ensuring that retail markets are accessible and secure and Directive 2004/39/EC on *markets in financial instruments*[166] sets up a comprehensive regulatory regime for the organised execution of investor transactions by stock markets, other trading systems and investment firms.

3. Different Regulatory Approaches Put to Test

a. Electronic Commerce Directive (2000/31/EC)

As just mentioned above, the aim of the e-commerce directive is to set up a comprehensive legal framework for all services provided remotely, usually for payment, by electronic means between enterprises and enterprises and consumers. Such services include *inter alia* the following on-line activities: entertainment, marketing, advertising, internet access and databases services. The directive only applies to service providers[167] established in the European Union. The directive contains two major types of provision, the first under Chapter I laying down the applicable law for service provision un-

---

164 Due to their extensive number only Directive 2006/48/EC of the banking sector is discussed. Others, thus, such as the Financial Conglomerates Directive (2002/87/EC) or Directive 2001/24/EC on the reorganisation and winding up of credit institutions are left aside.

165 Current Directive 2006/48/EC (entered into force on 20 July 2006 and is applicable since 1 January 2007) recasts Directive 2000/12/EC which has replaced the consolidated Directives 73/183/EEC, 77/780/EEC, 89/646/EEC, 89/299/EEC, 89/646/EEC, 89/647/EEC, 92/30/EEC and 92/121/EEC. There are other legislative acts relevant in the field of banking which are not mentioned here, such as for instance Directive 2000/46/EC on the taking-up, pursuit of and prudential supervision of the business of electronic money institutions or Council Directive 97/5/EC on cross-border credit transfers. For a listing of EC-financial services legislation, see: *Hemetsberger et al.* (2006) and *Usher* (2000).

166 Amending Directives 85/611/EEC, 93/6/EEC, Directive 2000/12/EC and repealing Directive 93/22/EEC.

167 Art 2 (b) of the Directive: Any natural or legal person providing an information society service.

der the coordinated field[168] and Chapter II providing for harmonisation measures.

aa. Taking up, Pursuit and Control of the Service Activity

The Directive's scope affects the free movement of e-commerce services without establishment as well as the freedom of establishment for e-commerce service providers. To this respect it rehulates the taking up and the pursuit of a service activity.[169] These phases of the service provision include, on the one hand authorisation, qualification, and notification procedures and requirements concerning the behaviour of the service provider, the quality or content of the service including those applicable to advertising and contracts and requirements concerning the liability of the service provider on the other hand. For these phases Art 3 (2) 2000/31/EC requires the Member State in which the service provision is received (host state) to leave its restrictive regulation unapplied.[170] In fact the stipulation of non-appliance of the host State's legal order as far as restrictive, combined with the possibility of derogation for certain policy reasons (see this section below) represents a formulation of the General Prohibition on Restrictions System as under today's Treaty and case-law based system. The main difference compared to today's general prohibition system under the Treaty and case law actually lies within the quantity of derogations admitted. Further evidence shall be delivered below under section III.I.5.b. "Excursus: The Country of Origin Principle and the Sys-

---

168 According to Art 2 (i), the coordinated field comprises the taking up of the activity of an information society service, such as requirements concerning qualifications, authorisation or notification, and the pursuit of the activity of an information society service, such as requirements concerning the behaviour of the service provider, requirements regarding the quality or content of the service including those applicable to advertising and contracts, or requirements concerning the liability of the service provider.

169 Art 2 (i) 2000/31/EC. Various clauses, excepting different subject matters from the directive's scope, such as its Art 1 (5) and the Annex ("*Exceptions from Article 3*"), have to be kept in mind but cannot be further analysed in the present context.

170 Art 3 (2) reads: "*Member States may not, for reasons falling within the coordinated field, restrict the freedom to provide information society services from another Member State*".

tem of General Prohibition on Restrictions – A Terminological Clarification".

As the directive's coordinated field comprises – according to Art 2 (i) 2000/31/EC – all aspects of the taking up and the pursuit of an e-commerce service activity there has been uncertainty whether the prohibition on restrictions system is also relevant for private international law related to e-commerce services.[171] This has to be denied due to Art 1 (4) 2000/31/EC, stipulating that the "*Directive does not establish additional rules on private international law*". The general prohibition thus only applies to those national laws, rules and regulations which are not subject to private international law norms. This leaves the prohibition's scope primarily open to national supervisory regulation relating to mandatory public law rules. The exclusion of private international law however does not affect its relationship to the general Treaty provisions and related case law under the free movement of services and freedom of establishment. Indeed private international law provisions still have to be measured against the general prohibition on restrictions under these two freedoms.

For those parts of the legal order affected by the general prohibition, it is not just the home state's legal order which is relevant for the taking up and pursuit of a service activity. The home state is simultaneously responsible for exercising control over the service provider's compliance with these rules.[172] The home state's control competence is exclusive, allowing the host Member State to interfere within certain limits only in case of home state's failure to act.[173]

The host Member State can derogate from the general prohibition rule and related home State control by applying its own legal order to a service, service provider or recipient in case that service prejudices or represents a serious and grave risk of prejudice to public policy, the protection of public health, public security, in-

---

171 For the different arguments brought forward in literature on this point, see for instance *Hellner* (2004).

172 Art 3 (1) of the directive states that "*each Member State shall ensure that the information society services provided by a service provider established on its territory comply with the national provisions applicable in the Member State in question which fall within the coordinated field*".

173 Art 3 (4) (b) and (5) 2000/31/EC.

cluding the safeguarding of national security and defense and the protection of consumers. The appliance of the own legal order must be proportionate and is legitimate only as far as necessary for the achievement of one of the before mentioned objectives.[174]. In comparison to today's possibilities of justifications under the general prohibition of restriction under the Treaty and case law, no overriding requirement of the general interest can be brought forward anymore. This signifies a far reaching reduction for the host Member State to evoke its own national legal order, especially under the light of today's open number of possible overriding requirements.

ab. Accompanying Measures

Beside the above presented core provisions of Directive 2000/31/EC, it includes several additional legislative measures aiming at harmonising Member States' laws within the coordinated field. These measures include that *"Member States shall ensure that the taking up and pursuit of the activity of an information society service provider may not be made subject to prior authorisation or any other requirement having equivalent effect"*[175], that *"Member States ensure that the service provider shall render certain information, easily, directly and permanently accessible to the recipients of the service and competent authorities"*[176], certain measures concerning commercial communication for information society services[177], the legal circumstances and admissibility of contracts to be concluded by electronic means[178] and the liability of hosting[179]. It is important to point out that these harmonisation measures equally apply to service providers and provision taking place without any cross-border element, thus not affecting any of the EC-fundamental freedoms.

b. Television Broadcasting Services

The Television Broadcasting Directive 89/552/EEC substantially amended by Directive 97/36/EC turns out to be similarly drafted as before discussed E-Commerce Directive. Consequently, only its

---

174 Art 3 (4) (a) 2000/31/EC.

175 Art 4 (1) 200/31/EC.

176 Art 5 2000/31/EC.

177 Art 6 *et seq* 2000/31/EC.

178 Art 9 *et seq* 2000/31/EC.

179 Art 12 *et seq* 2000/31/EC.

main features shall be high-lightened in the present section in order
to avoid redundancies. The Directive at hand constitutes the legal
framework for television broadcasting in the internal market. This
however only concerns the freedom to provide and receive broadcasting services and does not affect the freedom of establishment
for broadcasting service suppliers.[180] As regards the *taking-up and
pursuit* of television services, the Directive's Art 2a requires legislation (rules, laws, decisions etc) of the Member States where the
television broadcaster[181] is not established but provides its broadcasting services not to be restrictive (for possible derogations see
below).[182] According to Art 2 (1) 97/36/EC, broadcasting services
have to comply with the legislation of the Member State where the
broadcaster is established, has its head office and editorial decisions
are taken, only.[183] The host Member States has to this regard leave
its restrictive legislation unapplied. Additionally, the home Member
State is – in principle – exclusively competent for *supervision* on a
Community wide level, too.

This all is only true as far as restrictions are enacted *"for reasons which fall within the fields coordinated by this Directive"*.
Whereas the coordinated field under the E-Commerce Directive is
defined by generally referring to the taking-up and pursuit of an
information society service – besides marginal exceptions –, the
Television Broadcasting Directive follows a different structure. It
indeed coordinates the taking-up and pursuit only with respect to
certain aspects of broadcasting services, such as the content of
television programmes[184], television advertising and sponsorship[185]

---

180 This must be deduced from the fact that the Directive's central provi-
     sions – Art 2 and 2a – only concern the free movement of services.
     See also Recital 44 of Directive 97/36/EC.

181 For a definition of broadcaster see Art 1 (b) 89/552/EEC.

182 Art 2a reads to this regard: *"Member States shall ensure freedom of
     reception and shall not restrict transmissions on their territory of
     television broadcasts from other Member States (…)."*

183 Art 2 reads to this regard: *"Each Member State shall ensure that all
     television broadcasts transmitted by broadcasters under its jurisdic-
     tion comply with the rules of the system of law applicable to broad-
     casts intended for the public in that Member State."*

184 Art 4–9 89/552/EEC.

185 Art 10–21 89/552/EEC.

and the protection of minors and public order[186] (*coordinated field*). Similarly to the E-Commerce Directive presented before, Art 2a in connection with Art 2 thus enshrine – as regards the coordinated field – a general prohibition on restriction. Likewise to the E-Commerce Directive also the current Directive's general prohibition on restrictions – with its limited scope on certain aspects of broadcasting – only concerns national supervisory regulation relating to mandatory public law rules, not private international law.

Even though if a national restrictive measure of the host Member State fell under the coordinated field, it could still be upheld and thus *derogate from the general prohibition on restrictions* as regards the taking-up, the pursuit and the supervision of the broadcasting service under the conditions laid down in Art 2a 97/36/EC. It primarily states that derogation is possible in case the foreign television broadcaster includes programmes which do not adequately protect minors as circumscribed in the Directive's Art 22 or contain incitement to hatred on grounds of race, sex, religion or nationality and the home Member State does not or not sufficiently exercise its supervision powers. In case the broadcasting provider fails to comply with the home Member State rules in the course of exercising the free movement of services and the home Member State does not succeed in stopping it to do so, the host Member State can introduce and enforce its national legislation, too.[187]

Besides, the Directive at stake contains elaborate rules harmonising the coordinated field, however leaving Member States the possibility to enact stricter rules for broadcasting services under their jurisdiction (minimum harmonisation duty for home Member States). National restrictions affecting other aspects of cross-border broadcasting services in the Internal Market, thus, must not be measures against the Directive's standards, such as the limited possibilities of exceptions from the general prohibition system , but at those of general Treaty rules and case-law.

c. Financial Services – Credit Institutions

ca. Introduction

The EU financial services industry has been one of the first economic sectors increasingly focusing on European-wide cross-border

---

186 Art 22 and 23 89/552/EEC.

187 Art 2a (2) 89/552/EEC.

activities. From a legal perspective, their business activity has initially been Treaty-based – on the free movement of services and the
freedom of establishment – only. Soon, however, the relevant market players had to realise that the EC-primary legal framework
alone did not satisfy their business needs. Indeed, the basic Treaty
rules on the freedom to provide services and establishment did not
mean that a financial service undertaking trading lawfully in one
Member State was able to operate in another Member State without
facing a considerable additional amount of rules and complying
with the host State's local rules.[188] This legal shortcoming led to
extensive EC-secondary legislation in the field of financial services,
including credit institutions, insurance companies and investment
funds[189]. The relevant legislation – with its core acts Directive
2006/48/EC relating to the taking up and pursuit of the business of
credit institutions, Directive 2002/83/EC concerning life insurance[190], Directive 73/239/EEC on the taking-up and pursuit of the
business of direct insurance other than life assurance[191] and Directive 2004/39/EC on markets in financial instruments – is founded
on both, the freedom of establishment and the free movement of
services, and follows similar regulatory concepts in all these three
fields of financial services. The basic technique chosen was to
abandon the idea of progressive harmonisation of regulatory standards for the admission of the service provider (credit institution
etc) into other Member States' markets. Instead the introduction of
the Country of Origin Principle for the taking-up of the service
business was chosen. This has become known as the "*European
Passport*" for financial services.[192] The "European Passport" however is limited to the taking-up of the business (authorisation requirements) and does not apply to the exercise of the respective
freedom and the supervision process. Within the latter two a similar
regulatory technique as within the E-Commerce and the Television
Broadcasting Directive is adopted: Today's general prohibition on

---

188 *Usher* (2000), 90. Case C-222/95, *Parodi v. Banque de Bary*, ECR
      1997, I-3899.

189 They mainly consist of Undertakings for Collective Investment in
      Transferable Securities (UCITS).

190 OL L 345, 19/12/2002, 1–51.

191 OJ L 228, 16/08/1973, 3–19.

192 *Dalhuisen* (2000), 818 *et seq.*

restrictions system with specific modifications. Due to their principal analogousness only one of the financial services legislation – namely the business of credit institutions – shall be exemplarily analysed in the following section.

cb. The Business of Credit Institutions
under EC-Secondary Legislation

Although there also exists other relevant EC-secondary legislation affecting the business of credit institutions in the Internal Market[193], above mentioned Directive 2006/48/EC[194] is the essential instrument as regards the taking-up, the pursuit and the supervision of credit institutions[195] operating in a cross-border context based on the free movement of services and the freedom of establishment.

The *taking-up of the business of credit institutions* is regulated under the Directive's Art 6 *et seq.* It enshrines that all Member States must oblige credit institutions to obtain an authorisation – which depends on several requirements prescribed in the Directive such as initial capital, reputation, adequate infrastructure and systems, the shareholders and members structures, the management body and place of the head office of credit institutions and programme of operations and structural organisations[196] – before commencing financial services activities as defined under the Directive's Annex I.[197] Annex I includes all major service activities regularly exercised by credit institutions, such as "*acceptance of deposits and other repayable funds, lending, financial leasing,*

---

193 For a comprehensive analysis of the EC-law relating to the business of credit institutions before 1992, see: *Griller* (1992). For a compilation of relevant EC-law, see: *Gerster et al.* (2006).

194 Legal basis as stated in the directive: in particular first and third sentences of Art 47 (2).

195 A credit institution is defined under Art 4 (1) 2006/48/EC as "*(a) an undertaking whose business is to receive deposits or other repayable funds from the public and to grant credits for its own account*" and "*(b) an electronic money institution within the meaning of Directive 2000/46/EC* ". Art 1 (1) states that "*this Directive lays down rules concerning the taking up and pursuit of the business of credit institutions, and their prudential supervision.*"

196 Art 9 *et seq* 2006/48/EC.

197 Art 14 2006/48/EC: Every authorisation shall be notified to the European Commission, which shall be published in the Official Journal of the European Communities.

money transmission services, guarantees and commitments" and others. This authorisation has to be issued by that Member State where the credit institution as a legal person[198] has its registered head office.[199] Once granted, the authorisation has to be accepted in and the credit institution admitted to every other Member State's national market in order to exercise the freedom of establishment[200] and to provide services according to Art 23 2006/48/EC.[201] It namely states that host Member States must ensure that *"the activities listed in Annex I may be carried on within their territories (…) either by the establishment of a branch or by the way of the provision of services, by any credit institution authorised and supervised by the competent authorities*" of the home Member State. It thus defines that credit institutions are to be *"authorised and supervised by the competent authorities*" of the home Member State only. This formulation – non appliance of the own legal order and mandatory exertion of the host Member State's legal order – represents the first and only example of the Country of Origin Principle (CoOP) in existing secondary EC-legislation ("European Passport"). It further includes the supervision by the home Member State with respect to the authorisation. It is clear from the text however that this CoOP is limited to the authorisation of credit institutions as defined under Title II (Art 6 – 22) 2006/48/EC, comprising *inter alia* initial capital, reputation, adequate

---

198 In case the credit institution is not a legal person it must have its head office there.

199 Recital 10 of Directive 2006/48/EC. The authorisation shall not be granted or withdrawn in case a credit institution has opted for the legal system of one Member State for the purpose of evading the stricter standards in force in another Member State within whose territory it carries on or intends to carry on the greater part of its activities.

200 It is important to stress the fact that the Directive's scope under the freedom of establishment only covers legally dependent branches, not legally independent subsidiaries.

201 Art 24 2006/48/EC substantially corresponds to Art 23 but takes into account the special situations of financial institutions which are undertakings other than credit institutions, the principal activity of which is to acquire holdings (Art 4(5) 2006/48/EC). In the following text only credit institutions will be considered, although most of the provisions applicable to them are equally valid for financial institutions.

infrastructure and systems, the shareholders and members structures, the management body and place of the head office of credit institutions and programme of operations and structural organisations.

The *exercise of the business* of credit institutions *post-authorisation* in the host Member State either by means of the freedom of establishment of a branch or by the freedom to provide services is similarly structured. The credit institution also has to notify its intention to its home Member State authorities.[202] This notification then has to be communicated by the home State authorities to those of the host Member State. The latter has to indicate which of its national rules and laws shall apply – *"in the interest of the general good[203],"* – to the pursuit of the business of the credit institution in accordance with the powers transferred to it under Art 29 – 37 2006/48/EC (*"Powers of the competent authorities of the host Member State"*).[204] Beside these rules and laws – which have to be notified to the credit institution, the affected Member States, the European Commission and the Banking Advisory Committee – the *host* Member State's national legal order may not restrict the foreign service provider[205].[206] Consequently, the Directive adopts within the rules of exercise for credit institutions the Treaty's and case law's general prohibition on requirements. The decisive difference, however, lies within the fact that the host Member State has to define in advance which national restrictive legislation it wants to uphold. This deprives it of the possibility to enact any national restriction possibly justified through an overriding requirement of

---

202 Art 25 (1) 2006/48/EC.

203 The notion of "general good" can be equated with the above introduced terminology of "general interest".

204 Art 26 (1) 2006/48/EC.

205 Following from the above said, this is only true insofar as activities of Annex I are concerned.

206 Although in the securities and insurance industries regulation concerning the pursuit of the business, which means concerning the service itself instead of the service provider, is much more extensive, *post-authorisation* regulation is still relevant for the banking industry. This is especially true as regards more sophisticated banking services, such as in the areas of derivates and mortgage credit. See *Dalhuisen*, (2000), 718.

the general interest (=interest of the general good) at any later point of time without prior notification.

As far as *supervision* is concerned, Directive 2006/48/EC principally empowers the Member State which has issued the credit institution's authorisation, in other words the home Member State. For that purpose the Directive includes detailed minimum provisions on what supervision has to consist of and how it must be exercised.[207] The home State is principally competent for supervision of the financial institution in case of both, establishment of a branch as well as exercise of the freedom to provide services.[208] Besides, the *host* Member State remains competent as supervisory power under the following two constellations: Firstly, as regards branches under the freedom of establishment the host Member State is exclusively competent for the supervision of those rules and laws which it has lawfully applied to the foreign financial institution's branch in the interest of the general good.[209] Secondly, the host Member State may exercise supervisory power in case the financial institution does not comply with the rules and laws of the home Member State either under the freedom to provide services or of establishment and the home Member States fails to fulfill its supervisory obligations.[210] The host State's supervisory action must be necessary to prevent that institution from initiating further transactions within its territory. The presented regulation concerning the supervision powers equates the Treaty and case law-based status quo under the general prohibition on restrictions. Also under the latter those rules, laws etc lawfully applied by the home Member State are to be supervised by that State only.

Above presented provisions of Directive 2006/48/EC concerning all three phases of a credit institution's business – taking-up, pursuit and supervision process – only apply as far as supervisory regulation relating to mandatory public law rules are concerned. Consequently private international law norms, such as the

---

207 Art 40 – 149 2006/48/EC.

208 Art 40 2006/48/EC insofar states: "*The prudential supervision of a credit institution (…) shall be the responsibility of the competent authorities of the home Member State, without prejudice to those provisions of the Directive which give responsibility to the competent authorities of the host Member State.*"

209 Art 26 (1) 2006/48/EC.

210 Art 30 *et seq* 2006/48/EC.

law applicable to credit contracts, remain unaffected by the current Directive's regulatory content.

d. Summary

The regulatory technique chosen within the three EC-secondary legislative acts introduced before – E-Commerce, Television Broadcasting and Credit Institutions Directive – resemble each other to a large extend. All three affect the taking-up, the exercise and the supervision of the respective service provision by adopting the general prohibition on restrictions system as known under today's case law. The only, but decisive difference compared to today's case law lies within the extend of the possibility for the host Member State to justify prohibited restrictions. While under today's Treaty and case law based system an open-ended quantity of requirements of the general interest can principally be evoked, the secondary legislation at stake drastically curtails this possibility. The E-Commerce Directive, for instance, merely permits justification for restriction(s) through reasons of public policy, health and security and the Television Broadcasting Directive only acknowledges the protection of minors and the prevention of incitements to hatred on ground of race, sex and so on and so forth. Additionally, all three secondary legislative acts only relate to supervisory regulation relating to mandatory public law rules, not private international law and contain substantive harmonisation provisions. All establish detailed requirements which need to be respected by the home Member State when authorising and thus letting a service provider taking up its business. And they foresee minimum standards as regards the exercising and the content of supervision.

Beside this common approach one important exception has to be noted[211]: The Credit Institutions Directive stipulates for market access regulation (authorisation requirements) under both modes of supply, the freedom of establishment and the free movement of services, the Country of Origin Principle. For further details on the distinction between the System of General Prohibition on Restrictions and the Country of Origin Principle see below section III.I.5.b.

---

211 Another exception concerns the regulation of the exercise of the business of credit institutions in the context of the freedom of establishment under the Credit Institutions Directive which takes over all justifications through an overriding requirement of the general interest of today's case law.

III. The Services Directive (SD) – A Legal Analysis

A. Introduction

1. The Notion of the "Service Directive (SD)"

When referring to the "Services Directive (SD)", this paper means the version of the directive as published in the Official Journal of the European Union L 376/36, 27.12.2006: Directive 2006/123/EC of the European Parliament and of the Council of 12 December 2006 on services in the internal market. In contrast, Draft Services Directive 2004 ("DSD 2004") means the proposal for a Directive of the European Parliament and of the Council on services in the internal market, COM(2004) 2 final/3 of 5 March 2004. Draft Services Directive 2006 ("DSD 2006") means the amended proposal for a Directive of the European Parliament and of the Council on services in the internal market, COM(2006) 160 final of 4 April 2006.

2. The Directive's Structure and Main Regulatory Content

For the purpose of a simplified understanding of the detailed analysis of the Directive in the chapters to come, its overall structure shall be briefly outlined in this section. From a formal point of view, the Directive is organised in eight chapters – *"General Provisions"* (I), *"Administrative Simplification"* (II), *"Freedom of Establishment for Services Providers"* (III), *"Free movement of services"* (IV), *"Quality of Services"* (V), *"Administrative Cooperation"* (VI), *"Convergence Program"* (VII) and *"Final Provisions"* (VIII) – and subdivided in 46 Articles (Art 1–46). Besides, 118 recitals (Recital 1–118) complete the legal text.

From a substantial point of view the Directive aims at facilitating transnational service provision in the EU-Internal Market by eliminating existing legal and other barriers, preventing new ones to be established, and enhancing legal certainty for service providers and consumers.[212] Service provision is understood as any self-employed economic activity, normally provided for remuneration.[213] Although the Directive is meant to be horizontal as regards its

---

212 See below under section III.D. the analysis of the Directive's subject matter.

213 For a detailed definition of the term *"service"*, see below section III.E.1.

scope, many types of services are excluded from it, either because they are already part of EC-secondary legislation (such as financial services) or because they shall be regulated in separated acts in the future (such as healthcare services) or simply because they are considered to be politically too sensitive (such as services provided by notaries.) The Directive principally follows the existing legal structure of the EC-Treaty. It grasps cross-border services activities through distinguishing between those service providers moving from one Member State to another one in order to become established there for the purpose of service provision – covered by the freedom of establishment – and those providers returning to their country of origin after the accomplished provision – covered by the free movement of services.[214] These two freedoms are reshaped through the Directive's central Chapters III (*"Freedom of establishment for providers"*) and IV (*"Free movement of services"*). While the Directive's stipulations under Chapter III principally merely codify today's regulatory system under the Treaty and the ECJ's case law, Chapter IV reduces the host Member State's possibilities for a lawful introduction of restrictions. Both ways of service provision in the internal market are additionally enhanced through the introduction of provisions on administrative simplification (Chapter II) and administrative cooperation (Chapter VI). While under Chapter II mainly procedural provisions are enshrined, Chapter VI on administrative cooperation stipulates the division of supervisory powers as regards the exercise of the free movement of services. Issues of consumer protection are addressed through Chapter V on the Quality of Services. The Directive concludes with Chapter VII on Convergence Program, most notably containing a Member States' screening duty regarding potential barriers to service provisions in their legal orders, and Chapter VIII on Final Provisions.

B. The Directive's Naissance – The Political and Legal Background

1. The Political Intention

For understanding the Directive's basic regulatory approach it is essential to refer to the history and reasons for its naissance first. The relevant starting point dates back to the Lisbon Extraordinary

---

214 Compare the Directive's subject matter under Art 1 (1).

European Council from 23 to 24 March 2000[215], where the Council's conclusions set the bold target for the European Union to become the most competitive and dynamic, knowledge-based economy in the world by 2010. To achieve this ambitious goal, the Union must – beside others, but primarily – improve the framework conditions for Europe's services industries, especially by enhancing the functioning of the internal market for services. This will essentially determine the continuing success of the European economy. To this regard the Council invited the Commission to propose a comprehensive internal market strategy to remove barriers to services.

To this respect the Commission submitted the *"Internal Market Strategy for Services"* in 2000[216] which represented a continuation of the Single Market Action Plan from 1997 and the Strategy for Europe's Internal Market.[217] The core declaration therein called for clarifying whether *"there are unjustifiable and preventable barriers preventing services being bought or sold across borders"* and for developing *"legislative measures to dismantle remaining barriers and prevent the emergence of new ones"*. The Commission consequently published a report on *"The State of the Internal Market for Services"*[218] in 2002 as *"a basis for actions that will be launched at a second stage in 2003"*.[219] This report was the last formal and public action of the Commission before the issuance of the first proposal of a Services Directive in January 2004. It identified those obstacles most impedimental in the Commission's eyes to the functioning of an internal market for services. Any evaluation concerning the achievement of the Directive's initial purpose must thus be measured against this report. It shall therefore be analysed in depth.[220]

---

215 DOC/00/8.

216 European Commission, An Internal Market Strategy for Services, COM(2000) 888 of 29.12.2000.

217 COM(1999) 624 final of 24.11.1999.

218 COM(2002) 441 final of 30.7.2002.

219 *Ibidem*, 5.

220 For the purpose of analysis the report will be summarised in the sections to come focusing on the most relevant aspects for the present study.

2. Identified Obstacles to the Service Provision in the EU-Internal Market According to the "State of the Internal Market for Services" Report

a. Introduction

It shall be preliminarily remarked that the *"State of the Internal Market for Services"* report is based on an horizontal approach covering a large variety of service activities and analyses the entire business process of service activities ranging from establishment of the service provider (if established abroad), use of inputs necessary for the provision of the service, promotion, distribution and selling of services to the after-sales phase. The report thus covers the whole range of difficulties perceived as obstacles by the providers and users of services, but – and this is essential – *"does not at present seek to assess whether they are compatible with Community law. This question will form part of the second stage of the strategy which will propose solutions*[221]*"*, ie the proposed Services Directive.

Bearing this constraint in mind the Commission structured its report by first dividing the identified barriers in two groups, namely legal and non-legal barriers.[222] It secondly tried to systematise the barriers of the first group by analyzing *"the Common Origin of the Legal Barriers"*.[223] Finally it assessed the impact of the barriers on the European economy.[224]

b. Identified Barriers

ba. Legal Barriers

The identified barriers, especially the legal ones, shall be looked at more closely. The term "legal barriers" *"covers all obstacles to the development of service activities between Member States deriving directly or indirectly from a legal constraint and which are liable to prohibit, impede or otherwise render less advantageous such activities"*.[225] Following the business process, the report identifies as legal barriers relating to the *establishment of service providers*

---

221 COM(2002) 441 final of 30.7.2002, 5.

222 *Ibidem*, 14 *et seq.*

223 *Ibidem*, 45 *et seq.*

224 *Ibidem*, 55 *et seq.*

225 *Ibidem*, 14.

"monopolies and other quantitative restrictions on access to activities", *"nationality or residence requirements"*, *"authorisation and registration procedures"*, *"restrictions on multidisciplinary activities"*, *"legal form and internal structure of economic operators"*, *"professional qualifications"* and *"conditions governing the exercise of service activities"*[226]. Barriers relating to the *use of inputs necessary for the provision of services* have been put forward in connection with *"posting of workers"*, *"use of employment agencies or temporary workers from other Member States"*, *"cross border use of business services"*, and *"cross border use of equipment and material"*.[227] In connection with the *promotion of services* the following barriers are mentioned: *"Authorisation, registration and declaration procedures"*, *"bans on commercial communications"*, *"content of commercial communications"*, *"form of commercial communications"* and *"non-commercial communications"*.[228] The barriers listed in the report concerning the *distribution of services* are substantially the same as those relating to the establishment of service providers.[229] This is the case since the barriers to the "distribution of services" do not relate to the distribution services *strictu senso* but are those encountered in the cross-border provision of all services. In this context, the term "distribution of services" can thus be equated – in principle – with the exercise of the free movement of services under Art 49 *et seq* EC. Barriers within the phase of *sale of services* are linked directly or indirectly to the transaction in question. They embrace the *"formation and content of contracts"*,

---

226 It is important to mention that the „*conditions governing the exercise of service activities*" are only those which substantially affect and negatively influence the service provider's decision for establishment abroad.

227 *Ibidem*, 21–27.

228 *Ibidem*, 27–29.

229 *Ibidem*, 30–35: Barriers listed are: *"Monopolies and other quantitative restrictions on access to activities"*, *"nationality or residence requirements"*, *"authorisation and registration procedures"*, *"restrictions on multidisciplinary activities"*, *"legal form and internal structure of economic operators"*, *"professional qualifications"* and *"conditions governing the exercise of service activities"*. Additionally the barrier *"restriction on the receipt of services"* is mentioned.

"*price setting, payments, invoicing and accounting*", "*taxation*"[230], "*reimbursement, subsidy or aid to the service recipient*" and "*public contracts and concessions*".[231] As regards barriers to the *after sales aspects of services* "*liability and professional indemnity insurance of service providers*", "*debt collection*", "*provision of after-sales services*" and "*legal redress*" are cited.

In the following some *practical examples* for the before listed barriers within the single stages of the business process shall be given:[232] Examples for barriers in the phase of *establishment* of the service provider and the distribution of services are "*differences in practices and requirements for establishing a company, requirements for authorisation to provide services within a national territory, requirements concerning a physical outlet for service provision, differences in logistics, warehousing, conditions for the retail trade, postal services, home delivery, requirements for an access to infrastructure allowing the reception of services and lack of confidence in delivery systems*". Examples for barriers in the stage of *use of inputs* necessary for the provision of services are "*differences in practices and requirements for labor services recruitment, cross-border information on local skills availability, use of financial services by companies, provision of funding services, and differences in access to business and professional services*". Exemplary barriers within the *promotion of services* represent "*differences in how companies are permitted to use advertising, sales promotion, public relation and sponsorship services and the regulation of disclosure requirements*". Barrier examples for the *sale of services* process are "*national pricing regimes and health, safety and security concerns*". As regards the *after-sales support* barriers appear as rules for "*in-house customer services and customer complaint handling, extra-judicial redress mechanisms outside the firm, cross-border judicial redress systems and liability issues*".

bb. Non-Legal Barriers

All those barriers which can not be directly or indirectly derived from a legal constraint are defined as non-legal. The report men-

---

230 The payment and reimbursement of VAT is one of the problems most frequently cited in relation to the cross-border provision of services.

231 European Commission, COM(2000) 888, 35–40.

232 The examples are taken from: European Commission, COM(2000) 888, 6.

tions two categories, those resulting from a *"lack of information"*, such as missing knowledge on the fundamental principles of the internal market, and those related to *"language and cultural diversity"* between Member States.[233]

3. The Common Reasons of the Legal Barriers
– Member States' Failure and Structural Shortcomings

In order to evaluate any Community (legislative) measure aiming at eliminating the above presented barriers to service provision in the internal market, their common origin must be analysed. Only a strategy focusing on erasing the origin of the identified barriers will face lasting and sustainable success. The Commission's report names three reasons, namely the *"lack of mutual trust between Member States"*, the *"protection of national economic interests"* and the *"resistance to modernisation of the national legal frameworks"*.[234]

The *lack of mutual trust between Member States* regularly concerns the quality of the legal system of another Member State, founded on a lack of transparency and administrative co-operation between the Member States and in certain fields from a lack of harmonisation of the national rules, reflected in an excessive disparity between the levels and ways of protection of the general (public) interest guaranteed by the national systems. The *defense of interests of the national economy* remains firmly anchored in most of the Member States. The established case law of the Court, according to which *"measures constituting a restriction of the free provision of services cannot be justified by objectives of an economic nature such as the protection of national undertakings"*, is consistently violated.[235] In most cases Member States are willing to change their protectionist attitude only when being individually convicted by the Court. The third reason of origin for the malfunctioning of the service provision between Member States named by the Commission represents the *"resistance to modernisation of the national legal frameworks"*. Certainly, to a certain degree, the resistance to modernisation can also be explained by and founded on the other two reasons, the lack of mutual trust and the protection of national economic interests. It can nonetheless constitute an

---

233 European Commission, COM(2000) 888, 42–45.

234 *Ibidem*, 53–55.

235 Case C-164/99, *Portugaia Construções*, ECR 2002, I-787.

autonomous reason for a Member State's failure to fully adopt its national legal order to today's EC-legal framework.

It is important to underline at this point of the analysis process that beside the three reasons mentioned in the Commission's report a number of other, additional reasons should be considered in the author's point of view. While the Commission's report merely names reasons for which Member States are to be blamed directly, the present section suggests that there is also a quantity of structural reasons which can not be explained by a Member State's bad faith. The *weak system of enforcement of the internal market law*, allowing Member States to uphold their restrictions more easily, represents one of the structural reasons. Indeed the report criticises the lack of monitoring duties for Member States regarding judgments of the Court in proceedings against different Member States.[236] Moreover the treatment on a case-by-case basis and the poor effectiveness of penalties for infringements of the law of the internal market encourage Member States to postpone necessary adjustment initiatives of their national legal orders until being directly questioned by the Court. This explains why many of the above reported legal barriers still exist, although they have already been subject to judgments of the Court in the past. Another reason of the latter kind can be concluded from an interpretation of the report and a corresponding memo, summarising the main content of it.[237] The law of the internal market for services is to a high degree founded on the

---

236 *"The weak monitoring of the judgments of the Court by the national authorities does not always allow them to identify the need to modify their national legislation. (…) It seems that few Member States engage in any real active and systematic monitoring of all judgments concerning other Member States in order to assess the needs in terms of adjusting their own legislation."*

237 MEMO/02/178 of 31.7.2002. It reads under the relevant question *"Why can't most of these problems be dealt with under the infringements procedure?"* (3): *"Experience shows that often Member States, which are compelled to change their law, following an infringement procedure and a Court judgment just replace existing barriers by the introduction of new ones which means that service providers face new problems and a new infringement has to be brought. Furthermore, the rapidly evolving nature of markets and regulation, which means that new barriers are constantly being created, other actions are needed to complement infringement actions in order to create greater legal certainty."*

Treaty and the corresponding case law of the Court. Consequently EC-law for cross-border service provision predominantly consists of general principles formulated in the Treaty and an active role of the Court seeking to apply these principles case by case. Secondary legislative instruments, such as directives or regulations, have been rarely introduced and regularly govern only specific types of services.[238] Due to this absence of detailed horizontal regulation for service provision in the Internal Market, Member States are more likely to be uncertain about the actual legal framework and consequently tend to observe it less than necessary. This *missing transparency of the EC-law for service provision in the internal market* is especially manifest when taking into account the rapidly evolving and changing complexity of case constellations under today's highly advanced service industry. A last reason has to adopt a historical perspective and take into account the long standing tradition of Member States' legal orders to legislate and provide for a regulative framework for service provision. Especially with a view to techniques developed in the EC's legislative context for cross border service provision focusing on far reaching restrictions for applying the host Member State's legal order, they face a fundamental change in *legal culture*. Consequently Member States are highly suspicious on refraining from pursuing one of their most essential functions, namely the establishment and the protection of an effective market place, consumer, etc, by unconditionally conferring it to other Member States.

C. Purpose, Regulatory Approach and Addressees of the Services Directive

The SD is the linear follow-up initiative to the before analysed report on the "*State of the Internal Market for Services*".[239] Accordingly, Art 1[240] on the Directive's *purpose* lays down that the "*Di-*

---

238 Electronic communication services, networks and associated facilities services are for instance regulated in detail by Directives 2002/19/EC, 2002/20/EC, 2002/21/EC, 2002/22/EC and 2002/58/EC of the European Parliament and of the Council.

239 See the Directive's Recital 3: "*The report from the Commission on "The State of the Internal Market for Services" drew up an inventory of a large number of barriers which are preventing or slowing down the development of services between Member States (…)*".

240 When quoting articles without mentioning their legal source in the following course of the study they always refer to the SD.

rective establishes general provisions facilitating the exercise of the freedom of establishment for service providers and the free movement of services (…)". Recital 5 specifies the purpose of the Directive to enhance "*the legal certainty necessary for the exercise in practice of those two fundamental freedoms of the Treaty*". As to its *regulatory approach*, the Directive preliminarily states that the identified barriers "*cannot be removed solely by relying on direct application of Articles 43 and 49 of the Treaty, since, on the one hand, addressing them on a case-by-case basis through infringement procedures against Member States concerned would, especially following enlargement, be extremely complicated for national and Community institutions, and, on the other hand, the lifting of many barriers requires prior coordination of national legal schemes, including the setting up of administrative cooperation.*"[241] Accordingly, the Directive shall "*establish a general legal framework which benefits*" and eliminates "*a wide variety of services*", simultaneously starting a "*process of evaluation, consultation and complementary harmonisation*".[242] As to its *addressees* "*the Directive is addressed to the Member States*".[243] It affects however all service providers and recipients established in a Member State.[244]

D. Methodological Structure and Structural Outlook

In the following the main provisions of the Directive will be presented, analysed and brought into relation with the current legal framework. This will be carried out – after having introduced the Directive's subject matter and scope of application – by trailing the economic procedural reality: The provisions concerning the exercise of a service activity through establishment abroad (freedom of establishment) shall be launched separately from those regulating the provision of services abroad for a temporarily limited period of time (free movement of services). Under both analytical categories the following structure shall be maintained: Firstly, the Directive's legal text shall be interpreted and summarised, secondly an ap-

---

241 Recital 6.

242 Recital 7.

243 Art 46.

244 This follows from the Directive's scope under Art 2 (1): "*This Directive shall apply to services supplied by providers established in a Member State*". See definition of "provider" and "recipient" under Art 4 (2) and (3).

praisal shall point out major problem fields and inconsistencies and
thirdly the provisions shall be set in relation with today's legal
framework, thus providing for a comprehensive presentation of
major changes within EC-internal market law for transnational service provision. Within this presentation, the author will focus on a
combined perspective concerning access to, exercise of and control
over the service provider and provision.

E. Subject Matter and Scope of Application (Art 1–4)

1. The Legal Text

a. Subject Matter and Scope of Application

In accordance with the Directive's purpose and regulatory approach
under the recitals cited before, Art 1 and 2 define its subject matter
and scope. Accordingly, the Directive establishes *"general provisions facilitating the exercise of the freedom of establishment for
service providers and the free movement of services, while maintaining a high quality of services"* and applies *"to services supplied
by providers in a Member State"*.[245] Art 4 – providing for a definition of all relevant legal terms used in the Directive – is of specific
importance for a clarification of the before used terminology. To
this respect "service" is defined as *"any self-employed economic
activity, normally provided for remuneration, as referred to in Article 50 of the Treaty"*. "Provider" shall mean *"any natural person
who is a national of a Member State, or any legal person, as referred to in Article 48 of the Treaty, established in a Member State,
who offers or provides a service"*, whereas being *"established"*
signifies *"the actual pursuit of an economic activity, as referred to
in Article 43 of the Treaty, by the provider for an indefinite period
and a stable infrastructure from where the business of providing
services is actually carried out"*.

b. Exceptions to the Scope of Application

The above presented, *horizontally defined scope* is significantly
limited through exceptions laid down in Art 1 (2)-(7), Art 2 (2) and
(3) as well as through Art 3.

Firstly, Art 2 (2) defines that the Directive shall *not apply to
certain types of services*. These are non-economic services of general interest, financial services, electronic communication services,

---

245 A clear distinction between above mentioned "purpose" and current
"subject matter" cannot be drawn on the basis of the Directive.

services in the field of transport, services of temporary work agencies, healthcare services, audiovisual services, gambling services, services connected with the exercise of official authority, social services, private security services and services provided by notaries and bailiffs.[246] Secondly, Art 2 (3) does not exclude a certain type of service but *"the field of taxation"*. Thirdly, Art 1 (2)-(7) exclude from the Directive's scope the *"liberalisation of services of general economic interest"*, *"privatisation of public entities providing services"*, *"the abolition of monopolies"*, *"measures to promote cultural or linguistic diversity or media pluralism"*, Member State's *"criminal law"*, *"labor law"*, *"social security legislation"* and *"the exercise of fundamental rights"*. These articles define certain implications or issues or areas of law which the Directive may *not* have or deal with. Accordingly the Directive only applies to cross-border service activities which do not lead to or affect the liberalisation[247] of services of general economic interest reserved to public or private entities or the privatisation of public entities providing services (Art 1(2)), the abolition of monopolies or state aid granted by Member States covered by Community rules on competition (Art 1 (3)) and the protection and promotion of cultural or linguistic diversity or media pluralism (now Art 1 (4)). Besides, the Directive does not apply to matters of labor law (Art 1 (6)), social security legislation (Art 1 (6) and to all questions related to the exercise of fundamental rights Art 1 (7). Art 1 (2)-(7) thus do not define certain types of services not being affected by the Directive, but potentially affect all types of services falling under the Directive's scope. The Directive namely does not apply to services principally comprised by its scope in case its application would lead to or affect one of the implications or issues listed before. Fourthly, the provisions on the *"relationship with other provisions of Community law"* under Art 3 have relevance for the Directive's scope of application, too. Art 3 (1) generally enshrines that Community acts governing specific aspects of services, specific sectors or professions of service provision shall prevail in case of conflict with the Directive.[248] To this

---

246 Art 2 (2) (-a)-(l).

247 Liberalisation has to be understood in this context as the opening up to free market's competition.

248 Those parts of the free movement of services and the freedom of establishment related to service provision which are not regulated either by the Directive or any other secondary Community legislation

extend Art 3 (1) exemplary lists certain of such Community acts, namely Directive 96/71/EC (posting of workers), Regulation (EEC) 1408/71 (application of social security schemes), Directive 89/552/EEC (television broadcasting activities) and Directive 2005/36/EC (recognition of professional qualifications). In the fifth place, Art 3 (2) excludes the rules of private international law from the Directive's scope, including *"those which guarantee that consumers benefit from the protection granted to them by the consumer protection rules laid down in the consumer legislation in force in their Member State"*.

2. Appraisal

a. Services of General (Economic) Interest

Art 2 (2) leaves *"non-economic services of general interest"* outside the Directive's scope. Simultaneously, Art 1 (2) states that the Directive *"does not deal with the liberalisation of services of general economic interest, reserved to public or private entities"* and Art 1 (3) enshrines that Member States remain free *"to define in conformity with Community law, what they consider to be services of general economic interest"*. Two questions arise in this context: In the first place, what are services of general interest, in other words what are the boundaries set by Community law, and how can non-economic and economic ones be delimitated from each other? This is equally important for Directive's Art 16 which is not to be applied to "services of general economic interest".[249] And in the second place, what actually does the *"liberalisation"* of services of general economic interest mean?

As to the first question it has to be noted that defining the term "services of general interest" is necessary in the context of before mentioned Art 1 (2) and especially of Art 16. Art 16 namely exempts services of general economic interest from the Directive's stipulations on the free movement of services. Although the term "services of general interest" is used in the Treaty's Art 16 and 86 (2) it is neither defined there nor in any secondary legislative act. According to the Commission's understanding the term refers to *"services of an economic nature within the Member States or the*

---

remain determined by the EC-Treaty and the corresponding case law. This follows from Art 3 (3).

249 Art 17 (1).

Community subject to specific public service obligations by virtue of a general interest criterion. The concept of services of general economic interest thus covers in particular certain services provided by the big network industries such as transport, postal services, energy and communications. However, the term also extends to any other economic activity subject to public service obligations."[250] Although no consistently used terminology can be identified, the ECJ adopts a similar point of view.[251] As regards the differentiation between "economic" and "non-economic" services of general interest the defining criteria are the same as compared to other types of service activities. All services that correspond to an economic activity within the meaning of the case-law of the Court relating to Article 49 of the Treaty are covered by the Directive without distinguishing between services of general interest and other types. As elaborated above services correspond to an economic activity in case they are *"normally provided for remuneration"*. Decisive for classifying remuneration is that the economic activity is being performed in order to receive an economic value in return. It is essential that the remuneration constitutes an economic equivalent for the service rendered and does not just represent a negligible contribution to the costs.[252] Consequently those services delivered without an economic purpose are not covered.[253] The applicability of this general rule to services of general interest has been confirmed by the ECJ by stating that *"any activity consisting in offering goods and services on a given market is an economic activity"*.[254] Taking the legally speaking non-binding Commission definition together with the binding Court parameters, any activity in the sense of Art 49 EC subject to a public service obligation normally provided for remuneration can constitute a service of the general interest. According to above cited Art 1 (3), this represents the legal framework under which Member States are free to actually define a certain service activity as one of the general interest.

---

250 Green Paper on Services of General Interest, COM 2003(270), 16. Equally see: Communication from the Commission – Services of General Interest in Europe, COM 2000(580).

251 Case C-475/99, *Ambulanz Glöckner*, ECR 2001,8089 para 21.

252 Case C-263/86, *Belgium v. Humbel*, ECR 1988, 5365.

253 Case C-159/90, *Unborn Children*, ECR 1991, I-4685, 4740 paras 25 *et seq.*

254 Joint Cases C-180–184/98, *Pavel Pavlov*, ECR 2000, I-6451.

As to the second question, the Directive does not define the term *"liberalisation"*. Neither does the ECJ. The Treaty uses it within its Art 40, 51(2), 57(2), 133(1) and Art 52 without though providing for a definition. Literature has elaborated two possible definitions, mainly stemming from Art 52 EC: The first understands liberalisation in the context of services as *"the removal of all barriers to cross-border service provision"*, whereas the second has a broader understanding thus comprising all *"measures aiming at facilitating the free movement of services including acts of coordination"*.[255] However both definitions are not applicable to Directive's Art 1 (2) since the Directive explicitly pursues both aims, the removal of all barriers and facilitation of the free movement of services. And it does this also with regard to services of general economic interest as they are not excluded from the Directive's scope. Consequently, "liberalisation" in the present context has to be understood more narrowly, namely as a synonym for the "abolition of monopolies". This interpretation is in conformity with Art 1 (3), prohibiting the abolition of monopolies for services other than services of the general interest, as well as with Recital 8.[256] To conclude, Art 1 (2) excludes the Directive's application to Member States' measures which relate to a monopoly of a service of the general interest.[257]

b. Impact of the Non-Services Related Exceptions

As analysed above the Directive's scope is not just limited by excluding certain types of services but also through defining certain consequences or issues the Directive may not have or touch upon.

---

255 *Troberg / Tiedje* (2003), para 4 *et seq* with reference to the OECD-definition.

256 Recital 8: *"It is appropriate that the provisions of this Directive concerning the freedom of establishment and the free movement of services should apply only to the extent that the activities in question are open to competition, so that they do not oblige Member States either to liberalise services of general economic interest or to privatise public entities which provide such services or to abolish existing monopolies for other activities or certain distribution services."*

257 A similar *telos* is pursued by Art 15(4), stating that requirements *"in the field of services of general economic interest"* shall only be evaluated *"insofar as the application of these paragraphs does not obstruct the performance, in law or in fact, of the particular task assigned to them"*.

This latter way of restricting the Directive's scope has two consequences: Firstly, due to its horizontal nature, many aspects and parts of service provisions principally included are finally not to be measured against the Directive's provisions. This makes it difficult to predict the "real" scope of application. Secondly, central provisions of the Directive, such as Art 16 providing for a general prohibition on restrictions within the free movement of services, are in fact limited through the design of the Directive's scope. Member States can thus use the argument of implication or affected issue to apply their national restrictive regulation to services included in the Directive's scope. These arguments will be referred to as *Chapter-I-reasons of justifications* contrasting them to the reasons of justification stemming from Chapter IV on the free movement of services. Consequently, when assessing the effectiveness of, for example, Directive's Art 16 and comparing it with today's legal framework not just those exception clauses directly relating to Art 16 but also those of horizontal nature referring to the Directive's scope of application have to be considered.

c. The Scope of Application and National Regulation

The following shall establish a scheme of practical evaluation which kind of national regulation concerning cross-border service provision has to be measured against the Directive.

1) Is the type of service exposed to the national regulation included in the Directive's scope
(not excluded by Art 2 (2))?
↓ Positive:
▼ 2) Is the national regulation part of criminal, labor, social security or taxation law or is related to and based on fundamental rights provisions?
↓ Negative:
▼ 3) Does the national regulation relate to the realisation of one of the implications under Art 1 (2)-(6), such as for example the protection of cultural diversity?
↓ Negative:
▼ >>> The national regulation has to meet the Directive's regulative impositions.

d. Excursus: Directive 2005/36/EC on the
Recognition of Professional Qualifications
and Its Impact on the SD's Scope of Application

As enshrined in above cited Art 3 (1) of the SD the provisions of Directive 2005/36/EC (henceforth "Professional Qualifications Directive") prevail over the SD in case of conflict. Although this is only an exemplary application of the general *lex specialis* rule to the field of professional qualifications enshrined in Art 3, it is of exceptional importance for the understanding and the practical functioning of the SD. To this respect, two reasons can be brought forward: First, professional qualification issues arise in the context of nearly all services sectors. In contrast to the equally under Art 3 named television broadcasting directive for instance, professional qualifications are not limited to a certain service sector. Second, the question which professional qualification requirement is needed in a Member State primarily concerns the phase of access to an activity. This is the most crucial phase from an EC-Internal Market perspective. Indeed, national legislation on professional qualification requirements is a major source of limiting the free access to the cross-border taking up of services activities under both the freedom of establishment as well as free movement of services. Consequently one of the central sources of discrimination and impediment to the free movement of services and the freedom of establishment, the regulation of professional qualification requirements, remain outside the SD's scope of application. This directive thus substantially narrows the effect of the SD on MS's legal orders and impacts on its overall importance.

To go into the details, professional qualifications requirements can become relevant under both, the freedom of establishment and the free movement of services. For this reason, the SD exempts qualification issues from both of these principal sections. On the one hand it states in its Art 17 (6)[258] that *"Art 16 does not apply to matters covered by Title II of the Professional Qualification Directive."* This exempts all questions of professional qualification requirements for service providers offering their service under a regulated profession in the framework of the free movement of services.[259] To put it differently, the law- or unlawfulness of the

---

258 Art 17 (6) is the central exemption clause of the SD's Chapter IV on the "Free Movement of Services".

259 Regulated profession as defined under Art 3 (1) 2005/36/EC.

host Member State's legislation on professional qualification requirements applied *vis-a-vis* a foreign service provider admitted
under the free movement of services and principally falling under
the SD's scope of application is to be assessed on the basis of the
Professional Qualifications Directive only. On the other hand, and
although not explicitly enshrined in the SD but following from Art
3 (1), the same is true for Member States' legislation on professional requirements for service providers acting under the freedom
of establishment.

e. The Scope of Application: Examples

According to the SD's structure, its scope of application has been
negatively defined in the present study, thus primarily establishing
those circumstances which lead to a non-application of the Directive. In order to facilitate the understanding of its scope of application, principal service sectors to which the SD is fully or partly
applicable shall be exemplarily listed in the following: Firstly, services which are primarily provided to business, such as management consultancy, certification and testing, facilities management,
including office maintenance, advertising services, recruitment
services, and the services of commercial agents; Secondly, services
provided to both , business and consumers, such as legal or fiscal
advice services, real estate services, such as estate agencies, construction services, including the services of architects, distributive
trade services, trade fairs organisational services, car rental and
travel agency services; Thirdly, services principally relating to
consumers only comprise tourism services, including tour guides,
leisure services, sport centres and amusement parks, as well as
household support services.[260]

---

260 See *European Commission*, Single Market News, No 44 January
2007, 8.

F. Chapter III: The Freedom of Establishment
for Service Providers (Art 9–15)

1. The Legal Text[261]

a. The Definition of Authorisations and Requirements

The Directive's provisions on the freedom of establishment contain
two basic regulatory concerns: Firstly, Member States' *"authorisation schemes"* for the *"access to a service activity or the exercise
thereof"* are addressed to under Art 9–13 and, secondly, *"requirements prohibited or subject to evaluation for the access to or the
exercise of a service activity"* are regulated under Art 14–15.

The terminological difference between *"authorisation
schemes"* and *"requirements"* is decisive for a delimitation of the
different regulatory contents. The term "requirement" can be
equated with the term "restriction" from the ECJ's case law[262], thus
describing every Member State's measure *"liable to hinder or make
less attractive the exercise of fundamental freedoms"*.[263] The term
"authorisation", in contrast, applies to cases concerning *"inter alia,
the administrative procedures for granting authorisations, licences,
approvals or concessions, and also the obligation, in order to be
eligible to exercise the activity, to be registered as a member of a
profession or entered in a register, roll or database, to be officially
appointed to a body or to obtain a card attesting to membership of
a particular profession."*[264] This signifies that "requirements" ter-
minologically also cover "authorisations" since they are also liable
to hinder or make less attractive the exercise of the freedom of establishment. In the scope of the Directive however, "authorisations"
are separately regulated, thus constituting *lex specialis*.

---

261 It shall be indicated that the provisions of the Directive's Chapter V
     on the quality of services are principally also applicable in the con-
     text of the freedom of establishment. Within the study at hand, they
     are however integrated in the presentation on Chapter IV on the free
     movement of services.

262 This follows when comparing the definition of "requirement" under
     Art 4 (7) with the established case law of the Court.

263 Case C-55/94, *Gebhard*, ECR 1995, I-4165, para37.

264 Recital 39.

b. Authorisations

The section on authorisations is divided into three parts, the first one describing *if* an authorisation scheme can be lawfully applied by a Member State at all (Art 9), the second determining the substantive conditions for granting authorisations (*what*) (Art 10–12), and the third one *how* authorisation schemes have to be applied procedurally (Art 13).

Art 9 (1) allows the Member State to make "*access to a service activity or the exercise thereof*" only *subject to an authorisation* if the "*need for an authorisation scheme is justified by an overriding reason relating to the public interest*", if it is the only possible measure to achieve the underlying aim and if the authorisation scheme is non-discriminatory. Under Art 9 (2) in connection with Art 41, the Member States have to notify every authorisation scheme in the sense of Art 9 (1) they uphold to the Commission and justify its lawfulness. This is a provision common to several parts of the Directive, such as for example in connection with requirements upheld under Art 16 (see below section III.H.5). In case Art 9 allows Member States to maintain authorisation schemes, Art 10 sets the *criteria for granting authorisations* under such schemes. It includes that the criteria imposed are "justified by *an overriding reason relating to the public interest*" (necessity) (Art 10 (2) (b)), are non-discriminatory (Art 10 (2) (a)), proportionate (Art 10 (2) (c)), clear and unambiguous (d), objective (e), made public in advance (f), transparent and accessible (g) and that the overriding reason is not already satisfied through requirements and controls of the provider's home country (Art 10 (3))[265]. Besides, Art 11 (1) establishes that the granted authorisations shall principally be issued for an unlimited period of time[266], whereas Art 12 governs the particular case that only a limited number of authorisations for a given activity is available (a "*selection from among several candidates*" becomes necessary).

If Member States are allowed to introduce authorisation schemes and if they apply these schemes to the providers in a man-

---

265 The criteria of home-host-State-comparison is correct from a systematic point of view, since under the current Treaty and case law based system this comparative element also applies to regulation relating to market access, *ie* "authorisation", only. See above section II.B.3.d.db.

266 Art 11 (1) (a)-(c) defines certain exceptions to that principle.

ner consistent with the provisions established above under Art 10–
12, Art 13 defines the *(formal) procedures* to be used in this context. Accordingly, Member States shall guarantee that the authorisation procedures are *"clear, made public in advance and guarantee that application will be processed as quickly as possible"* (Art
13 (1), (2)). Member States have to fix and publish the time period
they consider necessary for the procedure in advance and in case
they fail to response timely, the authorisation shall be deemed to
have been granted *ex lege* (Art 13 (3)-(4)), ie automatically.[267]

c. Requirements

Under this section, the Directive distinguishes between two types of
requirements. First, it names those *requirements* under Art 14 (1)-
(8) which are *unconditionally forbidden* to be applied by Member
States. These concern *"discriminatory requirements based directly
or indirectly on nationality"*. " *Having an establishment in more
than one Member State"*, *"restrictions on the freedom of a provider
to choose between a principal or a secondary establishment"*,
*"conditions of reciprocity with the Member State in which the pro-
vider already has an establishment"*, *"case-by-case application of
an economic test"*, *"the direct involvement of competing operators
in the granting of authorisations"*, an obligation to participate in a
financial guarantee or insurance structure of the host State and an
*"obligation to have been pre-registered for a given period in the
registers"* held in the host Member State's territory are mentioned
as examples.[268]

Secondly, Art 15 lays down a screening-duty for the Member
States as regards certain non-discriminatory *requirements*. They are
admissible in principle (Art 15 (1)(2)), however only as far as they
are indeed applied in a non-discriminatory way (Art 15 (3)). The
requirements to be looked after are *"quantitative or territorial restrictions"* (Art 15 (2)(a)), specific legal form requirements (b),
shareholding requirements (c), particular provider's qualification
related requirements (d), *"ban on having more than one establishment in the territory of the same State"* (e), minimum number of
employees requirements (f), *"fixed minimum and/or maximum tariffs with which the provider must comply"* (g), and obligations to

---

267 This rule can be derogated through *"overriding reasons relating to
the public interest"*, (Art 13 (4) second sentence).

268 Thus, the following list is not exhaustive.

provide combined services (h). Existing and planned requirements falling under Art 15 must be notified to the Commission in the mutual evaluation report (Art 39), explaining why they meet the criteria of non-discrimination, including necessity and proportionality (Art 15 (5)). As regards envisaged requirements, Art 7 gives the Community the possibility to take a decision *"requesting the Member State in question to refrain from adopting them or to abolish them"*.

2. Appraisal: Chapter III – A Fundamental Definition Dilemma

As repeatedly stated, the Directive at hand aims at facilitating the exercise of the freedom of establishment on the one hand and the free movement of services on the other hand. The freedom of establishment for service providers shall be addressed through the before presented Chapter III. It is thus clear that the Directive does not engage in facilitating the freedom of establishment under Art 43–48 EC in general, but only as far as *"access to a service activity or the exercise thereof"* are concerned.[269] In other words only the freedom of establishment for service providers and provision shall be referred to. In order to determine which economic activities in the context of the freedom of establishment are comprised by Chapter III, the definition of the term *"service activity"* in this context is crucial. Under Art 4, as explained above under section III.E., "service" means *"any self-employed economic activity, normally provided for remuneration, as referred to in Article 50 of the Treaty"*. Art 50 EC considers "services" *"to be services within the meaning of this Treaty where they are normally provided for remuneration, in so far as they are not governed by the provisions relating to freedom of movement for goods, capital and persons"*. According to the Treaty the "freedom of persons" includes the free movement of workers and the freedom of establishment.[270] Consequently "services" are only "services" in the meaning of Art 50 EC as long as they are not comprised by – *inter alia* – the freedom of establishment. As a result Directive's Art 4 covers only those "services" which are not part of the freedom of establishment. In other words, every economic activity falling under the EC-Treaty law's understanding of the freedom of establishment cannot fall under the

---

269 Art 9 (1) and Art 14.

270 See the Treaty's Title III in connection with Chapters 1–3 including Art 39–55 EC.

Directive's definition of "services". This signifies that no "service activity" under Chapter III would ever be grasped by this Chapter. Chapter III namely applies to service provision under the freedom of establishment only. And every service activity related to the freedom of establishment is – according to the Directive's own definition – not a service activity in the sense of Art 4 and thus Chapter III. This would leave no field of application to Chapter III and would make its inclusion into the Directive's text senseless. It consequently has to be concluded that the legislators did not intend that outcome. What they wanted to do is to apply the Directive's provisions under Chapter III to those constellations where an economic activity constitutes an exercise of the freedom of establishment in the Treaty's sense but simultaneously represents a service activity in an economic meaning.[271] The term "service activity" under Chapter III has thus to be defined separately from the general definition under Art 4. It has to be resorted to the Treaty's scope of application of the freedom of establishment by including only those possible constellations with a non-physical output. The resulting legal framework for service providers making use of the freedom of establishment shall be presented after the next section on "Administrative Simplification" which is of decisive importance in the present context. It equally applies to service provision through establishment and the free movement of service.

G. Chapter II – Administrative Simplification (Art 5–8)

1. The Legal Text

As mentioned before, Chapter II primarily legislates for a simplification of "*the procedures and formalities applicable to access to a service activity and to the exercise thereof* [272]" in case of establishment of the service provider or its temporary cross-border supply. To this regard, Chapter II affects three different fields of Member States' legal orders, namely their organisational, procedural and

---

271 Compare for instance Recital 5 ("*It is therefore necessary to remove barriers to the freedom of establishment for providers in Member States (…).*") in connection with Recital 36 ("*The concept of 'provider' should cover any natural person who is a national of a Member State or any legal person engaged in a service activity in a Member State, in exercise either of the freedom of establishment (…).*").

272 Art 5 (1).

substantive administrative law. Chapter II shall be analysed by following this segmentation.

a. Organisational Administrative Law

As regards the Member States' organisational administrative law, Art 6 (1) obliges Member States to establish *"points of single contacts"*. They shall enable service providers to complete all administrative procedures and formalities needed for access to and exercise of a service activity at one administrative body only.[273] Art 6 (2) underlines that this provision *"shall be without prejudice to the allocation of functions and powers among the authorities within national systems"*. Consequently where several authorities at national, regional or local level are competent, one of them or a newly established one shall assume the role as point of single contact in the sense of a coordinator, without though gaining additional substantive competences *vis-à-vis* other authorities.[274] Against this background, it shall be repeated that Art 10 (4) under Chapter III (Freedom of Establishment for Providers) requires Member States to restructure their administrative organisation, too. This is insofar true as authorisations for access to or exercise of a service activity shall have validity throughout the whole national territory. However, only those authorisations granted in case the service provider is making use of the freedom of establishment are concerned.

b. Procedural Administrative Law

Art 8 obliges the Member States to ensure that administrative procedures relating to access to a service activity and to the exercise thereof can be easily completed from across borders three years after entry into force of the Directive.[275] It signifies that these procedures can be accomplished without any personal, physical contact between the applicant and the authority. This shall be guaranteed through the mandatory introduction of *electronic administrative communication means* – predominantly internet based ones – for all

---

273 Art 6 does not require the Member States to generally introduce single points of contact, but only for service providers engaged in a cross border service activity under the Directive's subject matter (Art 1) and scope (Art 2).

274 See Recital 48: *"The creation of points of single contact should not interfere with the allocation of functions among competent authorities within each national system."*

275 See Recital 52.

necessary procedures.[276] It concerns service provision in the frame-work of the freedom of establishment and the free movement of services. It does not preclude Member States from additionally adopting other methods to improve cross-border administrative procedures. Art 8 (2) exempts *"the inspection of premises on which the service is provided or of equipment used by the provider"* or the *"physical examination of the capability or of the personal integrity of the provider or of his responsible staff"* from the obligation to facilitate easy cross-border completion of the relevant procedures. Besides, Art 8 (3) gives the Community the competence to shape rules coordinating the compatibility of the Member States' renewed administrative procedures.

c. Substantive Administrative Law

The Member State's substantive administrative law has to be ad-justed through Chapter II's Art 5 (3) and Art 7.

Firstly, Art 5 (3) prescribes that a service provider's or recipi-ent's document related to an administrative procedure applicable to access to and exercise of a service activity proving that a require-ment has been satisfied, must be recognised by all other Member States' administrative authorities (*unconditional recognition of documents*). In other words, any document which is recognised in Member State A to prove the fulfillment of certain requirements has to be recognised in Member State B to prove the corresponding requirements. To this end, Art 5 (3) second sentence lists non-ex-haustive examples of forbidden, additional preconditions for recog-nition, such as *"to require that a document from another Member State be produced in its original form, or as a certified copy or as a certified translation"*. Member States can however impose addi-tional requirements on the service provider or recipient for recogni-tion of their documents *"in cases provided for in other Community instruments"* listed under Art 5 (4)[277] *"or where such a requirement*

---

276 This might comprise a combination of the already existing Internal Market Information (IMI)-System (primarily authority-to-authority communication) and the SOLVIT-System (primarily citizen-to-au-thority communication).

277 Art 5 (3) lists *inter alia* certain articles of Directive 2005/36/EC on the recognition of professional qualifications and Directive 98/5/EC to facilitate practice of the profession of lawyer on a permanent basis in a Member State other than that in which the qualification was ob-tained.

is justified by an overriding reason relating to the public interest".
"Overriding reasons relating to the public interest" are defined
under the Directive's Art 4 (8) meaning *"reasons recognised as
such in the case law of the Court of Justice".*

Secondly, Art 7 (1) necessitates the Member States to include
into their substantive administrative laws the right of service providers and recipients to obtain certain types of information. Such
information rights comprise *inter alia "requirements applicable to
providers established in their territory"*, *"the contact details of the
competent authorities"* and *"the means of and conditions for ac-
cessing public registers and databases on providers and services".*
The Member States' duties are further specified under Art 7 (2)-(6)
including to *"keep the information up-to date, to respond as quickly
as possible to any request for information or assistance or to make
the information available in other Community languages".*

2. Appraisal

Firstly, with regard to the *organisational administrative law*, it has
to be noted that the EC principally has no competence to arrange
the Member States' organisational structures according to the
Court's settled case law.[278] Those national administrative organisational structures, however, which impede the free exercise of the
fundamental freedoms and thus breach the relevant Community law
can be subject to EC-legislation.[279] Under this criterion the introduction of the single points of contract as well as the nation-wide
validity of granted authorisations can be justified.[280]

Secondly, the title of Art 8 – *"procedures by electronic means"*
– is misleading. Art 8 does not primarily concern electronic procedures but requires the Member States to guarantee *procedures*
which can be completed from across-borders without any physical
contact. For this purpose Art 8 wants the Member States to intro-

---

278 Case 96/81, *Commission v Netherlands*, ECR 1990, 1791, para 12.
Nevertheless the Community has already issued in April 1997 a rec-
ommendation on improving and simplifying the business environment for business start-ups, including single points of contact: OJ L
145, 5.6.1997, 29; compare also Recital 48.

279 Case C-128/89, *Commission v Italy,* ECR 1990, I-3239. For the
cooperation duties of national administrative bodies resulting from
EC-law, see: *Sydow* (2004), 23 *et seq.*

280 To the same conclusion: *Schliesky* (2005), 890.

duce in any case an electronic, internet based infrastructure for the completion of the relevant procedures. It leaves it open to Member States, however, to find additional solutions to reach the envisaged aim. For this reason Art 8 (3) reserves for the Community the power to legislate in detail on the realisation of cross-border usable administrative procedures.

The practical importance of Art 5 (3) on *substantive administrative law* – such as the obligation for mutual recognition of certificates – is very much restricted through its system of exemptions. This system comprises the possibility of justification through an overriding requirement of the public interest which corresponds to the notion of an overriding requirement of the general interest under today's system of general prohibition on restrictions. It therefore acknowledges a wide and unlimited variety of justifications for the non-appliance of the obligations under Art 5 (3).

Thirdly, the *right to information* under Art 7 is equally important but difficult to transpose into national law. It is important because cross-border administrative procedures require even more information than purely national operations. And it is difficult to transpose since it exists independently from the underlying subject field of the administrative legal order. It thus has to be transposed into national laws in a horizontal manner.

H. A Modified Legal Framework for the Freedom of Establishment for Service Providers through the Directive's Chapters II and III

This section shall answer the question which essential changes the Directive's stipulations under Chapter II and III will bring to the law on the freedom of establishment for service providers. It shall thus outline the impact of the above presented provisions on today's existing legal framework by focusing on the access to, the exercise of and the supervision of service provision through establishment.

On the one hand, it can be claimed that the provisions on the freedom of establishment for service providers under the SD largely remain consistent with the present system of general prohibition on restrictions. The central aspects of this system – the principal prohibition of all discriminatory requirements, the justifiability of non-discriminatory requirements and the open-ended number of possible justifications through an overriding requirement of the general interest – are purely upheld in this part of the Directive.[281] As regards

---

281 Especially under Art 9(1), 10(2), 14(1) and 15(2).

the supervision of service providers established abroad the legal framework remains consistent, too.

On the other hand, major innovations, however, can be identified: Firstly, Chapter III contains an extensive *codification of past ECJ's case law*. This is especially true for the prohibited requirements under Art 14, such as for instance the prohibition on having an establishment in more than one Member State. This will force Member States to implement the respective ECJ's rulings indirectly and will enhance legal certainty for service providers. Secondly, the introduction of a *screening process and a subsequent notification duty* by giving the Commission a veto possibility under Art 9 (2) and 15 (7) – both in connection with Art 41 – are unknown in EC-Internal Market law so far, at least for such an horizontal scope. As this screening and notification duty applies to authorisation schemes under Art 9 as well as to those requirements listed under Art 15 it will ease the Commission's capability of identifying possible violations of the Directive's and the Treaty's stipulations concerning service providers.

Taking the provisions on administrative simplification of Chapter II into account innovations are even more obvious. As regards the *points of single contracts* (Art 6) they represent a new mechanism in EC-law. In contrast to mere information points as established under the E-Commerce Directive[282], these single points of contract act on behalf of the service provider through substantially coordinating the necessary steps within the relevant national authorities. Also the introduction of *administrative procedures conducted by electronic means* enabling full, non-physical contact with the relevant authorities (Art 8) is a new instrument of realising the Internal Market for Services. Even as regards substantive administrative law, namely the unconditional recognition of documents and the stipulation of information rights for providers represent remarkable improvements compared to the legal status quo.

Finally, both, Chapter II and III do not apply to questions of professional qualifications. As elaborated above under section III.E.2.d., service providers acting under the freedom of establishment fall under the regulatory regime of Directive 2005/36/EC as far as national requirements for professional qualifications by the home or host State are concerned.

---

282 2000/31/EC.

I. The Free Movement of Services (Chapter IV, Art 16–21)
Including the Provisions on Quality of Services (Chapter V, Art 22–
27) and Administrative Cooperation (Chapter VI, Art 28–36)

1. Introduction

Chapter IV on the free movement of services is divided in two sections, Section 1 on the *"Freedom to Provide Services and Related Derogations"* and Section 2 on the *"Rights of Recipients of Services"*. According to several cross references within these two sections, Chapter VI on *"Administrative Cooperation"* is inextricably linked to them. Indeed, Chapter VI governs major aspects concerning supervision[283] of cross-border service provision and shall consequently be presented in a combined perspective. The Chapter on Quality of Services (V) is divided in provisions representing *lex specialis*-rules to the freedom to provide services and in stipulations concerning the rights of recipients. It follows that Chapter V shall be integrated into the analysis of Section 1 and 2 under Chapter IV.[284] Besides, it has to be pointed out that the provisions of Chapter II "Administrative Simplification" presented above are equally applicable in principle within the context of the free movement of services.

---

283 According to the definition in Recital 106 supervision comprises activities *"such as monitoring, fact finding, problem solving, enforcement and imposition of sanctions and subsequent follow-up activities"*.

284 Only one provision under Chapter V – namely Art 26 on the "Policy on Quality of Services" – seems to relate to the question of quality of services in its proper sense. As it mainly contains merely legally non-binding declarations of intent it shall be left aside in the present study. It shall be pointed out that – beside Art 24 on commercial communications by the regulated professions – all provisions of Chapter V equally apply in the context of the freedom of establishment under Directive's Chapter III. For details see Recital 97.

2. Chapter IV and V – The Free Movement of Services Including the Provisions on the Quality of Services: The Legal Text and Appraisal

a. Section 1 – The Freedom to Provide Services

aa. The General Prohibition on Restrictions

Art 16 (1) represents the central provision for the facilitation of the freedom to provide services under the free movement of services, installing a general prohibition on Member States' restrictions. It enshrines that Member States are obliged to *"respect the right of service providers to provide services in a Member State other than that in which they are established"*. To this end Member States shall *"ensure free access to and exercise of a service activity within"* their territory. According to Art 16 (1) third sentence *"free access to and exercise of a service activity"* shall mean that host Member States shall not impose *"any requirements"*, *"neither directly nor indirectly discriminatory"*[285] on the service provider. According to Art 3 (3) the provisions of the Directive shall be applied in accordance with the rules of the Treaty on the free movement of services. Consequently, as elaborated above under section III.F.1.a. – "The Definition of Authorisations and Requirements", "requirement" defines every Member State's measure *"liable to hinder or make less attractive the exercise of fundamental freedoms"*, such as obligations, prohibitions, conditions or limits provided for in legislative acts of the Member States, of professional bodies or in administrative practice.[286] This general prohibition of any requirement burdening the service provider directly or indirectly (through requirements imposed on the recipient) is further substantiated through Art 16 (2). It stipulates in a non-exhaustive manner requirements forbidden to be introduced by the host Member State, including establishment (a) or authorisation (b) obligations, a ban on the providers infrastructural plans (c), obligatory

---

285 It is important to mention that this does not affect the Member States' possibility to enact discriminatory requirements in case they are justifiable by one of the reason of Art 45 TEC (public order, health and security). This follows from the Directive's Art 2 (i).

286 See also Art 4 (7) which explicitly exempts *"rules laid down in collective agreements negotiated by the social partners"* from the definition of requirement.

application of specific provider-recipient contractual arrangements
(d), an obligation on the provider to possess service activity related
identity documents (e), requirements concerning the use of equipment and material necessary for the service provision (f), and any
restrictions imposed on the service recipient, such as authorisation
requirements or discriminatory limits on the grant of financial assistance (g).[287] Besides, Chapter V on the quality of service contains
– as indicated above –other explicitly prohibited requirements:
Those which oblige providers to exercise a given specific activity
exclusively or which restrict the exercise jointly or in partnership of
different activities ("*multidisciplinary activities*").[288]

> *ab. Exceptions from the General Prohibition on Requirements –*
> *Reasons of Justification and Mutual Evaluation (Art 39 (5))*

The general prohibition on restrictions contains three categories of
exceptions, firstly under Art 17, secondly under Art 16 (1) and (3)
and thirdly under Art 18.

Art 17 generally excludes *certain types of services* from the
scope of application of the general prohibition on restrictions under
Art 16 (1). As Art 17 does not exclude these services from the entire Chapter on the Free Movement of Services, the provisions under current Chapter IV apart from Art 16 (1), such as those on the
freedom to receive services, remain fully applicable. Art 17 comprises on the one hand those *services* being completely or partly
regulated in existing secondary legislation, including "*matters covered by the posting-of-workers-Directive*[289]*, Directive on the protection of individuals with regard to the processing of personal data
and on the free movement of such data*[290]*, Directive to facilitate the
effective exercise by lawyers of freedom to provide services*[291]*, Title
II of Directive 2005/36/EC*[292] *as well as requirements in the Member State where the service is provided which reserve a service
activity to a particular regulated profession, Council Regulation on
the coordination of social security systems*[293]*, Directive on the*

---

287 Art 16 (2)(g) refers to Art 19.

288 Art 25 (1).

289 Directive 96/71/EC.

290 Directive 95/46/EC.

291 Directive 77/249/EEC.

292 See section III.E.2.d.

293 Council Regulation 1408/71.

rights of citizens of the Union and their family members to move and reside freely within the territory of the Member States[294]*, Art 21 of the Convention implementing the Schengen Agreement, Council Regulation on the supervision and control of shipments of waste*[295]*, the Directives on copyright, neighbouring rights, industrial property rights*[296]*, and Directive on statutory audit of annual accounts and consolidated accounts*[297]*."* On the other hand certain *subject matters* are exempted without any reference to existing secondary legislation but being *considered politically sensitive*: These are *"services of general economic interest*[298]*, acts requiring by law the involvement of a notary, the registration of vehicles leased in another Member State, the activity of judicial recovery of debts, provisions regarding contractual and non-contractual obligations, including the form of contracts, determined pursuant to the rules of private international law."* Professional rules on commercial communications by the regulated professions are equally excepted from the general prohibition under Art 16 (1).[299] This is also true for cases where Member States require from service providers under the present framework of the free movement of services a document from another Member State to be produced in its original form or certified copy.[300]

The second possible derogation from the general prohibition on restrictions stipulated under Art 16 (1), gives Member States the possibility to impose requirements necessary for reasons of (1) *public policy*, (2) *public security*, (3) *public health* and (4) *the pro-*

---

294 Directive 2004/38/EC.

295 Council Regulation 259/93.

296 Directive 87/54/EEC and Directive 96/9/EC.

297 Directive 2006/43/EC.

298 The following services are exemplarily mentioned: *"Postal services"* as covered by Directive 97/67/EC, *"electricity services"* as covered by Directive 2003/54/EC, *"gas services"* as covered by Directive 2003/55/EC, *"water distribution and supply services"* and *"water waste services"* and *"treatment of waste"*.

299 This follows from Art 24 (1) under Chapter V (*"Quality of Services"*).

300 This is stipulated under Art 5 (3).

tection of the environment under *Art 16 (1)*. These requirements must additionally be non-discriminatory and proportionate.[301]

Last but not least, *Art 18* (*"Case-by-Case Derogations"*) allows the host Member State to impose requirements on the service provider for *reasons relating to the safety of a service*. These requirements can be discriminatory or non-discriminatory. Compared to those requirements under Art 17 and 16 (1) they have to fulfil – apart from proportionality – certain additional criteria in order to be lawfully imposed. Firstly, the envisaged requirement in the field of the service's safety has not been subject to Community harmonisation, secondly the envisaged requirement guarantees a higher level of protection than a comparable measure taken by the Member State of establishment would do and thirdly the host Member State has to observe certain procedural obligations under the *"Mutual Assistance"*-procedure of Art 35, such as close cooperation with the home Member State and the Commission when imposing a service's safety related requirement.

In connection with these admissible restrictions, Art 39 (5) obliges the Member States to submit a report to the Commission after the expiry of the transposition period to identify those requirements which they consider to be still applicable under Art 16 (1) and giving reasoning. Equally, Member States must communicate in a similar report any new requirement they are planning to introduce as well as any changes.

b. Section 2 – Rights of Recipients of Services

According to Art 19 *"Member States may not impose on a recipient requirements which restrict the use of a service supplied by a provider established in another Member State"*.[302] This stipulation addresses the recipient of the service provision resident in a different Member State than the service provider. This includes both, the State in which the recipient is established (resident) and that where

---

301 The stipulation in Art 16 (3), repeating the before mentioned reasons of justification and adding "employment conditions" is considered to be redundant as a drafting mistake resulting from the evolutionary history of DSD 2006 as it only repeats the before mentioned reasons. "Employment conditions" are in the present study covered by the Chapter-I-reasons of justification, including labour and social law.

302 By way of illustration the following restrictions are named under Art 19 (a) and (b): Authorisation or declaration obligations and discriminatory limits on the grant of financial assistance.

the recipient crosses to on a temporary basis only for the reception of the service. Furthermore, Art 21 engages the Member State of establishment (residence) of the recipient to provide him with certain information concerning essential questions of cross-border services reception.[303] Additional recipient's rights are – as mentioned above – specified under Art 22, 27 and 23 of Chapter V relating to the quality of services. In the first place, providers are obliged to keep certain information, such as for instance their place of registration / residence, available to the recipient.[304] This information must be supplied by the provider on his own initiative, must be easily accessible (also by electronic means) and has to appear in any of the provider's information document.[305] Special information duties under Art 27 (1) concern contact details in case of dispute, in particular a postal address, fax number or e-mail address and telephone number, to which all recipients can send a complaint or request for information about the service provided. Certain additional information – for example as regards regulated professions, a reference to the professional rules applicable in the Member State of establishment and how to access them – are to be delivered by the provider in case of recipient's request only.[306] In the second place, providers are obliged to subscribe to professional liability insurance in order to protect the recipient (or a third person) from risks to health, safety or financial security. The insurance can also be contracted in the provider's home Member State as long as it fully covers the described risks.[307]

c. Appraisal

This section's assessment focuses on the Directive's regulatory structure for the freedom to provide services and its possible derogations (section III.I.2.a.), thus leaving aside the recipients rights (section III.I.2.b.) to a large extend. To this regard five aspects which appear contradictive or need further clarification shall be pointed out: Firstly, the relationship between Art 17 (15) exempting from Art 16's scope of application *"contractual and non-contrac-*

---

303 For instance general information on redress in case of dispute with the foreign provider [Art 21 (1) (b)].

304 For details, see: Art 22 (1) (a)-(b).

305 Art 22 (2).

306 Art 22 (3).

307 Art 23 (1) and (2).

tual obligations, including the form of contracts, determined pursuant to the rules of private international law" and Art 3 (2) stipulating the non-applicability of the Directive on *"private international law, in particular rules governing the law applicable to contractual and non contractual obligations"* remains unclear. It thus appears advisable to entirely delete Art 17 (15). This would not change anything in substance, but provide for greater structural coherence. Secondly, Art 17 (2) reveals a similar problem as it anchors Art 16's non-applicability to matters covered by the Posting of Workers Directive. Art 1 (6) namely states that the Directive does not apply to *"labour law"* and *"social security legislation"*. And the Posting of Workers Directive principally includes nothing else than provisions in the field of labour and social law. Consequently also Art 17 (2) should be eliminated. Thirdly, as regards the exclusion of *"services of general economic interest"* by Art 17 (1) reference shall be made to the appraisal and the terminology above under section III.E.2.a. As elaborated there, Member States remain free to determine what they consider to be services of general economic interest within the parameters set out by Community law. As Art 17(1) represents an exception clause to the central provision of Art 16, the remaining margin for Member States' discretionary power through their definition competence could threaten the effectiveness of Art 16. Indeed it could represent a window of opportunity for Member States to justify restrictive measure contradictive to Art 16 by claiming them to be services of general economic interest.[308] Fourthly, the relationship between Art 16 and Art 17 (6) excluding *inter alia "matters covered by Title II of Directive 2005/36/EC "* shall be examined. As introduced above under E.2.4., the Professional Qualifications Directive (2005/36/EC) lays down provisions on the access to and pursuit of a regulated profession by means of the free movement of services (Title II) and the freedom of estab-

---

308 Respective Recital 70, stating that *"for the purposes of this Directive, and without prejudice to Article 16 of the Treaty, services may be considered to be services of general economic interest only if they are provided in application of a special task in the public interest entrusted to the provider by the Member State concerned. This assignment should be made by way of one or more acts, the form of which is determined by the Member State concerned, and should specify the precise nature of the special task"* does not bring any additional clarity.

lishment (Title III).[309] A *"regulated profession"* is defined as every professional activity access to which or the pursuit of which is subjected to the possession of specific professional qualifications as stipulated by legislative, regulatory or administrative means in the host Member State.[310] Since a large majority of today's service activities are bound to professional qualifications, including all types of attestation of professional competence (eg certificates) and / or experience, Art 17 (6) excludes the majority of service activities from the Directive's stipulations under the free movement of services, thus applies to them only those provisions of Title II of the Recognition of Professional Qualifications Directive. What is thus the essential regulatory content of Title II? Title II's Art 5 in connection with its Art 4 principally enshrine the System of General Prohibition on Restrictions as regards the access to a service activity (market access)[311] whereas it stipulates the applicability of the host Member State's legal order as regards all rules relating to the exercise of the service activity.[312] Comparing these regulations with the SD's approach it is apparent that the Professional Qualification Directive goes beyond as far as market access is concerned. The applied version of the System of General Prohibition on Restrictions namely does not foresee any reason of justification.[313] It however remains behind with respect to rules of exercise since it does not anchor the general prohibition on restrictions but gives the host Member State the possibility of applying its entire subject-matter related legislative framework to the service provider and provision with respect to professional qualification legislation. To conclude, the SD's stipulations on the free movement of services are indeed inapplicable to a key aspect of market access regulation, *ie* professional qualifications, for a great majority of service activities falling under the Professional Qualifications Directive. Last but not least

---

309 Art 1 2005/36/EC.

310 Art 3(1)(a) 2005/36/EC.

311 This follows from the wording that *"Member States shall not restrict, for any reason relating to professional qualifications, the free provision of services in another Member State"*.

312 Details as provided for in Art 6, 7, 8 and 9 of Title II 2005/26/EC shall not be considered in the paper at hand.

313 "Going beyond" and "remaining behind" refers to the amount of additional legislation stemming from the host Member State B a service provider from its home Member State A has to adjust to.

section III.E.2.b. as analysed above shall be briefly recalled. It emphasises that all those exceptions to the Directive's scope under its Art 1 and 2 not relating to a specific service activity but founding on certain consequences or issues the SD may not have or touch upon, could also be evoked as means of justifying a restrictive national measure by identifying it as lying outside the Directive's scope. Accordingly, Member States can claim that a national requirement is "justified" as it relates to or prevents the *"liberalisation of services of general economic interest"*, *"privatisation of public entities providing services"*, *"the abolition of monopolies"*, *"measures to promote cultural or linguistic diversity or media pluralism"*, Member State's *"criminal law"*, *"labor law"*, *"social security legislation"*, *"field of taxation"*, *"private international law"*, *"the exercise of fundamental rights"* and *"consumer protection"* rules laid down in the Member States' consumer legislation.[314] As a consequence, these *Chapter-I-reasons of justification* – in contrast to those under Chapter IV – are additional to those under Art 16 (1) (b) concerning public policy, public security, public health or the protection of the environment.

3. Chapter VI – Administrative Cooperation (Art 28–36): The Legal Text and Appraisal

a. Introduction

Chapter VI's main regulatory aim is to guarantee that *"Member States give each other mutual assistance and put in place measures for effective cooperation with one another in order to ensure the supervision of providers and the services they provide"*.[315] For this purpose Chapter VI primarily provides for delimitation of competence concerning supervision in the event of temporary movement of a provider to another Member State under Chapter IV on the free movement of services. Nevertheless, it also applies to general mutual assistance procedures in this case and under the Directive's Chapter III on the freedom of establishment and several other stipulations under different Chapters. The following analysis shall dominantly focus on the first constellation, however mentioning main aspects of the second, too.

---

314 Art 1 (2)-(6), Art 2 and Art 3 (2).

315 Art 28 (1).

b. Supervision under the
Free Movement of Services (Chapter IV)[316]

According to Art 30, the *Member State of establishment (home state)* is principally competent[317] and equally obliged[318] to exclusively supervise the service provider and the service delivered in another Member State. In case factual check and controls are necessary, the home Member State shall request the authorities of the Member State where the service is provided (host state) to act on his behalf.[319] The latter may also conduct these activities on its own initiative, even if it lacks supervisory power. They must however be *"not-discriminatory, not motivated by the fact that the provider is established in another Member State and proportionate"*. The host Member State, in contrast, is only exclusively competent for supervision in case it lawfully may derogate from the general prohibition on requirements under Art 16.[320] This Member State is thus in charge of supervision if those types of services under Art 17 are at stake, or if requirements are necessary for the reasons of public security, health, policy, protection of the environment as listed under Art 16 (1), or if a requirement is necessary for the safety of a service fulfilling the conditions of Art 19.[321] Additionally, the host Member State is also responsible for supervision in case it can uphold a national requirement due to a Chapter-I-reason of justification as elaborated under section III.I.2.c. above.

Apart from the types of services under Art 17, the host Member State is however not exclusively competent for the supervision of the entire service process including access to and exercise of it, but only as regards the compliance with the respective requirement it is

---

316 Supervision of the service provider and the service can principally be carried out either by the State of establishment (home state, Art 30) or by the State where the service is provided (host state, Art 31) or by both of them.

317 Art 30 (1).

318 Art 30 (2).

319 Mind that this request can also be put the other way round, namely the host Member State may request the state of establishment to undertake necessary checks, inspections and investigations [Art 29 (2)].

320 Art 31 (1).

321 For details, see above section II.I.2.a.ab.

allowed to apply.[322] All aspects apart from that relevant requirement may only be supervised by the host Member State after being invited to do so by the home state, or on its own initiative under the conditions stipulated before, respectively.[323]

c. General Provisions on Mutual Assistance and Cooperation

Art 28 lays down a general framework for mutual assistance between the Member States, also applicable to the freedom of establishment and other Directive's provisions. It obliges them to install *"liaison points"*[324] handling all the inter-State communication, satisfy *"information requests"* by other Member States[325], open their national registers in which providers have been entered for consultation of other Member States' authorities[326] and inform the Commission about cases where other Member States do not fulfil their obligations on mutual assistance[327]. Besides, Art 32 allows Member States to inform the Commission and all other States about any service activity *"that could cause serious damage to the health or safety of persons or to the environment"* ("alert mechanism"), Art 33 stipulates a *mutual information duty* for Member States on *"disciplinary or administrative actions or criminal sanctions and decisions concerning insolvency or bankruptcy involving fraud "* related to service providers, and Art 34 foresees the establishment of *"an electronic system for the exchange of information between Member States"*.

4. The Freedom to Provide Services and Administrative Cooperation – The Combined Regulatory Framework

To sum up, the host Member State has to consider the following steps under the (partly) new legal framework for answering the question which legal order shall apply to the access to and exercise of a cross-border service activity within their territory.[328] Firstly – after having checked the principal applicability of the SD – it shall

---

322 Art 31 (2).

323 Art 31 (3) and (4).

324 Art 28 (2).

325 Art 28 (3)-(6).

326 Art 28 (7).

327 Art 28 (8).

328 It shall be assumed that Member States have checked the principal applicability of the Directive especially under Art 1, 2 and 3.

assess whether the service activity is exempted from Chapter IV's scope through Art 17, listing all excepted services. Secondly – if this is not the case – it has to check whether its national provision represents a requirement in the above established sense.[329] Thirdly, it must consider whether this requirement is one of those under Art 16 (2) unconditionally forbidden. Fourthly, if the national measure constitutes a requirement which is not unconditionally forbidden it shall evaluate whether it is (a) applied in a non-discriminatory and (b) proportionate way and whether it is necessary for reasons of public policy, public security, public health, protection of the environment or – under specific circumstances listed under Art 18 (1) – safety of the service. Besides it can also be necessary for one of the Chapter-I-reasons of justification as introduced above under the last paragraph of section III.I.2.c. above. If it is necessary, the requirement can be applied on the service provider and provision. If not, the national requirement must not be upheld and the service provider is not bound by the home Member State's legal order to this respect. It remains however bound by the host Member State's legal order in case it foresees regulation for that case.

As far as the home Member State lawfully applies its legal order it is equally and exclusively competent for its supervision. Under those circumstances where the host Member State cannot affect its legal order and the service provider remains bound by the home Member State's legal order only, it is also the latter which is exclusively competent for supervision. The following graphic illustrates this analysis framework:

1) Is the SD principally applicable?
↓ Positive:
2) Is the service activity exempted from Chapter IV's scope through Art 17?
↓ Negative:
3) Is the national provision a requirement in the above established sense?
↓ Positive:
4) Is the requirement unconditionally forbidden according to Art 16 (2)?

---

329 This will most frequently to be answered with "yes", following the herein argued position that a foreign legal order already represents a requirement.

↓ Negative:
▼ 5) Is the requirement applied in a (a) non-discriminatory, (b) proportionate way, (c) necessary for reasons of public policy, security, health, protection of the environment, (under the specific circumstances listed under Art 18 (1)) safety of the service, or a Chapter-I-reason of justification?
↓ Positive:
▼ >>> The national requirement can be upheld and must be respected by the foreign service provider.

5. The Freedom to Provide Services under the Directive's Design – A Conclusion

a. Introduction

Evaluating which changes the before discussed chapter on the free movement of services and its related chapters on the quality of services and administrative simplification and cooperation will bring to the present legal situation requires to focus on one, most significant aspect, namely the applicable law for access to and exercise of a service provision. Before approaching this comparison, however, a summary of the already existing regulatory models for cross-border service provision in EC-law shall be offered. This excursus shall especially focus on the difference between the Country of Origin Principle and the General Prohibition on Restrictions System. A theoretical foundation appears to be of specific importance in the present context as there does not exist terminological coherence in literature.

b. Excursus: The Country of Origin Principle, the System of General Prohibition on Restrictions and the Country of Destination Principle - A Terminological Clarification

According to the authors' point of view, three different regulatory systems as regards the regulation of cross-border service provision are enshrined in primary and secondary EC-Law[330], namely the Country of Origin Principle (CoOP), the System of General Prohibition on Restrictions (GPoR)[331] and the Country of Destination Principle (CoDP).

---

330 This also takes into account secondary legislation in the stage of a draft thus not having legally binding force.

331 A frequently heard but in the present study contested argument is that the CoOP is already enshrined in today's Treaty based ECJ-case law

As regards the term *Country of Origin Principle* it has been firstly advocated as a regulatory concept in EC-Law[332] within the DSD 2004. The following quotes thus exhaustively specify the terminological formulation of the so-called CoOP: The DSD 2004 reads in Art 16 (1) and (2) that *"Member States shall ensure that providers are subject only to the national provisions of their Member State of origin which fall within the coordinated field"*, that this paragraph *"shall cover national provisions relating to access to and the exercise of a service activity"* and that , *"the Member State of origin shall be responsible for supervising the provider and the services provided by him, including services provided by him in another Member State"* (CoOP-Version 1). The second formulation of the CoOP is to be found in the Credit Institutions Directive with regard to authorisation.[333] It defines that credit institutions are to be *"authorised and supervised by the competent authorities"* of the home Member State only and that they may carry on their activities *"either by the establishment of a branch or by way of the provision of services"* in the host Member State (CoOP-Version 2).[334] As far as the *System of General Prohibition on Restrictions* is concerned also different versions are in force so far (only some of them shall be listed): Firstly, the ECJ's case law defines it by declaring illegal every host Member State's requirement *"liable to prohibit or otherwise impede the activities of a provider of services established in*

---

and thus just a synonym for the GPoR: *Brouwer* (2004); *Kluth /Rieger* (2006), describing the CoOP as a *"product"* of the ECJ's jurisprudence. Arguing against a congruency of these concepts, eg: *Fichtner* (2006).

332 Already before in 1985 the Commission's "White Paper on Completing the Internal Market" (COM (85) 310, paras 102–103) mentioned the *"home country control principle"*.

333 2006/48/EC – see above section I.D.3.c. – The CoOP is substituted in Recital 10 by the combined terms of *"principles of mutual recognition and home Member State supervision"*. The CoOP is to be equally found in the other secondary legislation relating to financial services as specified above under the before mentioned section.

334 A third formulation was included in the abandoned proposal for a Directive of the European Parliament and the Council concerning unfair business-to-consumer commercial practices in the Internal Market (the Unfair Commercial Practices Directive, COM (2003) 356 final) which will be explained immediately below.

another Member State"[335] except it can be justified by an overriding requirement of the general interest or a reason related to public policy, security or health (GPoR-Version 1). Secondly, the Television Broadcasting Directive and the E-Commerce Directive enshrine that home Member States "*shall ensure that (…) all broadcasters under their jurisdiction comply with the rules of the system of law applicable to broadcasters*" and that host Member States "*shall not restrict*" access to or exercise of the service activity on their territory beside it is justified by certain exhaustively specified requirements of the general interest (GPoR-Version 2). Thirdly, the Professional Qualifications Directive equally stipulates that host Member States "*shall not restrict*" foreign service providers but contrarily foresees no possibility of justifying the application of that Member State's restrictive legislation (GPoR-Version 3). Fourthly, Art 20 and 21 of the Credit Institution's Directive gives the host Member State the possibility – as far as the exercise of the freedom of establishment and the free movement of services *post-market access* (= *post-authorisation*) are concerned – to "*indicate*" in advance "*the conditions under which, in the interest of the general good, the service activities must be carried on*" in its territory (GPoR-Version 4). Lastly the SD – as analysed during entire Chapter III above – contains another modification of the GPoR. It states that "*Member States shall not make access to or exercise of a service activity in their territory subject to compliance with any requirements*" which are not justified by certain specified reasons of justification (GPoR-Version 5). As a matter of fact this Version 5 appears to be similar to Version 2. As regards the *Country of Destination Principle* the most prominent example represents the Posting of Workers Directive.[336] Its Art 3 enshrines that with regard to most central provisions of labor law named in the Directive only the host Member State's legal order applies to employees posted by a service provider established in another Member State (the home Member State).

---

335 Case C-76/90, *Säger v Dennemeyer*, ECR 1991, I-4221, para 12. This formula has more than once been repeated in recent judgments, such as Case C-398/95, *SETTG*, ECR I-3091, 3119, para 16.

336 Directive 96/71/EC; for a general description, see: *Barnard* (1999), 172.

Comparing the different regulatory models[337] it shall be assumed that Member State A indicates that state which is left by a service provider to make use of the freedom of establishment or the free movement of services in Member State B. The CoOP is consequently defined by a mandatory and unconditional, thus extraterritorial, appliance of the legal order of Member State A in Member State B. The GPoR in contrast mandates the non-appliance of the legal order of Member State B under certain conditions, most commonly in case of its restrictive nature and non-justifiability. The CoDP instead sets up a mandatory and unconditional appliance of the Member State B's legal order to service provision in its territory originating from Member State A. This classification is in line with a classification developed by *Maduro*. He has established three different regulatory models, the home state model, corresponding with above established CoOP, the host state model, corresponding with the CoDP and the harmonisation model as mentioned in the sentence before. Besides, he acknowledges the today's EC-Economic Constitution, thus indirectly also the GPoR, as a mixture of these three models.[338]

c. The Regulatory System under the SD and Today's Legal Framework

Following the conclusions of the before presented excursus it has to be preliminarily noted that the SD purely codifies to a large extend the so far case-law designed system of general prohibition on requirements. This is insofar true as Art 16 principally prohibits all requirements on the free movement of services by the host Member State. The latter can only lawfully impose a requirement as long as it is non-discriminatory, proportionate and necessary. This is thus exactly congruent with today's case law. The difference however lies within the possible justifications for the imposition of a requirement deemed necessary by the host Member State. While under today's legal framework all Treaty based reasons (Art 55 in connection with 45 EC) and all overriding requirements of the general interest are acknowledged, Art 16 merely recognises those of public policy, public security, public health, the protection of the

---

337 The generally used measure of harmonisation in EC-secondary legislation also represents a regulatory model, however not further deepened within the present context.

338 *Maduro* (1998), 52 *et seq.*

environment, safety of the service as well as the above introduced
Chapter-I-reasons of justification. The latter comprise requirements
relating to or affecting *"liberalisation of services of general economic interest"*, *"privatisation of public entities providing services"*, *"the abolition of monopolies"*, *"measures to promote cultural or linguistic diversity or media pluralism"*, Member State's
"criminal law", *"labor law"*, *"social security legislation"*, *"field of
taxation"*, *"private international law"*, *"the exercise of fundamental
rights"* and *"consumer protection"*

Furthermore, the so far to be applied system of overriding requirements of the general interest – of course it remains in force
outside the Directive's and Chapter's IV specified scope – allowed
the acceptance of new overriding requirements by the Court. This
evolutionary possibility has absconded under the Directive.

Beside, Member States must implement Art 16 (2), prescribing
certain requirements to be unconditionally forbidden. These requirements codify past case-law decisions, thus giving them a generally binding force through EC-secondary legislation. Additionally
it has to be pointed out that the system of general prohibition on
restrictions as enshrined in the SD is combined with a screening
duty to be carried out by the Member States (Art 39 (5)), requiring
them to reach the Commission's consent for every existing and
future requirement as defined by Art 16 (1).

J. The Service Directive – A Summary of its Main Innovations

Maintaining the so far followed structure, cross border service provision through the *freedom of establishment* primarily faces
changes with regard to Member States' requirements. On the one
hand the SD lists several requirements unconditionally forbidden
(Art 14) and on the other hand certain requirements which are subject to compulsory evaluation by and notification to the Commission (Art 15). With regard to the *free movement of services*, a
stipulation of unconditionally forbidden requirements is equally
included (Art 16 (2)). In contrast, however, all requirements which
a Member State holds up, introduces or modifies have to be evaluated and notified to the Commission (Art 39 (5) in connection with
Art 16). Besides, the system of general prohibition on restrictions as
known under today's legal framework is modified by restricting
possible justifications to those explicitly or implicitly (Art 1 (2–6),
Art 2, Art 3 (2)) enshrined in the Directive. The delimitation of
supervisory powers in the context of the free movement of services

depending on whether and to which extend the host Member State can lawfully apply its legal order primarily codifies but simultaneously clarifies today's legal status-quo (Art 30, 31). As far as the *SD-provisions relating to both freedoms* are concerned, national administrative procedures are simplified through a general examination duty on behalf of the Member States considering the complexity of their administrative practice (Art 5), the establishment of points of single contract (Art 6) and of electronically manageable administrative procedures (Art 8) as well as through certain information duties *vis-à-vis* the service provider (Art 7). This simplification of national administrative procedures is additionally enhanced by a reinforced cooperation between the Member States' administrations. To this regard Member States must establish national liaison points and are obliged to cooperate and respond to questions stemming from another Member State's national administration (Art 28, 29). Also relating to both freedoms are the legal innovations in the field of service recipients' rights and related stipulations on the quality of services. They primarily oblige Member States to guarantee that their respective administrative bodies as well as those service providers established in their territory provide the service recipient (regularly the consumer) with specific information, such as the legal status of the provider (Art 21, 22).

IV. Conclusion – Evaluating the Directive's Main Innovations in the Light of Its Overall Aim and Purpose

The last section of the study in hand is devoted to connect today's legal status-quo for cross border service provision under the Treaty as well as under EC-secondary legislation with the SD. This shall help in answering the paper's fundamental question whether the SD meets it original expectations and aims. These expectations and aims have been best formulated in the Commission's report on *"The State of the Internal Market for Services"*[339], namely by identifying all obstacles currently hampering the internal market for services. These obstacles can be summarised in two points: the missing legal certainty and the abolition of concrete Member States' restrictions as listed in the report.

As to the first, an evaluation of the SD in the light of the present legal framework delivers an ambiguous result. On the negative

---

339 European Commission, COM(2000) 888, 42–45.

side of the coin, the SD's differentiation between the regulatory approach applicable to the freedom of establishment and that applicable to the free movement of services has to be named in the first place. So far, as demonstrated in Chapter II above, the basic principles of the system of general prohibition on restrictions have been the same within both freedoms. This is no longer true, since within the free movement of services the possibilities of justification are restricted to certain, in the Directive listed reasons and no longer open for new ones. Secondly, this is especially true since the delimitation between the two freedoms enshrined in the SD is based on the very flexible and currently changing criteria of the Court's case law further adding to the decrease of legal certainty. Thirdly, the limited Directive's scope makes it applicable to only some services and increases the complexity of the choice of the relevant law. In other words, the internal market law for services splits up in three different fields of application with three different set of rules: In the first place, there is the set of rules under the SD's stipulation on the freedom of establishment. Although it is following the system of general prohibition on restrictions of today's freedom of establishment, it additionally consists of a variety of other regulation as enshrined in the SD. In the second place, there is the set of rules under the Directive's free movement of services. And in the third place, there exist those rules as enshrined under today's Treaty based freedom of establishment and free movement of services and the corresponding secondary legislation. In this regard the *lex specialis* regulation by the Professional Qualifications Directive is important to mention. This directive excludes the applicable provisions of the SD from being applied in the crucial area of market access for service providers – in the question of professional qualifications – hereby undoubtedly limiting its potential effects. Continuing with the negative side of the coin concerning the aim of increased legal certainty, the failed system change with respect to the free movement of services has to be discussed in the forth place. By maintaining today's system of general prohibition of restrictions, Member States will continue to use their discretionary power to keep foreign service providers out of their national markets. The limitation of possible justifications is not helpful to this respect since on the one hand still many reasons can be legitimately brought forward (Chapter-I-reasons of justification!) and on the other hand it is still in the host Member State's hands to initially and potentially abusively interpret those reasons. Also relating to the reasons of justification in the framework of the free movement of services is the screening and notification duty. This legal instrument, however, is the first to be presented under the positive side of the coin. It indeed will enhance legal certainty, since Member States' restrictions have to be notified to the Commission, a procedure which will facilitate the work of the latter to bring Member States in compliance with the SD's stipulations. Secondly, under both freedoms certain national requirements are unconditionally forbidden. Although these articles represent a mere codification of the Court's case-law, they transform the – in principle – purely *inter-partes* applicable case-law into *erga omnes* legally binding force and consequently are to be welcomed.

This codification ("black-listing") of requirements can also be listed as a positive achievement under the second category, the abolition of concrete Member States' restrictions. Besides, the SD's stipulations on administrative simplification, namely the introduction of points of single contracts, the right to information and the procedures by electronic means will help service providers to eliminate unjustified restrictions to a large extend.

Summing up, the SD introduces certain improvements with regard to legal certainty as well as the abolition of concrete restrictions. The chance for a fundamental breakthrough for service providers and Europe's internal market in the field of services, however, is passed up due to the limited scope of application and, above all, the missed system change. Future legislative initiatives should thus primarily focus on these two aspects. Firstly, an extended scope of application should horizontally apply to all service sectors and all phases of the service provision not yet regulated in EC-secondary legislation. To this regard an integration of the Professional Qualifications Directive and an alignment of its regulatory principles to those of an enhanced second generation services directive would be essential. Secondly, a shift to a comprehensive Country of Origin Principle on the basis of the free movement of services would guarantee the required system change. According to the above (5.2.) introduced terminology, that principle would declare the host Member State's legal order inapplicable, making the home Member State's one the only relevant for the service provider abroad. The predominant problem linked to this approach is seen by many to lie within the *de facto* impossibility of Member States' authorities to know eventually 26 different legal orders so as to apply them properly. In the critics point of view this lack of knowledge would lead to a non-appliance of Member States' legal orders as soon as the service provider would move abroad and would signify an elementary erosion of national supervisory law in the service economy with all its potentially negative consequences. On this account, two additional regulatory instruments should accompany the introduction of the CoOP: In the first place, the introduction of the CoOP should be limited to the free movement of services leaving the freedom of establishment aside. Within it it should be applied to national requirements regulating market access or post-market access regulation substantially affecting market access only. In the second place, a second generation services directive must include an extended annex providing for a list of all national regulation to which the CoOP should be applicable. This list of national regulation should be detailed enough in order to allow national administrative authorities to actually apply it to foreign service providers. The Professional Qualifications Directive provides for an example for such a detailed an elaborated annex allowing the applicability of Member State A-law in Member State B by authorities of the latter. This innovative approach, however, requires a joint research effort by academia and practitioners. Especially the delimitation between regulation relating to the *post*-market access phase but substantially affecting market access and that without implications for a service provider's market access[340] as well as the design of the mentioned annex represent future research questions resulting from the present paper.

References

Catherine Barnard (1999), EC Employment Law, Oxford (Oxford University Press) 1999.

Catherine Barnard (2004), The Substantive Law of the EU, Oxford (Oxford University Press) 2004.

Carl Böhert / Dieter Grunow / Jan Ziekow (2005), Überprüfung ausgewählter Aspekte des Vorschlages zu einer Richtlinie des Europäischen Parlaments und des Rates über Dienstleistungen im Binnenmarkt KOM (2004), Speyer (Forschungsinstitut für öffentliche Verwaltung) 2005.

---

340 Compare above section II.B.3.c.

Onno Brouwer (2004), The Country of Origin Principle: Rulings of the European Court of Justice and its Impact on Legislation, in: European Parliament, Public Hearing of 11 November 2004 on the Proposal for a Directive on Services in the Internal Market and Consumer Protection, 52–55

Paul Craig / Gráinne de Burca (2003), EU Law. Text, Cases and Materials, Oxford (Oxford University Press) ³2003.

José Luiz Cruz da Vilaca (2002), On the Application of Keck in the Field of Free Provision of Services, in: *Mads Andenas / Wulf Henning Roth* (eds.), Services and Free Movement in EU Law, Oxford (Oxford University Press) 2002, 22–40.

Jan Hendrik Dalhuisen (2000), On International Commercial, Financial and Trade Law, Oxford (Hart) 2000.

Thomas Eilmansberger (1999), Zur Reichweite der Grundfreiheiten des Binnenmarkts, in: Juristische Blätter 121 (1999), 345–367 + 434–453.

Nikolai Fichtner (2006), The Rise and Fall of the Country of Origin Principle in the EU's Services Directive – Uncovering the Principle's Premises and Potential Implications (= Beiträge zum Transnationalen Wirtschaftsrecht, Vol. 54), Halle (Martin-Luther-Universität Halle-Wittenberg) 2006.

Cornelia Gerster et al. (2006), Kreditwirtschaftlich wichtige Vorhaben der EU, Berlin (Bundesverband Öffentlicher Banken Deutschlands) ¹⁴2006.

Stefan Griller (ed.) (1992), Banken im Binnenmarkt, Vienna (Service Fachverlag) 1992.

Jesper Lau Hansen (2002), Full Circle: Is there a Difference between the Freedom of Establishment and the Freedom to Provide Services?, in: *Mads Andenas / Wulf Henning Roth* (eds.), Services and Free Movement in EU Law, Oxford (Oxford University Press) 2002, 176–215.

Vassilis Hatzopoulos / Thien Uyen Do (2006), The Case Law of the ECJ Concerning the Free Provision of Services: 2000-2005, in: CMLRev 43 (2006), 923–991.

Michael Hellner (2004), The Country of Origin Principle in the E-commerce Directive – A Conflict with Conflict of Laws?, in: European Review of Private Law 12 (2004) No. 2, 193–213.

Walburga Hemetsberger / *Henning Schoppmann* / *David Schwander* / *Christoph Wengler* (2006), European Banking and Financial Services Law, The Hague (Kluwer Law) 2006.

Matthias Herdegen (2004), Europarecht, München (Beck) [6]2004.

Hans D. Jarass (2002), A Unified Approach to the Fundamental Freedoms, in: *Mads Andenas* / *Wulf Henning Roth* (eds.), Services and Free Movement in EU Law, Oxford (Oxford University Press) 2002, 138–175.

Wolfgang Kiemel (2003), Art 56 EG, in: *Hans von der Groeben* / *Jürgen Schwarze* (eds.), Kommentar zum Vertrag über die Europäische Union und zur Gründung der Europäischen Gemeinschaft, Baden Baden (Nomos) [6]2003.

Thorsten Kingreen (2003), Grundfreiheiten, in: *Armin von Bogdandy* (ed.), Europäisches Verfassungsrecht. Theoretische und dogmatische Grundzüge, Berlin (Springer) 2003, 640–682.

Thorsten Kingreen / *Rainer Strömer* (1998), Die subjektiv-öffentlichen Rechte des primären Gemeinschaftsrechts, in: Europarecht 33 (1998) No. 3, 263–290.

Winfried Kluth / *Frank Rieger* (2006), Die gemeinschaftsrechtlichen Grundlagen und berufsrechtlichen Wirkungen von Herkunftslandprinzip und Bestimmungslandprinzip, in: Gewerbe Archiv 52 (2006), 1–8

Henk Kox / *Arjan Lejour* / *Raymond Montizaan* (2004/2005), The Free Movement of Services within the EU, (= CPB Working Paper No. 69), The Hague, October 2004 (revised September 2005).

Koen Lenaerts / *Piet van Nuffel* (2005), Constitutional Law of the European Union, London (Thomson, Sweet & Maxwell) [2]2005.

Peter-Christian Müller-Graff (2003), Art 49 EGV, in: *Rudolf Streinz* (ed.), EUV/EGV, Munich (Beck) 2003.

Christoph Ohler (1996), Die Kapitalverkehrsfreiheit und ihre Schranken, in: Zeitschrift für Wirtschafts- und Bankenrecht 1996, 1801 *et seqq.*

Miguel Poiares Maduro (1998), We, the Court: The European Court of Justice and the European Economic Constitution, Oxford (Hart) 1998.

Albrecht Randelzhofer / Ulrich Forsthoff (2001), vor Art 36–55 EGV, in: *Eberhard Grabitz / Meinhard Hilf* (eds.), Das Recht der Europäischen Union, Munich (Beck) 2001.

Albrecht Randelzhofer / Ulrich Forsthoff (2004), Art 49/50 EGV, in: *Eberhard Grabitz / Meinhard Hilf* (eds.), Das Recht der Europäischen Union, Munich (Beck) 2004.

Georg Ress / Jörg Ukrow (2005), Art 56, in: *Eberhard Grabitz / Meinhard Hilf* (eds.), Das Recht der Europäischen Union, Munich (Beck) 2005.

John Antony Usher (2000), The Law of Money and Financial Services in the EC, Oxford (Clarendon) 2000.

Wulf-Henning Roth (2002), The European Court of Justice's Case Law on Freedom to Provide Services: Is 'Keck' Relevant?, in: *Mads Andenas / Wulf Henning Roth* (eds.), Services and Free Movement in EU Law, Oxford (Oxford University Press) 2002, 4–21.

Utz Schliesky (2005), Von der Realisierung des Binnenmarktes über die Verwaltungsreform zu einem gemeineuropäischen Verwaltungsrecht? Die Auswirkungen der geplanten Dienstleistungsrichtlinie auf das deutsche Verwaltungsrecht, in: Deutsche Verwaltungsblätter 2005, 887 *et seqq.*

Wolfgang Schön (1997), Europäische Kapitalverkehrsfreiheit und nationales Steuerrecht, in: *Wolfgang Schön* (ed.), Gedächtnisschrift für Brigitte Knobbe-Keuk, Cologne (Schmidt) 1997, 743 *et seqq.*

Rudolf Streinz (2003), Europarecht, Heidelberg (Müller) ⁶2003.

Gernot Sydow (2004), Verwaltungskooperation in der Europäischen Union. Zur horizontalen und vertikalen Zusammenarbeit der europäischen Verwaltungen am Beispiel des Produktzulassungsrechts, Tübingen (Mohr Siebeck) 2004.

Christian Tietje (2003), Niederlassungsfreiheit, in: *Dirk Ehlers* (ed.), Europäische Grundrechte und Grundfreiheiten, Berlin (de Gruyter) 2003.

Christian Tietje / Peter Troberg (2003), Art 43 EG, in: *Hans von der Groeben / Jürgen Schwarze* (eds.), Kommentar zum Vertrag über die Europäische Union und zur Gründung der Europäischen Gemeinschaft, Baden Baden (Nomos) ⁶2003.

Peter Troberg / Christian Tietje (2003), Art 52 EG, in: *Hans von der Groeben / Jürgen Schwarze* (eds.), Kommentar zum Vertrag über die Europäische Union und zur Gründung der Europäischen Gemeinschaft, Baden Baden (Nomos) [6]2003.

Peter von Wilmoswsky (2003), Freiheit des Kapital- und Zahlungsverkehrs, in: *Dirk Ehlers* (ed.), Europäische Grundrechte und Grundfreiheiten, Berlin (de Gruyter) 2003.

Lorna Woods (2004), Free Movement of Goods and Services within the European Community, Aldershot (Ashgate) 2004.

**Harald Badinger, Fritz Breuss,
Philip Schuster and Richard Sellner**

Macroeconomic Effects of the Services Directive

I. Introduction

Making the Single Market more dynamic has been identified as one
of the top priorities to improve the EU's growth performance.[1] In
contrast to manufacturing industries, where the Single Market appears to be working quite well[2], an assessment by the European
Commission[3] on the state of the internal market for services has
identified a large gap between the vision of an integrated European
economy and reality in service industries. There are still many impediments to the free movement of services in the EU. Particularly
for small and medium-sized enterprises, the bulk of service providers, entry barriers in new EU markets are often prohibitive. With
the Directive on Services in the Internal Market (SD) the European
Parliament and the Council aim at removing the remaining barriers
in this area to enable firms to exploit the full potential of cross-border services. This would be an important step forward in bringing
the EU closer to its Lisbon targets.

Previous studies suggest sizeable macro-economic effects of
the services directive in its original version (henceforth Draft Services Directive (DSD 2004))[4]. *Kox et al.*[5] econometrically estimate
the implications of the SD for the cross-border provision of services; their results suggest that (in the service industries investigated) intra-EU trade would increase by some 44 percent and intra-
EU FDI by some 26 percent. Copenhagen Economics[6] simulates the
effects of the SD using a computable general equilibrium (CGE)

1   *Sapir et al.* (2004).
2   *Badinger* (2007).
3   European Commission (2002).
4   European Commission (2004).
5   *Kox et al.* (2004/2005).
6   Copenhagen Economics (2005a).

model, assuming a reduction in tariff equivalents to the obstacles to cross-border provision of services (estimated in a first step). Their simulations suggest an increase in employment by around 600,000 persons and an increase in activity (value added) by some 1.1 percent.

This study supplements previous studies, using a simple econometric approach to estimate the economic effects of the SD through two channels: (i) the *trade channel* via the principle of "Free movement of services", and (ii) the *FDI channel* via the principle of "Freedom of establishment for service providers". For both channels we deduce its implications for the macro-economic performance, i.e. for productivity, employment, value added, investment and GDP. According to our calculations the finally agreed upon version of the Services Directive (henceforth SD 2006) could raise employment by 400,000 in the EU-25 and increase real GDP by around one percent in the medium to long run.

The remainder of this paper is organised as follows: Section II outlines the main transmission channels via which the SD is supposed to contribute to the Lisbon goal of more jobs and growth. Section III reports on previous studies by four European research groups on this topic. Section IV presents the own econometric estimates of the trade channel of the SD. Section V does the same for the FDI channel. In Section VI we evaluate the implications of the changes from DSD 2004 to SD 2006. The final Section VII summarises the results and outlines some policy conclusions.

II. The Services Directive and its Macro-economic Implications

Extending the (functioning of the) Single Market to service industries by implementing the four freedoms has no direct effects on growth and employment, but it is supposed to generate its effects mainly via an increase in trade, FDI and competition[7].

Figure 1 illustrates the main channels through which the Single Market may contribute indirectly to an improvement of macroeconomic performance. The abolishment of non-tariff barriers

---

7   For a more detailed discussion of the transmission channels of the Single Market and the effects on macro-economic performance, see *Griffith / Harrison* (2004), *Nicodème / Sauner-Leroy* (2004), and OECD (2003).

(reduction of administrative hurdles via implementing the SD 2006) leads to an increase in *intra-EU trade* (a consequence of a better exploitation of the "Free movement of services" principle) and an easier market access for foreign (EU) firms and therefore more *FDI* (a consequence of the "Freedom of establishment for service providers").

Apart from increasing competition, more trade is supposed to raise productivity mainly through three channels: the exploitation of economies of scale as a result of larger markets, international specialisation according to comparative advantages, and its contribution to the international diffusion of technology and knowledge.[8] This is the first transmission channel we will investigate. A related channel involving similar mechanisms is foreign direct investment (FDI). The effects of FDI are investigated separately.

More trade also implies more competition via the famous "pro-competitive effect" of free trade proposed by Bhagwati.[9] Whether more FDI leads to more competition as well is an open question.

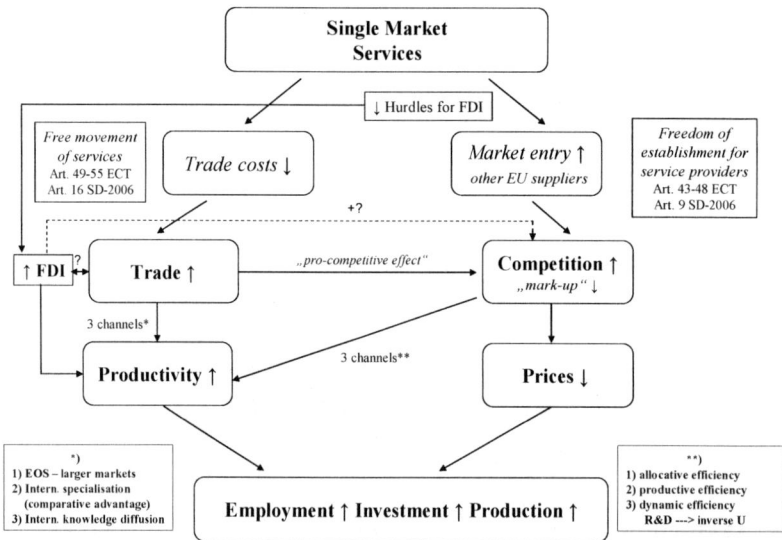

Fig. 1: The   Services   Directive   and   its   Macro-economic Implications

---

8   See *Frankel / Romer* (1999).

9   *Bhagwati* (1965).

Competition, in turn, increases productivity by bringing prices more in line with marginal costs, which reduces distortions of the price mechanism and enables a more efficient allocation of resources and higher productivity of the factors capital and labour (allocative efficiency); higher competitive pressure also increases the incentives for the management to organise work more efficiently and to reduce slack, as well as potential gains from exploiting increasing returns to scale as market size increases (productive efficiency). Finally, competition might also raise dynamic efficiency by increasing incentives for R&D activities and innovations and thereby boosting technological progress and growth of total factor productivity.[10] FDI is also supposed to lead to more productivity as well. This can be documented in particular in the transformation countries of Eastern Europe before they entered the EU.

An increase in competition will also reduce prices for two reasons: first, marginal costs go down as a result of higher productivity. Second, as a consequence of diminished market power, firms' mark-ups over marginal costs decrease as well. This reduction in prices increases the demand for services and thus also output. Whether the demand for production factors (employment and investment) ultimately increases, too, is a question that has to be answered empirically; it is conceivable that the growing demand for services can be met with a given (or even with a smaller) input of production factors as a result of the original increase in productivity.[11]

III. The Services Directive: Results of Four Research Groups

Most studies on the effects of the Single Market focus on manufacturing, and here in turn often only on selected industries where strong effects of the Single Market were to be expected. To date,

---

10 Recently, it has been suggested that there might be an inverse U-shaped relationship between competition and innovation (*Aghion et al.*, 2005), i.e. there could be an optimal degree of competition between too little and too much competition.

11 In a recent paper, *Nordhaus* (2005) shows that – in contrast to widely held views – the increase in productivity in US manufacturing has rather mitigated than caused the large reduction in employment in manufacturing, whose primary cause turns out to be the increase in productivity and decline in prices of international competitors.

there are results of four research groups in Europe on the economic impact of the SD (see table 1). One has to take into account, however, that the results of all these studies refer to the original proposal for a Services Directive by the European Commission in 2004[12] (DSD 2004) as compared to the final version of the directive (SD 2006).

(1) One of the first and most comprehensive studies – a first version was published already in 2004, the final version in 2005 – was that by Copenhagen Economics[13]. In a first step it made a survey on the administrative hurdles (regulatory barriers) hindering the full working of the single market for services along the lines of the documentation of administrative barriers carried out by the European Commission[14]. After translating these answers into an Internal Market Restrictiveness Index in Services (IMRIS) and aggregating it into seven sub indices (establishment, use of inputs, promotion, distribution, sales, after sales and non-legal) an econometric analysis studied two types of impact: rent creation and cost-creation. Both effects lead to higher prices, whereas the first results in higher profits and the latter in higher costs. Then these effects are converted into tariff equivalents and the consequences of the reduction of the IMRIS when implementing the DSD 2004 are simulated with a static computable general equilibrium (CGE) model (called GETEM) with imperfect competition covering all 25 EU Member States (EU-25). The most striking result that has received most attention is that the model predicts an economy-wide increase in employment by 0.3 percent that is 600,000 new jobs. Employment in services industries is predicted to go up by 0.5 percent and value added by 1.1 percent in the medium to the long run. Welfare (measured by private consumption) increases by € 37 billion or +0.6%. The elimination of the country of origin principle (CoOP) – estimated by Copenhagen Economics[15] in a special study for the UK government – would lower the effects by 10 percent.

---

12   European Commission (2004).

13   Copenhagen Economics (2005a).

14   European Commission (2002).

15   Copenhagen Economics (2005b).

Tab. 1: Macroeconomic Effects of the Liberalisation of the Services Market according to the DSD 2004: Results of Four Research Groups for EU-25

Research group (Methods)	Real GDP % (welfare)	Employ-ment % (persons)	Intra-EU trade in services %	Intra-EU FDI %
(1) Copenhagen Economics (2005a; 2005b) (CGE model – GETM)	+0.6 *) (€ 37 bn.) (without CoOP: -10%)	+0.3 (600,000) (without CoOP: -10%)	+5.0	-
(2) *O'Toole* (2005), Dublin (CGE model GTAP)	+0.5 (€44 bn.)	-	-	-
(3) *CPB*, The Hague (3a) *Kox et al.* (2004/2005) (Gravity models: trade, FDI) (3b) *Gelauff / Lejour* (2006) (WorldScan model: 5 Lisbon highlights) (3c) *Bruijn et al.* (2006) (WorldScan model)	- +0.2 +0.3 – +0.7 (without CoOP: +0.2 – +0.4	- 0.0 0.0	+30 – +60 (∅+44) +30.0 (+1.7% total EU trade) 30–60 (without CoOP: +20–+40)	+20 – +35 (∅+26) - - -
(4) *Breuss / Badinger*, EI, Vienna (2006) (Cross-section and panel econometrics)	+0.7 (€ 74 bn. 2005 PPS)	+0.3 (408,000– 816,000; ∅612.000)	Taken from CPB (2004/2005)	-

*) Refers to private consumption; CPB = Netherlands Bureau for Economic Policy Analysis; CoOP = country of origin principle; EI = Europainstitut at the Vienna University of Economics and BA.

(2) Also by applying a CGE model (GTAP model) *O'Toole*[16] reaches nearly the same welfare effects of the implementation of

---

16   *O'Toole* (2005).

the DSD 2004, namely € 44 bn. or +0.5%. However, in this static CGE model with perfect competition and fixed labour supply there are no overall employment effects due to the implementation of the DSD 2004.

(3) In several studies in the years 2004–06, the CPB (Centraal Planbureau – Netherlands Bureau for Economic Policy Analysis, The Hague) studied the impact of existing administrative hurdles in the EU Member States on the cross-border provision of services.

(3a) The core argument of *Kox et al.*[17] is that it is not only the degree of regulation in service industries, but also the heterogeneity of regulations across EU countries that hampers the free movement of services within the EU. Building on previous work by the OECD[18], *Kox et al.* develop an index for the policy-heterogeneity of regulation in service industries (with sub-indices), based on a bilateral comparison of 183 aspects of market regulation; they calculate that implementing of the DSD 2004 would reduce total EU policy heterogeneity by approximately 1/3 (see table 2).

Tab. 2: Expected Impacts of Proposed EU Measures in the SD on Intra-EU Policy Heterogeneity

Sub-index	Reduction
Regulatory and administrative opacity	66–77%
Explicit barriers to trade and investment	73–78%
Administrative burdens on start-ups	34–46%
Barriers to competition	29–37%
State control	3–6%
Overall heterogeneity indicator	31–38%

Source: *Kox et al.* (2004/2005), 32.

Subsequently, *Kox et al.* estimate the effects of regulatory heterogeneity on bilateral intra-EU trade in services and intra-EU FDI in services. For trade, they use a gravity model, the standard approach to estimating trade potentials; for FDI, the gravity model is slightly modified in line with the knowledge-capital model[19]. The indices of regulatory heterogeneity are used as explanatory variables in both models; then the effects of the SD's implementation

---

17   *Kox et al.* (2004/2005).

18   Particularly, *Nicoletti et al.* (1999) and *Golub* (2003).

19   *Markusen* (2002).

are simulated using the (significant) parameter estimates and the expected reduction of the respective indices. The sample comprises bilateral trade flows of the 14 old EU countries (Belgium and Luxembourg are aggregated) for the years 1999–2001. In the investigation of bilateral FDI stocks, three new Member States are also contained in the sample (Czech Republic, Hungary, and Poland), but here only the years 1998 and 1999 are considered. *Kox et al.* take the commercial services sector as an aggregate, where only those sectors are covered that are affected by the SD ("transport" and "travel", which together make up some 50 percent of total trade in services are excluded).

According to the results of the latest version of the study, the implementation of the SD would have the following effects: (1) Intra-EU trade in services increases by 44 percent (range: 30–62 percent with an average of +44 percent),[20] and (2) Intra-EU FDI in services increase by 26 percent (range: 18–36 percent with an average of +26 percent). The trade results are of similar magnitude in later CPB studies by *Gelauff / Lejour* and by *Bruijn et al.*[21]

(3b) *Gelauff / Lejour* with the Worldscan model of CPB – a static general equilibrium world model covering 19 EU countries explicitly, the rest EU, USA, rest OECD, non-OECD and 12 sectors, four of which are service sectors (transport services, other commercial services, research and development and other services) – study "Five Lisbon highlights" (the internal market for services, the reduction of administrative burdens, goals on improving human capital, the 3% target on research and development expenditures, and 70% target on the employment rate). The implementation of the DSD 2004 leads to an increase in real GDP in 2025 of cumulative 0.2 percentage points for the EU (+0.4 percent for Austria). The

---

20 Intra-EU trade covers about half of total trade in services. Consequently, the estimated effect on total trade in services is half of the effects given above. In terms of total intra-EU trade (including goods), the estimated effect corresponds to an increase by 2–5 percent. Out of total trade (goods and services) of the EU, only 20 percent consists of *trade in services*. The structure of trade in services (as of 2003) is as follows: 33% tourism/travel, 31% business services, 18% transport, 10% financial services, 3% telecommunication, 2% each construction and government services, 1% private services.

21 *Gelauff / Lejour* (2006), *Bruijn et al.* (2006).

overall employment effect is zero in this static CGE model. However, there are some reallocations between the 12 sectors used in the model (with negative employment effects in the sector "other commercial services").

(3c) *Bruijn et al.*[22], also using the Worldscan model, study the implications of the DSD 2004 and the SD 2006. In the original version the SD would result in an increase of real GDP in 2025 of +0.3 to 0.7 percentage points (again with zero overall employment effects). Excluding the CoOP would reduce the effects by 1/3 to an increase of real GDP of +0.2 to 0.4 percentage points.

(4) In an econometric study by *Breuss* and *Badinger*[23] using a cross-section and panel approach, the implementation of the DSD 2004 is estimated to result in the creation of on average 612,000 new jobs and an increase in real GDP by 0.7 percent. These effects – as all those of the other studies – apply only in the medium to the long-run. The methodology and the results of this study are explained in the following sections.

IV. Econometric Estimation of the
Trade Channel Effects of the Services Directive

The following sections describe the empirical analysis, the data used, the econometric methodology applied and the simulations of the macro-economic impact of an implementation of the SD. The results are based on *Breuss / Badinger* (2006) and hence rely on the impact of the DSD 2004. Finally, we make an evaluation how much the change from the country of origin principle (CoOP) to the country of destination principle (CoDP) – as drafted in the SD 2006 – might influence the overall results.[24]

A. The Implications for Competition and Productivity

1. Data Sources and Country Coverage

Our data set draws on several sources. Data except those on trade were taken and derived from the *60-Industry Database* of the Groningen Growth and Development Centre (GGDC, 2005) as well

---

22   *Bruijn et al.* (2006).

23   *Breuss / Badinger* (2006).

24   For a detailed discussion of the changes from a legal perspective see the contribution by *Maydell* to this volume.

as from the *Structural Analysis (STAN) Database* of the OECD. The latter source was particularly important for obtaining investment data needed to calculate investment ratios, capital stocks (and to derive estimates for mark-ups). Trade data were taken exclusively from the *Statistics on International Trade in Services* database of the OECD.

As far as country coverage is concerned, our initial approach was to use the EU-25, of course; it turned out, however, that even four of the EU-15 countries had to be excluded due to missing data (Denmark, Luxembourg, Ireland, and Portugal). For several specifications, particularly those requiring data on mark-ups, the cross-section dimension had to be further reduced since not all countries have data for real investment in all industries considered.[25] Nevertheless, the coverage is large enough to regard our results as representative, at least for the EU-15, and to a smaller extent for the EU-25. As control countries and to add observations, we also included Norway and the USA, two further OECD countries for which sufficient data were available. We checked the sensitivity of the results, when these two non-EU countries were excluded or when country dummies for the USA and Norway were used, and found that their inclusion makes no important difference to the results.

2. Industry Classification and Coverage of the Services Directive

We use the most detailed classification of service industries which our data sources permit. Restrictions are placed by all sources, also since the industry classifications used by the STAN and the GGDC data (International Standard of Industrial Classification) are not exactly the same as the one used in the OECD Statistics on International Trade in Services (Extended Balance of Payments Services Classification). Fortunately, the correspondences[26] turned out to be close enough to obtain a reasonable sub-classification of the service sector into 13 detailed service industries.

---

25   This is particularly true for BE, ES, IT, SE and UK.

26   See UN (2002).

Tab. 3: Composition of EU-15's Total Value Added (VA) and Employment (EMP) in 2002

	ISIC Rev3	VA (million euro)	EMP (1000)	VA	EMP
				(percent of total)	
TOTAL (ALL INDUSTRIES)	**01–99**	**9,233,547**	**170,059**	**100**	**100**
Agriculture, forestry, fishing	01,02, 05	146,731	6,993	1.59	4.11
Mining and quarrying	10–14	76,925	368	0.83	0.22
Manufacturing	15–37	1,707,667	29,409	18.49	17.29
Electricity, gas and water supply	40–41	191,940	1,017	2.08	0.60
Total services	45–99	7,110,284	132,272	77.00	77.78
Total services	**45–99**	**7,110,284**	**132,272**	**77.00**	**77.78**
Service industries included in estimation	**45– 749**	**5,006,293**	**81,730**	**54.22**	**48.06**
Construction SI01	45	561,000	11,803	6.08	6.94
Sale, maintenance and repair of motor vehicles and motorcycles; retail sale of automotive fuel SI02	50	166,110	3,786	1.80	2.23
Wholesale trade and commission trade, except motor vehicles and motorcycles SI02	51	424,100	7,430	4.59	4.37
Retail trade, except of motor vehicles and motorcycles; repair of personal and household goods SI02	52	425,910	14,920	4.61	8.77

Tab. 3: Composition of EU-15's Total Value Added (VA) and Employment (EMP) in 2002 (continued):

	ISIC Rev3		VA (million euro)	EMP (1000)	VA (percent of total)	EMP (percent of total)
Hotels & restaurants	SI03	55	256,440	8,275	2.78	4.87
Inland transport	SI04	60	202,410	4,460	2.19	2.62
Water transport	SI04	61	21,465	182	0.23	0.11
Air transport	SI05	62	39,098	388	0.42	0.23
(Supporting and auxiliary transport activities; activities of travel agencies)		63	135,580	2,094	1.47	1.23
Communications	SI06	64	259,080	2,645	2.81	1.56
Financial intermediation, except insurance and pension funding	SI07	65	333,090	3,284	3.61	1.93
Insurance and pension funding, except, compulsory social security	SI08	66	77,841	983	0.84	0.58
(Activities auxiliary to financial intermediation)		67	65,285	1,157	0.71	0.68
Real estate activities	SI13	70	928,360	1,713	10.05	1.01
Renting of machinery and equipment	SI09	71	110,360	531	1.20	0.31
Computer and related activities	SI10	72	185,330	2,299	2.01	1.35
Research and development	SI11	73	39,814	690	0.43	0.41
Legal, technical and advertising	SI12	741–3	469,550	6,628	5.09	3.90
Other business activities, nec	SI12	749	305,470	8,462	3.31	4.98

Tab. 3: Composition of EU-15's Total Value Added (VA) and Employment (EMP) in 2002 (continued):

	ISIC Rev3	VA (million euro)	EMP (1000)	VA	EMP (percent of total)
Service industries excl. from estimation	**75–99**	**2,103,991**	**50,542**	**22.79**	**29.72**
Public administration and defence; compulsory social security	75	601,680	11,915	6.52	7.01
Education	80	472,420	11,051	5.12	6.50
Health and social work	85	613,320	15,509	6.64	9.12
Other community, social and personal services	90–93	359,200	8,440	3.89	4.96
Private households with employed persons	95	57,371	3,627	0.62	2.13
Extra-territorial organisations and bodies	99	0	0	0.00	0.00

VA = value added at current prices, EMP = total persons engaged.

Source: Groningen Growth and Development Centre, 60-Industry Database, February 2005. Industries in parentheses are not included in our samples due to lack of data and correspondence with other data sources.

Table 3 gives a detailed overview of the composition of the EU-15's value added and employment by industry. Total services constitute 77 percent of value added or 78 percent of total employment. It should be added, however, that several service industries are not considered to be covered by the SD: these are typical non-market or government provided services (such as public administration, defence, health and social work, etc.). Together these industries make up 23 percent of total value added (or 30 percent of total employment), leaving service industries totalling 54 percent of total value added (or 48 percent in terms of total employment) to be potentially covered by the SD. These industries, referred to as SI01 to SI13, constitute our most comprehensive sample.[27]

From this sample, however, not all industries will be covered. First, transport (SI04, SI05) is excluded from the SD; the same is true for financial services (SI07, SI08). We also exclude travel (SI03) (though it is largely covered by the SD) for two reasons: first, to make our sample as consistent as possible with the *Kox et al.*[28] study that excludes travel from the estimates (which we will use in the simulation); second, travel turns out to be an outlier in the sense that results change significantly when it is added to the sample. (The relevance of the sample choice will be discussed in greater detail below.) Communication (SI06), which includes telecommunication, and construction (SI01) are partly excluded from the SD.

When the study by *Breuss / Badinger* (2006) was carried out it was uncertain how the revision of the DSD 2004 would result in a narrowing of the coverage of sectors.[29] This uncertainty was handled by applying the "LEGO approach", that means starting from the most comprehensive sample including all industries, and then excluding, step by step, industries which are not covered (or not fully covered) by the SD until a sample remains which closely coincides with the SD 2006. The final industry classification and the samples used are given in *table 4*.

---

27   For reasons of data availability two industries are not contained in our samples (supporting and auxiliary transport activities; activities of travel agencies as well as activities auxiliary to financial intermediation); together, they account for 2.18 percent of total value added.

28   *Kox et al.* (2004/2005).

29   See *Vogt* (2005) for an early discussion.

Tab. 4: Overview of Final Industry Classification and Samples Used in Estimation

(a) Detailed industries contained in full sample		Value added	Employ-ment
		Percent of total	
SI01	Construction	6.08	6.94
SI02	Trade and repair	11.00	15.37
SI03	Travel (hotels and restaurants)[1]	2.78	4.87
SI04	Water, land transport, etc.	2.42	2.73
SI05	Air transport	0.42	0.23
SI06	Post and telecommunications	2.81	1.56
SI07	Financial intermediation	3.61	1.93
SI08	Insurance and pension funding	0.84	0.58
SI09	Renting of machinery and equipment	1.20	0.31
SI10	Computer and related activities	2.01	1.35
SI11	Research and development	0.43	0.41
SI12	Other business activities	8.39	8.87
SI13	Real estate activities	10.05	1.01
(b) Samples used in estimation			
Sample A	All (SI01–SI13)	52.04	46.15
Sample B	A, excl. transport (SI04,SI05)	49.20	43.19
Sample C	B, excl. financial services (SI07,08)	44.74	40.68
Sample D	C, excl. travel (SI03)	41.97	35.82
Sample Da	D, excl. construction (SI01)	35.89	28.87
Sample Db	D, excl. communication (SI06)	39.16	34.26

Data refer to EU-15 and the year 2002.

Sources: GGDC-60 industry database (see table 3). Sample A does not include the industries in parentheses from table 3. 1) For SI03 ("Travel") no perfect correspondence could be achieved: trade data for SI03 include both hotels and restaurants as well as travel agencies, whereas SI03 for the other variables covers only hotels and restaurants (since activities of travel agencies and tour operators are only available aggregated with transport activities, and cannot be allocated accordingly).

To give some impression of the relevance of the respective samples, *table 4* shows the corresponding shares of the services industries contained in the samples in total value added and total employment. While we will use the "LEGO approach" and carry out the estimation for all samples, sample D, which is closest to both the study by *Kox et al.* and the coverage of the SD, is our preferred sample.

3. Methodological Issues

Our empirical analysis can be divided into three classes of empirical models which are all similar in their structure and motivated by the transmission channels of the SD illustrated in *figure 1*:

First, we explain *competition* (measured as mark-up ratio, i.e. the ratio of prices over marginal costs[30]) by domestic market size (in terms of population) and trade (more precisely, the ratio of imports to production) to figure out the likely "pro-competitive effect" of the increase in trade triggered by the SD:

$$Markup_{ik} = \mu_k + \varphi \ln m_{ik} + \tau \ln Pop_i + u_{ik}. \qquad (1)$$

Markup_{ik} is related to trade, measured as ratio of imports to production (*m*) and country size, measured by population (*Pop*); *i* (*k*) refers to country (service industry). Obviously, imports are endogenous in (1), e.g. as a results of reverse causality. High mark-ups may act as signals for profit opportunities and thus attract foreign competitors. We use the geographical share of the import ratio to instrument for imports in (1) as constructed in *Badinger / Breuss* (2005) – using a gravity model approach – to get a robustness check and to ensure that our least squares results are not driven by endogeneity (see below for a more detailed discussion).

Our second group of models investigates the link between *productivity* (measured in terms of value added per hour worked) and domestic market size and trade. This should help us to assess the first important channel of the SD, the direct effects of trade on productivity. The basic specification used is similar to the study by *Frankel / Romer*[31] who, however, use aggregate data and a large sample of countries. As far as the direct effects of *trade on productivity* are concerned, the results are disappointing. In contrast to

---

30   We calculate the country- and industry specific mark-up (*Markup_{ik}*) as the ratio of value added to the sum of capital costs and labour compensation according to: $Markup_{ik} = VA_{ik}^{nom} / (W_{ik} + K_{ik}R_{ik})$; where VA_{ik}^{nom} is nominal value added, W_{ik} is labour compensation (both taken from OECD STAN Database), and $K_{ik}R_{ik}$ is the capital stock times the user costs of capital.

31   *Frankel / Romer* (1999).

aggregate estimates as in *Frankel / Romer* and industry estimates for manufacturing in *Badinger / Breuss*[32], we do not obtain a direct effect of trade on productivity for any of the samples of service industries considered[33]. Therefore this (direct) channel is omitted from our analysis. Instead we consider the indirect channel from competition to productivity, using:

$$\ln Prod_{ik} = \mu_k + \delta Markup_{ik} + \tau \ln Pop_i + u_{ik}. \qquad (2)$$

Productivity (*Prod*) measured by output per hour worked is related to competition (*Markup*) and market size (*Pop*).

The third group of models tries to examine the relation between *economic performance* (productivity, employment, investment) and market size and competition. These models are similar in spirit to the approach taken by Griffith and Harrison (2004) and follow the equation:

$$Perform_{ik} = \mu_k + \delta Markup_{ik} + \tau \ln Pop_i + u_{ik}. \qquad (3)$$

Perform (macro-economic performance) is identified by three macro-economic variables: (i) Productivity (Prod), (ii) Employment (L), and (iii) Investment (sk = investment ratio).

Endogeneity is likely to be a problem in all models: trade is endogenous with respect to productivity and competition, and competition is likely to be endogenous with respect to performance (particularly productivity). Previous studies with similar specifications suggest that least squares estimates are not far off (or often tend to underestimate the effects). Nevertheless, we check the robustness of the results using instrumental variable (IV) techniques, thereby exploiting the exogeneity of geography.[34] The basic mes-

---

32   *Badinger / Breuss* (2005).

33   In a more recent attempt, *Badinger / Breuss* (2006) found a relationship between aggregate trade in services and productivity at the country level.

34   In particular, we use the fact that aggregate "proximity" of a country and industry is an important determinant of both trade and competition (through trade and threat of entry). Ideally, these proximity measures would be constructed from (industry-specific) geographical trade shares calculated from the estimates of bilateral gravity models including geographical variables only (as suggested by *Frankel / Romer*, 1999). Such an approach was chosen in a similar setting for manufacturing industries by *Badinger / Breuss* (2005). For service

sage of this exercise is that the least squares estimates are not misleading.

We use *two approaches*: a *cross-section approach* referring to
averages of the period 1995–2000, and a *panel approach* covering
the period 1978–2002. The advantage of the cross-section approach
is that it refers to more actual data and that geography-based (i.e.
time-invariant) instruments can be used to address endogeneity
concerns. Here, the advantage of the panel estimates lies in the use
of much more observations; a disadvantage is that we are forced to
rely on the least squares estimates; this is not too much of a problem, however, in light of the small differences between the least
squares and the IV results in the cross-section analysis.

4. Estimation Results

As to the industry dimension, we always start from the most comprehensive sample A, including all industries, and then, step by
step, exclude industries not covered by the SD until we arrive at
sample D. The results in *table A1* in the appendix report only the
results for the preferred sample D.

As we did not find a significant direct relationship between
trade and productivity for service sectors we endorse the indirect
channel according to equation (1), namely between *competition* and
productivity. The results are documented for Sample D in *table A1*
in the appendix (the last three columns).

Regarding the relationship between *competition* and *economic
performance*, results correspond more closely to the theoretical
presumptions. *Table A1* in the appendix illustrates some key regression results, referring to sample D. The main results can be summarised as follows:

For our preferred sample D (see *table 4*) we can identify indirect effects of the SD on the economic performance via an increase
in competition. We find both economically and statistically significant effects of trade on competition (mark-ups), and of competition
on productivity, employment and investment. More trade leads to

---

industries at the level of disaggregation used here, however, bilateral
trade data are not available; hence, we use an auxiliary approach and
construct the instruments for trade and competition for a sample of
services industries from industry-specific proximity measures for
manufacturing industries from *Breuss / Badinger* (2005).

more competition (lower mark-ups) which is associated with higher productivity as well as higher employment, investment and output.

The IV results of our cross-section estimates tend to be higher than the least squares estimates. While the IV results should be treated with caution since only an auxiliary approach can be used for the construction of instruments, they nevertheless suggest that the least squares estimates are not fundamentally misleading.

The results of the least squares panel estimates are in line with the results from the cross-section models, though the panel results suggest a somewhat smaller magnitude of the effects.

As far as the relevance of the sample choice is concerned, it should be noted that the results are not completely robust for all samples given in *table 4*. As far as transport services are concerned, adding them to sample D hardly affects the results. This is not true for financial services; results are sensitive to adding this industry so that the results for sample D cannot be extended to financial services without qualification.

A further point that deserves some discussion is the exclusion of "travel" from our preferred sample. On principle, travel (including hotels and restaurants, catering, as well as activities of travel agencies and tour operators, tourist assistance activities) is covered by the SD, but we nevertheless excluded it from the estimation for two reasons: first, to make our industry coverage as consistent as possible with the study by *Kox et al.* who excluded travel as well; second, "travel" (SI03) turned out to be an outlier in the estimation in so far as the results changed significantly when travel was added to the estimation. There is no fully convincing explanation for this phenomenon: particularly pronounced measurement problems in this industry may be one explanation; another issue is that competition in travel industries exhibits several idiosyncratic characteristics (as the role of local, region-specific amenities); a further point (at least for the regressions including trade) is that for this particular industry there is only a rough correspondence between our trade and production data.

B. Simulation of the Macro-economic Implications of the Services Directive via the Trade Channel

Figure 2 illustrates our finding that the main channel through which the SD will contribute to macro-economic performance is an increase in competition. To obtain an assessment on the likely magnitude of these effects we need to quantify: (1) the likely increase in competition as a result of the SD, and (2) the magnitude of the effects of competition on performance.

Fig. 2: Simulation of the Effects of the Services Directive – via the Trade Channel

1. Effects of the Services Directive on Competition

As a benchmark estimate of the likely effects of the SD on competition, we use our estimation results for the link between imports and competition, together with the trade effects of the SD according to *Kox et al.*[35] As already mentioned above, they estimate that due to the implementation of the DSD 2004 the overall heterogeneity indicator will decline by 1/3 (see *table 2*) and this will increase intra-EU trade (in the industries covered by the SD) by 30 to 62 percent; in our simulation we focus on their central estimate of 44 percent. Note that our estimates refer to total rather than intra-EU trade. Since intra-EU trade in services accounts for around half of total trade in services, we assume that the SD will increase total trade in services by some 22 percent.[36] The average of our estimates for our preferred sample D (see *table A1* in the appendix) suggests that an increase in imports by one percent reduces mark-ups by 0.127 percentage points.

This implies that an increase in trade (imports) by 22 percent will translate into an increase in competition, i.e. a reduction in mark-ups by some 2.5 percentage points. It should be borne in mind, however, that the SD will enhance competition not only through an increase in trade but also by making market entry easier and increasing the threat of entry. Against this background we interpret the mark-up reduction of 2.5 percentage points as a lower bound; as an upper bound we will use a mark-up reduction of 5 percentage points (which also corresponds to the effects obtained

---

35   *Kox et al.* (2004/2005).

36   Hence, we assume that the effects estimated by *Kox et al.* (2004/2005) are fully realised in terms of additional trade; it is conceivable that part of this additional intra-EU trade is simply substituted for extra-EU trade, yielding a smaller increase in total trade.

using the coefficient from the cross-section IV estimates).[37] As a central estimate for the simulation, we use a mark-up reduction by 3.75 percentage points.

2. Effects of Competition on Productivity, Employment, and Investment

Our estimates provide us with a range of coefficients for the effects of competition on productivity, employment and investment. Again, we focus on our preferred sample (D), but still we have three estimates: least squares and IV from the cross-section, and least squares from the panel. As a benchmark, we decided to use the average of the three estimates; as a consequence, the following coefficients are used in the simulation:

- semi-elasticity between productivity and mark-ups: -0.214,
- semi-elasticity between employment and mark-ups: -0.225,
- semi-elasticity between investment and mark-ups: -0.145.

Together with the assumed increase in competition (reduction in mark-ups) by 2.5 to 5 percentage points this will provide us with a range of estimates regarding the effects of the SD on productivity, employment, investment and value added.

3. Simulation Results of the Economic Impact of DSD 2004

Table 5 summarises the results of the simulation for the EU as a whole. Note that our estimation is carried out only for eleven EU countries due to limited data availability, but throughout we calculate the results for the EU-15 and EU-25 countries, too.

The simulation suggests that in the service industries considered (sample D, see table 4), productivity in terms of value added per hour worked will go up by 0.53 to 1.07 percent (central estimate: 0.80 percent), employment by 0.56 to 1.13 percent (central estimate: 0.85 percent). Taken together, this implies an increase in value added by 1.10 to 2.20 percent (central estimate: 1.65 percent). The investment ratio is predicted to rise by 0.36 to 0.73 percentage points (central estimate: 0.55 percentage points).

---

37   This upper bound implies a relative reduction in mark-ups by 10 percent; this is still clearly below the mark-up reduction in manufacturing as a result of the Single Market according to the estimates by *Badinger* (2007).

Tab. 5: Economic Effects of the Services Directive – Estimates for the EU

	Min.	Central	Max.
Increase in competition (red. in mark-ups in percent)	-2.5	-3.75	-5
Increase in productivity (percent)	0.53	0.80	1.07
Increase in employment (percent)	0.56	0.85	1.13
Increase in value added (percent)	1.10	1.65	2.20
Increase in investment ratio (percentage points)	0.36	0.55	0.73
Absolute increase in employment (in 1000)			
EU-11	323.6	485.3	647.1
EU-15	343.1	514.7	686.2
EU-25	408.0	612.0	816.0

Bearing in mind that the share in total value added of the industries considered makes up some 42 percent (EU-15, 2002 see *table A1* in the appendix), the central estimates imply an aggregate GDP effect of 0.69 percent. Combining the relative effects on employment with the employment figures for the EU-11 and the EU-15 (sample D, values for 2002, see *table 2*), employment in service industries of the EU-11 is predicted to increase by some 485,000 persons, or by 515,000 persons in the EU-15: extrapolating the results to the EU-25 using the ratio of aggregate employment in the EU-25 to aggregate employment in the EU-15 (1.19), the predicted increase in employment for the EU-25 amounts to 612,000 persons. *Table 6* shows the absolute changes in employment by country based on the central estimates.

Comparing our aggregate estimates with the CGE simulations by Copenhagen Economics[38], we find surprisingly similar results. The estimated increase in employment by Copenhagen Economics amounts to around 600,000 persons, which is very close to our central estimates for the EU-25; the increase in value added in service industries according to Copenhagen Economics amounts to 1.1 percent, which is also in the range of our estimates.

---

38   Copenhagen Economics (2005a).

Tab. 6: Absolute Employment Effects of the Services Directive –
Estimates by Country

		Minimum	Central	Maximum
AUT	Austria	7.0	10.6	14.1
BEL	Belgium	8.4	12.5	16.7
DEU	Germany	76.6	114.9	153.2
ESP	Spain	32.2	48.3	64.4
FIN	Finland	4.1	6.2	8.2
FRA	France	49.2	73.7	98.3
GBR	United Kingdom	66.8	100.2	133.6
GRC	Greece	6.7	10.0	13.3
ITA	Italy	46.0	69.0	92.0
NLD	Netherlands	18.8	28.2	37.6
SWE	Sweden	7.8	11.8	15.7
DNK	Denmark	5.3	7.9	10.6
LUX	Luxembourg	0.7	1.0	1.4
IRL	Ireland	3.7	5.5	7.3
PRT	Portugal	9.9	14.9	19.9
EU-15	European Union (15)	343.1	514.7	686.2

The same pro-competitive effect is assumed for each country here, i.e. the variation is only due to the different levels of employment in sample D across countries.

There is no reason to assume that changes in competition have fundamentally different effects across countries. This was also confirmed when trying to estimate country-specific coefficients for competition in the models for productivity, employment and investment, which yielded implausible results. However, the SD is likely to have different effects on the degree of competition in the EU countries, depending on the current level of regulation and regulation heterogeneity in the respective country. *Kox et al.* (2004/2005) calculate country-specific changes of their regulation heterogeneity indices and use them to simulate country-specific effects of the SD on trade in services. Countries with a higher level of regulation (or more heterogeneity with respect to the other EU countries) will experience a larger opening up of markets and hence larger trade effects.

It is plausible to assume that the increase in imports relative to the EU average (implied by the country-specific estimates in *Kox et al.*[39] is a good indicator for the increase in market access due to the SD relative to the EU average and thus for the increase in competition relative to the EU average. *Table 7* shows the implied country-specific effects of the SD on productivity, employment, value added, investment and absolute employment, each of them based on the central estimate. Above average winners are Portugal, Denmark, Greece, Austria, and Italy; the effects in Germany, Spain, Finland, and France correspond roughly to the average EU effects, while Belgium, the Netherlands, Luxembourg, Ireland, Sweden and the United Kingdom gain less than the EU average. This is not a new result, of course, but an implication shared with the *Kox et al.* study.

It should be added that these figures are "bottom-line" results; potential reallocations between industries and countries are not investigated here. In particular, the fear of trade unions that the SD could lead to "social dumping" is not addressed in our study. On the one hand, the huge disparities in wage costs (roughly 1:10) could lead to an unbeatable comparative advantage of service providers from the new EU Member States of Eastern Europe. On the other hand, the old EU countries have a much stronger competitive edge in providing services when it comes to quality competition.[40]

From the productivity and employment performance one can deduce the effects of the implementation of the DSD 2004 on real GDP. Measured at 2005 PPS GDP in EU-25 would be higher by € 75 billion or by 0.7 percent.

---

39   See *Kox et al.* (2004/2005), 43.

40   For a related discussion, see *Vogt* (2005), 19.

Tab. 7: *Economic Effects of the Services Directive – Country-Specific Results*

	Pro-comp. effect rel. to EU av.*)	Competition percent	Productivity percent	Employment percent	Value added percent	Inv.ratio Perc. points	Employment 1000s
AUT	1.27	-4.77	1.02	1.08	2.10	0.69	13.4
BEL	0.84	-3.15	0.67	0.71	1.38	0.46	10.5
DEU	1.07	-4.01	0.86	0.90	1.76	0.58	122.8
ESP	1.02	-3.84	0.82	0.86	1.68	0.56	49.4
FIN	1.00	-3.75	0.80	0.85	1.65	0.55	6.2
FRA	1.02	-3.84	0.82	0.86	1.68	0.56	75.4
GBR	0.93	-3.49	0.75	0.79	1.53	0.51	93.4
GRC	1.55	-5.80	1.24	1.31	2.54	0.84	15.5
ITA	1.20	-4.52	0.97	1.02	1.98	0.66	83.1
NLD	0.84	-3.15	0.67	0.71	1.38	0.46	23.7
SWE	0.93	-3.49	0.75	0.79	1.53	0.51	11.0
DNK	1.32	-4.94	1.06	1.11	2.17	0.72	10.4
LUX	0.84	-3.15	0.67	0.71	1.38	0.46	0.9
IRL	0.84	-3.15	0.67	0.71	1.38	0.46	4.6
PRT	1.52	-5.71	1.22	1.29	2.51	0.83	22.7
EU-15	1.00	-3.75	0.80	0.85	1.65	0.55	514.7

*) Relative pro-competitive effect of the SD in the respective country corresponding to the relative trade effects estimated by *Kox et al.* (2005), 43. Since Belgium and Luxembourg are treated as aggregate in the study *by Kox et al.* (2004/2005), we assume the same value for both countries. The aggregate value for the EU does not correspond to the sum of country values due to mechanics of aggregation and averaging.

V. Econometric Estimation of the
FDI Channel of the Services Directive

As figure 1 illustrates there are two channels via which the reduction of regulation might relieve the cross-border provision of services: (i) via the principle of "Free movement of services" (SD 2006) implying more Intra-EU trade, more competition and hence a better macro-economic performance (see section IV) and (ii) via the principle of "Freedom of establishment for services providers" leading to more Intra-EU FDI flows.

In this chapter we deal with the second channel, the impact of the SD on foreign direct investment (FDI). This channel is not dealt with explicitly in the previous studies (see *table 1*), neither in the CGE model of Copenhagen Economics nor in the Worldscan model of the CPB. However, *Kox et al.*[41] estimate econometrically that the reduction of policy-heterogeneity by 1/3 would lead to an increase in Intra-EU-FDI stocks by 18–36 % (with an average of +26%). The aim of this chapter is to quantify directly the effects of regulations for FDI on FDI activity in services industries and furthermore to estimate the resulting impact on productivity.

We assume that FDI regulations affect all foreign investors in the same way, irrespective of their residences. Thus we do not include an index for heterogeneity as suggested by *Kox et al.* in our estimations but the FDI regulation index constructed by *Golub*[42]. As bilateral data on FDI flows or stocks are not (or at least not sufficiently) available at the industry level, we use an aggregate approach rather than a traditional bilateral gravity-type model. We follow a two step procedure: First, we estimate the impact of regulation on FDI stocks. Second, we relate productivity on FDI stocks to derive the macro-economic impact of SD's "Freedom of establishment for services providers". Using our estimates we simulate the change in productivity resulting from a reduction in FDI regulations by 1/3.

---

41   *Kox et al.* (2004/2005).

42   *Golub* (2003).

A. The Implications on FDI and Productivity

1. Data Sources and Country Coverage

The data sources used to estimate the effects of the SD on foreign direct investment and the impact of the change in foreign direct investment on productivity include the *60-Industry Database* of the Groningen Growth and Development Centre (GGDC) as well as the *International Direct Investment Statistics Database* of the OECD. The latter was mainly used to obtain data on FDI inward stocks for the individual service sectors, while the GGDC database provided us with data on average labour productivity and value added. Due to poor data on FDI stocks only four service sectors and eleven countries could be included in our analysis. As can bee seen from *table 8*, the four sectors included cover 28.25 percent of the value added and 36.05 percent of employment of all industries of the EU-15 in the year 2002. The sample comprises 11 EU countries: Austria, Czech Republic, Denmark, France, Germany, Greece, Hungary, Netherlands, Poland, Portugal and United Kingdom (three of which are new EU member states and transformation economies – Czech Republic, Hungary and Poland).

Tab. 8: Shares of Total Value Added (VA) and Employment (EMP) in 2002 of the Service Industries Included in the Estimation

			VA	EMP
		ISIC Rev3	(percent of total)	
Total		**1–99**	**100.00**	**100.00**
Total services		**45–99**	**77.00**	**77.78**
Service industries				
incl. in estimation			**28.25**	**36.05**
Construction	SI01	45	6.08	6.94
Distribution	SI02	50, 51, 52	11.00	15.37
Hotels & restaurants	SI03	55	2.78	4.87
Business services	SI04	741–3, 749	8.39	8.87
Service industries				
excl. from estimation			**48.75**	**41.73**

Data refer to EU-15. VA = value added at current prices, EMP = total persons engaged.

Source: Groningen Growth and Development Centre, 60-Industry Database, February 2005.

In order to maximise sample size, averages over the years 2000 to 2002 were taken for every variable except the FDI regulation index. FDI barriers within the EU were measured by the "FDI restriction indices" by *Golub*, based on the years 1998 and 2000. The index incorporates regulations on how much foreign equity is allowed in a specific sector, screening and approval and other restrictions. As can be seen from *figure 3*, within the covered sample of the four sectors (1 = construction, 2 = distribution, 3 = hotels & restaurants, 4 = business services), Austria seems to have the most rigorous restrictions on FDI while the Netherlands have the most liberal regime in this respect.

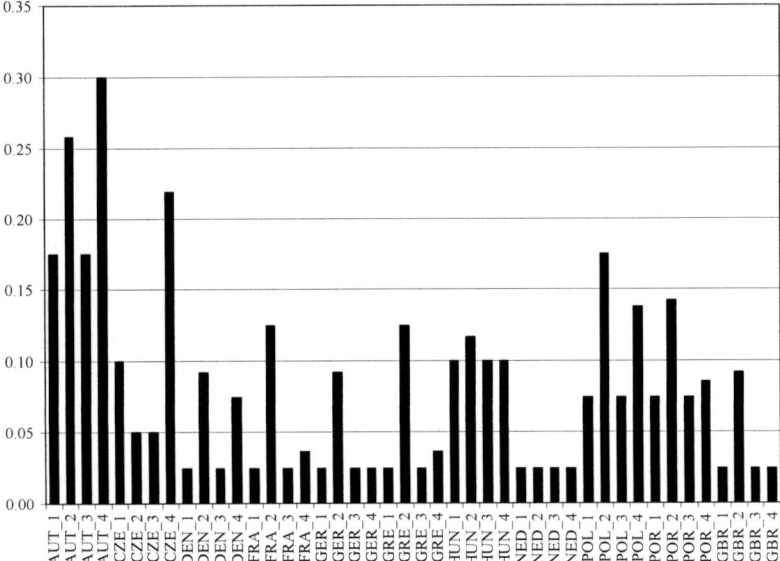

Fig. 3: Foreign Direct Investment Regulation Indices by Country and Industry, Source: Golub *(2003).*

2. Methodological Issues

The main problem arising in the estimation is the possible endogeneity of FDI stocks. It seems likely that productivity itself is an explaining factor for FDI stocks. Unfortunately, due to absence of bilateral FDI data we were not able to construct instruments as suggested by *Gao*[43]. However, *Gao* and *Frankel / Romer*[44] found evi-

---

43   *Gao* (2004).

dence that an ordinary least square estimation tends to underestimate the effects of FDI and trade on productivity. Therefore, we may assume that our OLS estimates are not misleading and may be interpreted with due care as a lower bound of the possible effect.

Our empirical analysis can be divided into two classes of empirical models which are similar in their structure (and also comparable to the approach for the analysis of the trade channel; see section IV). They are motivated by the transmission channels of the SD illustrated in *figure 1*:

First, we relate *foreign direct investment (FDI)* to domestic market size (in terms of population) and *regulation intensity for FDI*:

$$\ln FDI_{ik} = \mu_k^T + \mu_k^{NT} + \delta \ln Reg_{ik} + \tau \ln Pop_i + \varepsilon_{ik}, \qquad (4)$$

where FDI_{ik} is measured in terms of the inward FDI stock relative to value added (*i* denotes country and *k* industry); Reg_{ik} are the indices for FDI restriction for industry *k* in country *i*, and Pop_i is population of country *i*. The industry specific constants are allowed to differ between the transition (T) and non-transition economies (NT), to account for the fact that the transformation economies in Eastern Europe experienced a huge inflow of FDI in the 1990s (well above the "normal" FDI flows between industrial countries).

The second group of models tries to identify the impact of *FDI on productivity* using a specification similar to the one suggested by Gao[45]. He finds a significant positive effect of FDI-stock-to-GDP-ratio on real GDP per worker for a sample of non-oil producing developing countries. We depart from this specification in three respects. As in equation (2), productivity is defined as value added per hour worked; population is used as only control variable; and industry-specific constants are included, which are again allowed to differ between transition and non-transition economies.

$$\ln Prod_{ik} = \mu_k^T + \mu_k^{NT} + \delta \ln FDI_{ik} + \tau \ln Pop_i + \varepsilon_{ik}. \qquad (5)$$

3. Estimation Results

After removing one outlier (the Greek business services industry) from our sample, results for equation (4) are quite satisfactory and

---

44   *Frankel / Romer* (1999).

45   *Gao* (2004).

robust to changes in the specification. The second column in *table A2* in the appendix shows the summary of the cross-section estimation results. Our preferred specification includes only *Reg* and *Pop* as explanatory variables, consistent with the analysis of the trade channel. Aggregate measures of area, distance and language did not enter the empirical models at conventional significance levels.

On average, countries of the EU-15 have higher FDI inward stocks than transition countries, although only one constant term is significant at a 10 percent level (the interaction between the transition and the construction industry dummy, not displayed in *table A2*). Population, which serves as a control variable for size effects, has a negative effect on FDI inward stocks ratio, significant at a 5 percent level. On average, smaller countries are not only more open in terms of trade but attract also greater FDI stocks relative to value added than larger ones.

Turning to row 4 in *table A2*, we find an negative relation between the FDI inward stock ratio and the indices for FDI regulation. Since the Golub regulation index is inversely defined, reducing barriers to FDI by one percentage point in the service market leads to an increase in the ratio of FDI inward stocks to value added by 0.45 percent. This coefficient is statistically significant at the 5 percent level.

The third column in *table A2* reports the estimation results of equation (5), relating *average labour productivity (Prod)* to *FDI* and *market size*. In contrast to equation (4), results are not that robust to changes in the specification. Different factors explaining productivity (R&D ratio, capital labour ratio and labour compensation) have been included and tested along with FDI inward stocks, the central factor of our study. When estimating with UNCTAD FDI flow data, no significant effects of FDI on productivity can be found. The same is true when R&D ratios are included along with OECD FDI inward stocks. However, leaving aside R&D ratios, a marginally significant (10 percent level) positive impact of the FDI ratio on average labour productivity can be found. A 1 percent increase in the ratio of FDI inward stock relative to value added improves productivity by 0.15 percent. In the equation for the estimation of average labour productivity, population has a significant and positive impact. Finally, average productivity levels are significantly smaller in the three transition countries of our sample.

B. Simulation of the Macro-economic Implications of the Services Directive via the FDI Channel

We used the coefficient for FDI regulation of equation (4) and FDI inward stocks of equation (5) to simulate effects of the SD on FDI inward stocks and productivity, based on the assumption that its implementation leads to a reduction in barriers to FDI by 1/3 (the reduction in policy heterogeneity as a result of the SD according to Kox et al.[46]). *Figure 4* illustrates the channel through which the services directive may influence performance in terms of productivity.

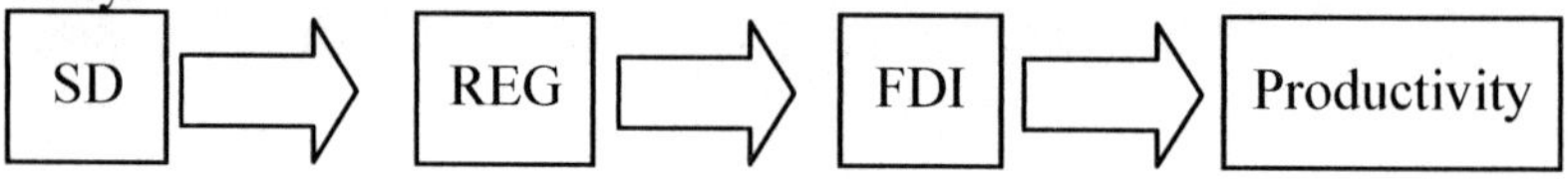

| SD | ⟹ | REG | ⟹ | FDI | ⟹ | Productivity |

Fig. 4: Simulation of the Effects of the Services Directive – via the FDI Channel

According to our estimates, the reduction of the barriers to FDI in service industries (*Reg*) by one third implies an increase in FDI inward stocks in the four observed services industries by 18.9 percent. These results are comparable to the lower bound estimates of *Kox et al.* (2004/2005), but as argued above the OLS estimates are likely to underestimate the effects.

This 18.9 percent increase in FDI inward stocks translates into an increase in average labour productivity by 2.8 percent. Assuming that the Services Directive does not affect the industries excluded from the sample (some 72 percent of value added), aggregate total productivity gains amount to 0.80 percent. Note, however, that these effects rely on calculations of *Kox et al.* assuming the implementation of the DSD 2004.

Economic theory on employment effects of FDI is ambiguous. Several trial regression, relating employment to FDI and including standard controls, did not yield robust results. We do not pursue this issue further here and assume that the stimulation of FDI via die implementation of the SD only leads to productivity and hence production effects. From the increase of productivity and zero employment growth one can deduce that the implementation of the DSD 2004 would lead to an increase in real GDP by 0.80 percent.

---

46   *Kox et al.* (2004/2005).

VI. Which Change in the Macro-economic Effects without the CoOP?

Two significant changes have occurred in the transition from the DSD 2004 to the SD 2006:

i.   The *country of origin principle* (CoOP) has been replaced by the *country of destination principle (CoDP)*. According to Copenhagen Economics[47], in a special evaluation for the UK government, this could reduce the economic effects by 10 percent. The CPB[48] estimates that the liberalisation effect could even be reduced by 1/3.

ii.   The SD 2006 has also diminished the sectoral coverage compared to the original proposal in the DSD 2004. More services sectors have been exempted.

Tab. 9: Macro-economic Effects of the SD 2006 as Compared to those of DSD 2004: EU-25

	DSD 2004	**SD 2006**
(I) Trade channel		
Employment	612.000	408.000
GDP, real	+0.7%	+0.5%
(II) FDI channel		
Employment	-	-
GDP, real	+0.8%	+0.5%
(III) Total: (I) + (II)		
Employment	612.000	408.000
GDP, real	+1.5%	+1.0%

Note: The figures are to be interpreted as medium to long-run effects.

An evaluation of how much the change from the CoOP to the CoDP affects the "Policy heterogeneity indices" or the "Indices of FDI restrictions" is very difficult. The SD 2006 involves a lot of exception clauses, allowing EU Member States to make restrictions only for reasons of public policy, public security, public health or the protection of the environment. How much EU Member States will make use of such restrictions and how much of them will pass the newly introduced "screening process" (Art. 41(5)) by the European Commission is an open question.

---

47   Copenhagen Economics (2005b).

48   *Bruijn et al.* (2006).

We therefore rely on the assumption that the watering down of the DSD 2004 by the SD 2006 will reduce liberalisation effects by 1/3. This translates into a proportionate reduction of the macro-economic effects, because it reduces both the old and new EU Member States potential to exploit their respective comparative advantages. The corresponding results are given in *table 9*.

VII. Policy Implications and Conclusions

Making the EU's Single Market more dynamic has been identified as one of the top priorities to improve the EU's growth performance. While the Single Market in manufacturing appears to be working quite well, there are still many impediments to the free movement of services in the Internal Market. Particularly for small and medium-sized enterprises, the bulk of service providers, entry barriers in new EU markets are often prohibitive. The Internal Market for Services should have been working since its inception in 1993. However, already seven years later in March 2000 on the summit of the European Council in Lisbon the heads of state or government had to conclude that in reality it did not. In the context of the "Lisbon strategy" it therefore asked the European Commission to design a global "Single Market Strategy" to make the Single Market working properly. A comprehensive report on the existing administrative and regulatory hurdles in the EU Member States[49] was the starting point for launching a Directive of the European Parliament and of the Council on Services in the Internal Market in February 2004 (DSD 2004). After an intensive public discussion in many EU Member States – mainly between the social partners – the European Parliament (EP) in February 2006 agreed upon a revised proposal which the European Commission in April 2006 followed closely. With some minor revisions and additions the directive passed the Council; after an implementation period of three years the SD 2006 will fully come into force in 2010.

This study builds on previous work on the economic impact of the SD (Copenhagen Economics, *Kox et al.*[50]) and investigates its economic implications using an alternative approach. In particular, we use a simple partial econometric framework to estimate the ef-

---

49   See European Commission (2002).

50   Copenhagen Economics (2005a), *Kox et al.* (2004/2005).

fects of the reduction in regulation due to the implementation of the SD via two channels: (i) via the trade channel and (ii) via the FDI channel.

Ad (i): *Trade channel:* More trade leads to more competition which is associated with higher productivity, higher employment, investment and output. Based on previous estimates of the trade effects of the SD by *Kox et al.*, and recognising that the SD increases competition also via easier market entry by reducing the start-up costs of firms, we assume that the SD leads to a reduction in mark-ups (in terms of value added) by 2.5 to 5 percentage points; this is smaller than the mark-up reductions in manufacturing due to the Single Market according to the estimates of *Badinger*[51]. Using this range of effects of the DSD 2004 on competition, we estimate its effects on productivity, employment, investment and value added. Results suggest that productivity in the service industries covered by the SD increases by 0.80 percent, employment by 0.85 percent (or by 612,000 persons in terms of the EU-25), and the investment ratio by 0.55 percentage points. Value added of the services covered will go up by 1.65 percent, which corresponds to an aggregate GDP effect of 0.7 percent. The elimination of the CoOP will reduce these effects by 1/3. All these effects, however, have to be understood as potentials, realised in the medium and long term.

Ad (ii): *FDI channel:* In contrast to other studies, we also explicitly analyse the impact of a reduction of regulations on FDI and the relationship from FDI to productivity. Regarding the productivity effects, we reach similar results in magnitude as for the trade channel.

Taking (i) and (ii) together we reach the following overall macro-economic effects of the SD 2006 for the EU-25: Employment will increase by around 400.000 persons and GDP increases by around 1 percent.

Some words of caution are advisable here: First, it should be noted that the results are not completely robust across all specifications, when additional service industries are included. Particularly sensitive industries turn out to be travel (covered by the SD) and financial services (not covered by the SD). There is no straightforward explanation for this discrepancy. While the choice of the preferred sample is well motivated and corresponds most closely to

---

51   *Badinger* (2007).

that used in previous studies and the coverage of the SD, this remains a qualification to our results which has to be borne in mind.

Second, there is considerable uncertainty with respect to the magnitude of the effects; this is not only true for the trade effects estimated by *Kox et al.* with a range from 30 to 62 percent, whose central estimate of 44 percent we use to get a benchmark estimate of the magnitude of the SD's pro-competitive effect. It should also be emphasised that our estimated coefficients regarding the effects of competition on productivity, employment and investment used in the simulation are point estimates with sizeable confidence intervals.

It is, however, reassuring that the evaluation of the SD with completely different methods (ours rely on a simple partial econometric approach; Copenhagen Economics and CPB apply comprehensive world CGE models) leads to quite similar conclusions concerning the magnitude of the effects on major macro-economic variables.

References

Philip Aghion / Nicolas Bloom / Richard Blundell / Rachel Griffit / Peter Howitt (2005), Competition and Innovation: An Inverted U-relationship, in: Quarterly Journal of Economics, 120 (2005) 2, 701–728.

Harald Badinger (2007), Has the EU's Single Market Programme Fostered Competition? Testing for a Decrease in Markup Ratios in EU Industries, in: Oxford Bulletin of Economics and Statistics (forthcoming).

Harald Badinger / Fritz Breuss (2005), Trade and Productivity: An Industry Perspective, (= EI Working Paper 66), Vienna (Europainstitut, Wirtschaftsuniversität Wien) 2005.

Harald Badinger / Fritz Breuss (2006), Trade and Productivity: An Industry and Aggregate Perspective. Europainstitut, Wirtschaftsuniversität Wien, unpublished manuscript, February 2006.

Jagdish N. Bhagwati (1965), On the equivalence of tariffs and quotas, in: *Richard E. Baldwin et al.*, (Eds.), Trade, Growth and the Balance of Payments: Essays in Honor of Gottfied Haberler, Amsterdam (North-Holland) 1965, 53–67.

Fritz Breuss / Harald Badinger (2006), The European Single Market for Services in the Context of the Lisbon Agenda: Macroeconomic Effects of the Services Directive, in: Deepening the Lisbon Agenda: Studies on Productivity, Services and Technologies (Lissabon vertiefen: Studien zu Produktivität, Dienstleistungen und Technologien), Federal Ministry of Economics and Labour of the Republic of Austria (BMWA), Vienna, January 2006, 79–108.

Roland de Bruijn / Henk Kox / Arjan Lejour (2006), The trade-induced effects of the Services Directive and the country of origin principle (= CPB Document No 108), The Hague, February 2006.

Copenhagen Economics (2005a), Economic Assessment of the Barriers to the Internal Market for Services. Final Report, 1 January 2005.

Copenhagen Economics (2005b), The Economic Importance of the Country of Origin Principle in the Proposed Services Directive. Final Report, 17 November 2005.

European Commission (2002), Report from the Commission to the Council and the European Parliament on the State of the Internal Market for Services, COM(2002) 441final of 30 July 2002.

European Commission (2004), Proposal for a Directive of the European Parliament and of the Council on Services in the Internal Market. COM(2004) 2final/3 of 5 March 2004.

European Commission (2006). Directive 2006/123/EC of the European Parliament and of the Council 12 December 2006 on services in the internal market, Official Journal No L 376/36 of 27 December 2006.

Jeffrey A. Frankel / David Romer (1999), Does Trade Cause Growth? in: American Economic Review, 89 (1999) No. 3, 279–399.

Ting Gao (2004), FDI, openness and income, in: The Journal of International Trade & Economic Development, 13 (2004) No. 3, 305–323.

Groningen Growth and Development Centre (2005), 60-Industry Database, February 2005, available at http://www.ggdc.net.

George M. M. Gelauff / Arjan M. Lejour (2006), The new Lisbon Strategy: An estimation of the economic impact of reaching five Lisbon Targets. Report prepared for the Enterprise and Industry Directorate-General of the European Commission (Industrial Policy and Economic Reforms Papers No. 1), The Hague (CPB), January 2006.

Stephen S. Golub (2003), Measures of Restrictions on Inward Foreign Direct Investment for OECD Countries (= OECD Economics Department Working Paper, No. 357), Paris, June 2003.

Rachel Griffith / Rupert Harrison (2004), The Link between Product Market Reform and Macro-Economic Performance (= European Economy, No. 209), European Commission Directorate-General for Economic and Financial Affairs, Economic Papers, Brussels, August 2004.

Henk Kox / Arjan Lejour / Raymond Montizaan (2004/2005), The Free Movement of Services within the EU, ((= CPB Document No 69), The Hague, October 2004 (revised September 2005).

James R. Markusen (2002), Multinational Firms and the Theory of International Trade, Cambridge/MA (MIT Press) 2002.

Joaquim Oliveira Martins / Stefano Scarpetta / Dirk Pilat (1996), Mark-up Ratios in Manufacturing Industries. Estimates for 14 OECD Countries (= OECD Economics Department Working Paper, No. 162), Paris, April 1996.

Gaëtan Nicodème / Jacques-Bernard Sauner-Leroy (2004), Product Market Reforms and Productivity: A Review of the Theoretical and Empirical Literature on the Transmission Channels (= European Economy, No. 218), European Commission Directorate-General for Economic and Financial Affairs, Economic Papers, Brussels, December 2004.

Giuseppe Nicoletti / Stefano Scarpetta / Olivier Boylaud (1999), Summary Indicators of Product Market Regulation with an Extension to Employment Protection Legislation. (= OECD Economics Department Working Paper, No. 226), Paris, December 1999.

William Nordhaus (2005), The Sources of the Productivity Rebound and the Manufacturing Employment Puzzle (= NBER Working Paper, No. 11354), Washington/DC, May 2005.

OECD (2003), Product Market Competition and Economic Performance. OECD Economic Outlook, No. 72, chapter 6.

OECD (2005), Economic Surveys: Euro Area. Vol. 11, September 2005.

Ronnie O'Toole (2005), The Services Directive: An Initial Estimate of the Economic Impact on Ireland, unpublished manuscript, Dublin, 28 February 2005.

André Sapir / Philip Aghion / Giuseppe Bertola / Martin Hellwig / Jean Pisani-Ferry / Dariusz Rosati / José Viñals / Helen Wallace (2004), An Agenda for a Growing Europe: The Sapir Report, Oxford (Oxford University Press (2004).

UN (2002), Manual on Statistics of International Trade in Services, United Nations.

Line Vogt (2005), The EU's Single Market: At Your Service? (= OECD Economics Department Working Paper, No. 449), Paris, October 2005.

164 Harald Badinger, Fritz Breuss, Philip Schuster, Richard Sellner

Appendix

Tab. A1: Competition and Performance in Service Industries: Least Squares and IV Results for Sample D

Dependent variable	Productivity			Employment		
	Cross-section[1]		Panel[2]	Cross-section[1]		Panel[2]
	LS	IV	LS	LS	IV	LS
Constant[3]	2.689	2.836	3.124	-4.934	-4.768	-2.799
Mark-up	-0.221**	-0.345**	-0.075***	-0.214**	-0.352***	-0.110***
	(-2.20)	(-1.77)	(-3.973)	(-2.20)	(-3.83)	(-3.813)
Pop	0.160***	0.163***	0.128***	1.011***	1.015***	1.005***
	(2.89)	(2.95)	(14.360)	(29.00)	(28.75)	(320.48)
m						
SE	0.464	0.469	0.438	0.368	0.375	0.395
R^2	0.805	0.802	0.791	0.974	0.973	0.966
Obs.	62	62	1271	61	61	1217

Tab. A1: (continued)

Dependent variable	Investment			Mark-ups		
	Cross-section[1]		Panel[2]	Cross-section[1]		Panel[2]
	LS	IV	LS	LS	IV	LS
Constant[3]	0.460	0.488	0.523	0.973	0.875	0.543
Mark-up	-0.147***	-0.171***	-0.124***			
	(-2.79)	(-2.88)	(-4.972)			
Pop	0.009	0.010	0.013***	0.011	-0.020	0.054***
	(0.84)	(0.86)	(4.685)	(0.22)	(-0.43)	(7.86)
m				-0.099	-0.234*	-0.044**
				(-1.51)	(-1.82)	(-2.64)
SE	0.156	0.156	0.191	0.395	0.415	0.480
R^2	0.723	0.722	0.653	0.309	0.239	0.218
Obs.	62	62	1221	57	57	700

Notes to Table A1: LS ... least squares estimates; IV ... instrumental variable estimates. 1) Cross-section estimates refer to the average of the period 1995–2000; the cross-section dimension comprises 13 countries (see section V) and 7 industries (sample D, see table 3). 2) Panel estimates are pooled estimates with industry dummies and time-specific fixed effects included and refer to period 1978–2002 (for longest time series). 3) Average of industry-specific constants. *** Significant at 1 percent; ** 5 percent, * 10 percent. T-values in parentheses are based on robust standard errors. Pop denotes population; m is the ratio of imports to production. Productivity is measured in value added per hour worked. L denotes total employment in persons. Investment is measured as the ratio of gross fixed capital formation over value added. Mark-ups is the ratio of prices over marginal costs. All variables except the investment ratio and the mark-up ratio are in natural logs. For more details on the estimation, see *Breuss / Badinger* (2005).

Tab. A2:Regulation, Productivity and FDI Inward Stocks per value added in Service Industries: Cross-section1) Least Squares

Dependent variable	FDI	Productivity
$Const.^{NT\ 2)}$	0.591	1.796
$Const^{T\ 2)}$	-0.151	0.561
Pop	-0.326**	0.149**
	(-2.628)	(2.444)
Reg	-0.454**	-
	(-2.333)	-
FDI	-	0.150*
	-	(1.771)
SE	0.733	0.382
R^2	0.825	0.751
Observations	43	44

Notes: 1) Cross-section estimates refer to the average of the period 2000–2002; the cross-section dimension comprises 11 EU Member States and 4 industries (see table 8). The cross-section estimations include interacting industry and transition country dummies. 2) Average of industry-specific constants for non-transition (NT) and transition (T) countries. *** Significant at 1 percent; ** 5 percent, * 10 percent. t-values in parentheses are based on robust standard errors. Pop denotes population; Reg are the *Golub* (2003) indices for FDI restriction for 1998/2003 and FDI is the total FDI inward stock per value added. Productivity is measured in value added per hour worked. All variables are in natural logs.

Andreas Pichler, Katharina Steiner,
Gerhard Fink, Peter Haiss*

Financial Integration in Europe:
Effects on Markets and Economic Growth

I. Abstract

The aim of this chapter is to identify problematic issues of the process of European financial market integration focusing on banking in order to draw lessons for the design of the integration process of other service industries. Particular focus will be put on the implica-

* The authors are indebted for helpful comments and input provided by the finance-growth nexus research group at the Europainstitut / Vienna University of Economics and Business Administration. The finance-growth nexus research group initially was supported by the Jubiläumsfonds of the Oesterreichische Nationalbank (project no. 8868).

tions of the (de)regulation-induced integration, on changing financial market structures, competition and efficiency in EU-15. This is of importance as the perception arises that integration and the single market for financial services per se are the ultimate objective of the EU's integration efforts. But, does the design of the financial integration process promote the growth impact that is needed to achieve the Lisbon economic goal? The value of this chapter lies in merging the law-finance view and the finance-growth nexus. We collect descriptive evidence and combine it with theoretical and empirical research results on financial market integration.

II. Introduction

The single market for financial services including banking, securities and insurance services is one of the main pillars of the Single Market in the European Union (EU). A regulatory framework has been adopted that is based on market discipline, supervision and risk-based capital guidelines. It aims at fostering financial integration and claims to raise competition, transparency and efficiency within the sector and beyond for the economy at large[1]. According to the European Central Bank (ECB)[2] "a market for a given set of financial services is fully integrated if all potential market participants with the same relevant characteristics

– face a single set of rules concerning these financial services,
– have equal access to these services without discrimination against comparable market participants,
– and are treated equally when they are operating in the market".

The ECB's definition of financial integration is based on the assumption that the law of one price holds. To put it differently, instruments, which generate identical cash flows, should be prized identically[3]. Consistent application of this definition leads to the perception that integration and thus the single market for financial services per se are the ultimate objective of the European Union's efforts. Implications on competition and efficiency of financial intermediation are not taken into account by this definition. Ac-

---

1   EC (2005a), EC (2005b), EC (2005c).

2   *Baele et al.* (2004).

3   *Hartmann et al.* (2003).

cordingly, the final stage of integration as described above also applies to an oligopoly or even a monopoly.

We challenge the view that integrated financial markets per se should be the surveyor's wooden rot for successful efforts towards integration and call for a re-opening of the debate on the effects of financial integration under different perspectives. In particular, considerations on the implications of financial integration on the efficiency of financial intermediation, investment and thus economic growth are of utmost importance regarding the European Commission's confession that the financial sector should significantly contribute to the Lisbon economic reform process[4].

Various studies and analyses[5] conducted by the European Commission (e.g. the Financial Integration Monitor) have put emphasis on the integration process focusing on correlation and convergence aspects and structural changes in ownership and concentration levels. Empirical evidence mostly highlights the varying degrees of integration among different market segments. Results on efficiency gains are mixed[6]. The question of the optimal design of financial market integration in terms of efficiency gains in financial intermediation has not been properly answered yet.

Other research has attempted to provide empirical and theoretical answers to the question of the overall impact of financial market integration on economic growth in the EU7. It is almost unanimously argued in ex-ante empirical analysis that financial integration would be a growth trigger. For example, London Economics[8] estimated in their studies commissioned by the European Commission that substantial further integration of European financial markets would lead to additional 1.1% increase in GDP growth in the long run in EU-15. But does the current design of the financial liberalisation efforts promote this growth impact?

---

4   EC (2005a), EC (2005c).

5   *Hartmann et al.* (2003), *Heinemann / Schüler* (2003), *Baele et al.* (2004), *Baele* (2006).

6   *Heinemann / Schüler* (2002).

7   *Catinat et al.* (1988), *Giannetti et al.* (2002), London Economics (2002), *Guiso et al.* (2004), *Mariani / Padoan* (2006).

8   London Economics (2002).

In the Lisbon economic reform process, the European Union lags far behind its goals to become the world's most competitive and most dynamic economic region. Job creation and economic growth have to be accelerated. Against this background, it is necessary to assess the effects induced by the process of financial integration. This need is also recognised in the revamped FSAP (Financial Services Action Plan). The following chapter attempts to touch upon these issues. We focus on banking and capital market integration, collect descriptive evidence and combine it with theoretical and empirical research results on financial market integration, the law-and-finance-view[9] and the discussion of the finance-growth nexus restarted by *King* and *Levine*[10] in 1993. We apply *Kane*'s[11] regulatory dialectic in arguing that market participants' reactions and counter-reactions to regulatory change may have fostered integration, but may also have made financial and/or real markets less efficient and thus have cost GDP growth. One of our main contributions lies in extending the hitherto rather institutional perspective and combining it with the research stream, which deals with the impact of finance on growth. Is financial market integration conducive to efficiency in the financial sector, efficiency in the real sector, and/or economic growth and stability? Answers to these issues are not only important for policy makers, supervisors and market participants in the European Union – but also beyond, as European integration is frequently taken as a role model for Asia and other regions.

The following fundamental questions arise and will be discussed in this chapter:

– Are the European financial markets integrated and have the measures aimed at promoting financial integration served the purpose? How has financial integration affected the sector's efficiency?

– Are the measures taken by the European Commission to integrate the financial markets really balanced? Do they create a level-playing field for all market participants or are some stakeholders given preferential treatment over others?

---

9   *La Porta et al.* (1998); *Beck et al.* (2001); *Arteta et al.* (2001).

10   *King / Levine* (1993).

11   *Kane* (1981).

- Does the current design of financial integration promote financial development? What are the implications for economic growth? Is the declining correlation between finance and growth in the European Union as discussed by *Rousseau* and *Wachtel*[12] a consequence of the integration process?

These are crucial issues as they add to the understanding of the implications of liberalisation and regulation on the efficiency of the European financial sector. Proper answers to these questions will help to redesign the process of financial integration in a way that fosters economic growth more strongly and thus contributes to the Lisbon economic reform process. The rest of the chapter progresses as follows: Section 2 briefly summarises the status quo of research within the law-finance and the finance-growth nexus. A detailed descriptive analysis of changing financial market structures and the impact on efficiency and different stakeholders in section 3 adds to the understanding of the effects of regulation-induced integration and highlights problematic issues of the process of financial integration. Focus will be put on EU-15 as the differing impact of financial integration on the European transition economies that joined the EU in 2004 calls for a separate analysis. Section 4 discusses the impact of financial integration on economic growth. Finally, it is the aim to draw lessons for the design of the integration process of other service industries.

III. The law-finance and the finance-growth nexus

Initiatives for European financial integration are inspired by economic theory and empirical evidence claiming that financial liberalisation is very likely to contribute to economic growth through e.g. increased efficiency in capital allocation[13] as *Gaspar, Hartmann* and *Sleijpen*[14] put it at the Second ECB Central Banking Conference in 2002. Liberalisation is based on various deregulations such as the liberalisation of prices, quantitative restrictions and capital controls. In the past decades, European financial integration has been shaped by regulations aimed at liberalising cross-border capital movements (e.g. the 'First Banking Directive'

---

12   *Rousseau / Wachtel* (2005).

13   *Pagano* (1993), *Levine* (1997), *Beck et al.* (1999).

14   *Gaspar et al.* (2003).

77/780/EEC[15]) and harmonising national legislations (e.g. Solvency Directive 89/647/EEC[16]). To put it differently, re-regulation at the supranational level, rather than deregulation characterises financial market integration[17]. The Monetary Union and the European enlargements in 1995 and 2004 also shaped the process of financial integration and account for different impacts across countries. To embed the analysis in economic theory, the following section offers a brief literature review focusing on the law-finance and the finance-growth nexus, i.e. the nexus between regulation, financial integration, financial intermediation and economic growth in the European Union.

A. Law-finance nexus

Empirical research on the law-finance nexus mostly focuses on large panel data sets including both developed and developing countries[18]. It is argued that strong institutions, the rule of law, and the quality of law enforcement exhibit positive influences on financial depth and economic growth. In high-income countries, evidence of strong positive effects of capital account liberalisation is fragile, according to *Arteta*, *Eichengreen* and *Wyplosz*[19]. It is rather the sequencing of trade and financial liberalisation and the elimination of major macroeconomic imbalances before financial liberalisation that are important for the effects[20]. With regard to the focus on European financial integration, the issue of the right timing and sequencing of reforms is of interest e.g. with respect to sector versus cross-border financial liberalisation.

Apart from the above-mentioned empirical research on the role of the institutional background in liberalising financial markets, few cross-country analyses have been conducted on the impact of regu-

---

15 EEC (1977): First Council Directive 77/780/EEC of 12 December 1977 on the coordination of the laws, regulations and administrative provisions relating to the taking up and pursuit of the business of credit institutions.

16 EEC (1989): Council Directive 89/647/EEC of 18 December 1989 on a solvency ratio for credit institutions.

17 *Griller* (1992).

18 E.g. *La Porta et al.* (1998), *Arteta et al.* (2001), *Beck et al.* (2003).

19 *Arteta et al.* (2001).

20 *Klein / Olivei* (2005), *Caprio / Summers* (1993).

lation on efficiency, also due to methodological difficulties[21]. *Buch* and *Heinrich*[22] argue that country-specific conditions (regulatory or demographic factors) exhibit a significant impact on the relative banking performance of European countries. For the USA, empirical analyses on the impact of regulation on efficiency of banking and financial markets were conducted.[23] These studies differentiated between local banks and banks operating at the national level. *Collender* and *Shaffer*[24] show that deregulation, particularly abolishing geographical restrictions,[25] led to an increase in efficiency for banks operating at the national level. Interstate mergers and acquisitions did not impair local economic growth. Empirical research on the link between (de)regulation and efficiency of banking in the process of European integration mostly provides positive evidence, but also highlights the impact of country-specific factors[26]. Price Waterhouse[27] commissioned by the European Commission, presented an ex-ante quantification of the effects of regulation based on assumptions of the likely movement of prices in an integrated financial market. According to their results, the gain in consumer surplus should materialise in the range of ECU 11–33 billion. According to Price Waterhouse[28], it is the "dynamic effect of economic integration and not simply the result of removing the costs of meeting some of the existing regulations" that leads to welfare gains. Accordingly, increasing competition plays a central role. But, the reliability of the quantification results is not very high[29]. First, a model of cost-reduction normally used for industrial goods was applied. In addition, lack of data and certain assumptions such as

---

21   *Nell-Breuning* (2005).

22   *Buch / Heinrich* (2002).

23   by e.g. *Collender / Shaffer* (2003), or *Stiroh / Strahan* (2003).

24   *Collender / Shaffer* (2003).

25   In 1994, deregulation (Riegle Neal Interstate Banking and Branching Efficiency Act) abolished any geographic restriction on banks in the US (*Collender / Shaffer*, 2003).

26   *Wagenvoort / Schure* (1999), *Dietsch / Lozano Vivas* (2000), *Iqbal Ali / Gstach* (2000).

27   EC (1988).

28   EC (1988).

29   *Frauwallner* (1992).

the uniformity of prices are problematic issues. *Nell-Breuning*[30] provides mixed evidence of the effect of European (de)regulation on banking and capital markets. The impact on capital markets is largely positive while banks are mostly negatively affected. These first results on the direct link between regulation and efficiency call for a detailed analysis of European financial integration on a sector and country level.

Integration shapes the financial market structure in terms of market vs. bank based systems[31] and concentration levels. *Boot, Dezelan* and *Milbourn*[32] focus on the effectiveness of regulation and capital requirements. With a theoretical industrial organisation model they show that it is of particular importance to create a level playing field for financial and non-financial institutions in order to achieve overall efficiency gains. *Buch* and *Heinrich*[33] empirically analyzed changes in the competitive structure induced by (de)regulation in a sample of 21 OECD countries between 1979 and 1999. They found that a stronger regulatory environment in more developed countries leads to lower market power and lower profits. With respect to EU membership, the Second Banking Directive has no significant impact on either overhead costs or profitability measures.

The previous discussion on the law-finance link follows the efficiency hypothesis and assumes causality from regulation to changes in the efficiency of financial intermediaries and the competitive structure of financial markets and thus differing impacts on economic growth. However, regulation is not a purely exogenous variable. Lobbying of different stakeholders has an impact on the design of regulations[34]. Regulation is influenced by current developments in financial markets and may often react only with a lag after changes in the market took place. *Beck et al.*[35] emphasise that the more rapidly the legal system is adapted to changes in the eco-

---

30   *Nell-Breuning* (2005).
31   For a literature review on the issue of market- versus bank-based systems see *Carettoni et al.* (2001).
32   *Boot et al.* (1999).
33   *Buch / Heinrich* (2002).
34   *Nell-Breuning* (2005).
35   *Beck et al.* (2001).

nomic structure, the more it will benefit the financial system and the growth process. *Kane's*[36] analysis on the "reactive" position of regulations is rather negative as far as efficiency is concerned. *Kane's*[37] regulatory dialectic describes the political processes of regulation and the economic processes of regulation avoidance as opposing forces, which continuously chase each other in a kind of vicious circle. Regulation may create unintended effects for the regulator due to regulation avoidance by the regulated. Regulatory avoidance creates so-called "regulation-induced innovation", which is not necessarily a particular advance in technical productivity and thus may not contribute to higher efficiency of the financial institutions, real investment and, thus, economic growth[38]. Regulatory arbitrage, i.e. the escape into less regulated fields and circumvention activities create political pressure for re-regulation, which affects the financial institution's efficiency and increases the social costs of enforcing regulation. With regard to European financial integration, one may raise the question how far Europe has been trapped in such a vicious circle of regulation, regulatory innovation and re-regulation.

B. Finance-growth nexus

Since the 1990s, research in development-economics has focused on the relationship between the financial sector and economic growth. Causality issues and the types of financial structure supportive for economic growth are still under discussion[39]. The "finance - economic growth" link may follow five causality patterns[40]: a leading role of the financial sector (supply-leading approach), a demand-following, a bi-directional link, negative causality from finance to growth, and no link[41]. Theories in support of a demand-

---

36   *Kane* (1981).

37   *Ibidem.*

38   *Ibidem.*

39   For research on market- versus bank-based financial systems and their impact on economic growth see e.g. *Bonin / Wachtel* (2002), *Demirgüç-Kunt / Maksimovic* (2002), or *Levine* (2002).

40   For a detailed analysis on the different causalities see *Blum et al.* (2002).

41   *Lucas* (1988), *Rodrik* (1998), *Blum et al.* (2002)

following role of the financial sector, such as *Robinson*[42], argue that the needs and developments in the real sector economy determine financial development. This is in line with the "New Institutional Economics arguing that institutions adjust to market imperfections in a way that maximises individual utilities"[43].

Goldsmith[44], *McKinnon*[45] and *Shaw*[46] were the first to report the contribution of financial sector liberalisation to economic growth, following the supply-leading theory. By applying larger country samples and time frames, *Beck, Levine* and *Loayza*[47] deepened the perception that the size and development of a financial system is strongly correlated with economic growth. *Demirgüç-Kunt* and *Detragiache*[48] confirmed *King* and *Levine's*[49] findings that financial development is positively correlated with output growth. If properly performed, capital allocation to real investment together with technological innovation may spur economic growth[50]. In general, cross-country studies[51] assume a supply-leading link between finance and economic growth, whereas time-series studies[52] provide unstable causality patterns.

The causal pattern may depend on the level of economic development and change over time[53]. In view of the following analysis of the interdependence between the financial sector (in terms of financial integration) and economic growth in the European Union, it is interesting to note that according to *Patrick*[54], financial sector development seems to follow demand in developed economies. But,

42   *Robinson* (1962).

43   *Blum et al.* (2002).

44   *Goldsmith* (1966).

45   *McKinnon* (1973).

46   *Shaw* (1973).

47   *Beck et al.* (1999).

48   *Demirgüç-Kunt / Detragiache* (1998).

49   *King / Levine* (1993).

50   *Levine* (1997).

51   e.g. *Beck et al.* (1999), *Edwards* (2001).

52   e.g. *Al-Tamimi et al.* (2001).

53   *Patrick* (1966), *Arteta et al.* (2001).

54   *Patrick* (1966).

his result was opposed by e.g. *Alesina, Grilli* and *Milesi-Ferretti*[55] and their analysis on 20 high-income countries, or by Edwards[56] who focused on capital account liberalisation and found cross-country evidence that financial liberalisation supported growth in high-income countries while it slowed economic development in low-income countries within the same timeframe (1975–1997). *Arteta et al*[57] also report a positive, but fragile correlation between more open financial markets and economic growth for countries with a high level of financial development if institutions and the rule of law are strong. *Hahn*[58] indicates that there is a robust and positive relationship between private credit and long-run growth, while this is not true for other segments of the financial sector. Recently, *Rousseau* and *Wachtel*[59] raised concerns about the robustness of findings in cross-country studies. While results from studies using data from the 1960s to the 1980s seemed robust, the basic structural relationship between finance and growth has changed during the last 15 years. In this context, the question arises whether financial market integration in the European Union has contributed to the empirically perceived decline in the relationship between finance and growth. In earlier years, a positive impact of financial market development on economic growth seemed to be taken for granted. However, as European integration made progress, this relation seemingly has disappeared, and according to *Fitzgerald*[60] a 'worrying potential for market failure' seems to have emerged from European integration. What are the reasons for this development? The following analysis intends to combine the discussed separate streams of research, the law-finance view and the finance-growth nexus to shed light on the effects of regulation-induced integration on financial development and its link to economic growth (Box 1). *Hartmann et al*[61] strengthen such an approach by arguing that "a

---

55   *Alesina et al.* (1994).

56   *Edwards* (2001).

57   *Arteta et al.* (2001).

58   *Hahn* (2004).

59   *Rousseau / Wachtel* (2005).

60   *Fitzgerald* (2005).

61   *Hartmann et al.* (2006).

comprehensive view on the financial system needs to go much beyond financial integration".

Box 1: Law-finance and Finance-growth-nexus - an overview of existing research
Law-finance
• impact of legal traditions (public vs. civil law) and strong institutions on financial market development (e.g. *La Porta* (1998); *Beck et al.* (2003); *Das* (2004))
• impact of (de)regulation on efficiency in banking and financial intermediation (e.g. *Kane* (1981); *Wagenvoort / Schure* (1999); *Dietsch / Lozano Vivas* (2000); *Collender / Schaffer* (2003); *Nell-Breuning* (2005))
• impact of (de)regulation on concentration levels (e.g. *La Porta* (1998); *Boot et al.* (1999); *Buch / Heinrich* (2002))
Finance-growth
• question of causality: supply-leading role of the financial sector for economic growth (e.g. *King / Levine* (1993), *Levine* (1997); *Demirgüç-Kunt / Detragiache* (1998); *Beck et al.* (1999); *Edwards* (2001))
• increasing concerns about the robustness of the positive, supply-leading role of the financial sector in developed countries (*Arteta et al,* (2001); *Manning* (2003); *Fitzgerald* (2004); *Rousseau / Wachtel* (2005)).
→ Necessity to combine both streams of research to find out about the impact of regulation-induced financial market integration on growth.

IV. European financial integration's consequences on performance, market structure, and efficiency

Three decades after the First Banking Directive[62] marked the starting point of European financial integration, the financial markets are still far from being integrated[63]. Although the (de)regulatory measures taken by the European Commission led to a single European wholesale market, retail markets are not significantly integrated. The European Commission continues to promote further

---

62   EEC (1977).

63   Perfect financial integration is given if national borders do not play any role for cross-border financial transactions (*Heinemann / Schüler*, 2002). For a detailed discussion on how to measure financial integration see *Heinemann / Schüler* (2002), *Beale et al.* (2004), or *Barros et al.* (2005).

integration, particularly in the retail markets, while the desirability of this process remains at question.

The following subsections will assess whether the implemented measures have served to integrate the markets and how the process affected market participants' efficiency. Changes in the performance and profitability of market participants will be examined under the aspect of two theoretical approaches: the Structure-Conduct-Performance (SCP) paradigm, which assumes that market structure determines the behaviour of market participants, which in turn exercises a significant influence on performance; and the efficiency theory, which aims at explaining changes in market participants' profitability with changes in the underlying efficiency figures. Competition and efficiency are often seen as closely related to each other in a sense that strong competition forces market participants to increase their efficiency. Profitability is linked to both competition and efficiency, as strong competition tends to reduce profitability while high efficiency may improve it[64].

Following the Structure-Conduct-Performance paradigm, we try to assess whether and to what degree the European financial markets are integrated and to identify changes in the intensity of competition and thus market structure with particular focus on banking. These changes and local competition have often been neglected but significantly affect profitability of banking and financial intermediation[65]. In the second subsection we try to find out whether the changes in market participants' profitability have been accompanied by changes in efficiency of financial intermediation, which in turn affect external financing for (real) investment and may thus have an impact on economic growth. In the third subsection we discuss whether integration and regulation were able to create a level playing-field for all market participants.

We aim at identifying effects of EU-wide regulation in the financial services industry on changes in structure and efficiency and on legal or institutional obstacles to integration where further initiatives are particularly needed.

Are the European financial markets integrated? Have the measures served the purpose?

---

64   *Bikker / Bos* (2004).
65   *Barros et al.* (2005).

Since the beginning of the European financial integration process in the late 1970s, the gradual change in financial structures has
been driven by diverse developments. *Llewellyn*[66] distinguishes
between developments at the country, European and global level.
At the country-level, local competitive pressures in sub-markets and
shifts in ownership patterns operate to induce further structural
changes. European integration factors include EU-wide regulation,
the introduction of the single monetary union and the impact of the
enlargement process. Policy-induced pressures operate at the global
(e.g. GATS), European and country-specific level, but may only
gradually have an impact on market-inherent factors such as cultural differences that might hamper integration. Altogether, it is the
combination of these factors that affects all aspects of financial
business and that is significant for changes in market structures and
integration. This needs to be considered when trying to disentangle
the impact of EU financial market regulations on the integration
process. In the following, changes in market structure with a particular focus on banking will be discussed before consequences for
other segments of the financial sector will be assessed.

1) Integration in banking: The introduction of the Single Currency and the European Monetary Union has acted as a catalyst for
financial integration in Europe – both within the Euro area and in
the non-participating EU countries – as it transferred monetary
policymaking to the European level and changed the ways of doing
business[67]. Recently, the following main issues shaped financial
integration in Europe: the adoption of new international financial
reporting standards (IFRS), the implementation of the Basel II ac-
cord, and the European Commission's FSAP and its follow-up, the
Green Paper on Financial Services Policy 2005–2010[68]. To put it
differently, measures aimed at liberalising cross-border business
were accompanied by stricter regulations causing different impacts
on the various market segments. Therefore, the degree of integration in the European financial services markets differs by market
segment. Corporate markets have made much more progress in
integration than retail markets, in which the need of proximity to

---

66   *Llewellyn* (2006).

67   *Gnan et al.* (2005), *Bernstein* (2006).

68   EC (2005d).

clients and long-term relationships shape the nature of competition[69]. The more transaction-based corporate markets could more
easily gain advantages through economies of scale, which led to a
faster consolidation and integration. The diverse degree of integration across the various market segments calls for an assessment of
the segments in which more integration is definitely needed and
achievable to allow for efficiency gains.

Tab. 1: Number of M&As in EU-25 banking sector

	2001	2002	2003	2004	2005 h1
Domestic M&As	93	75	73	60	22
Cross-border M&As	49	42	22	26	8
Total M&As	**142**	**117**	**95**	**86**	**30**

Source: ECB EU Banking Structures, October 2005.

Note: M&As of commercial banks, credit institutions, mortgage banks,
investment banks and merchant banks.

In banking, despite all progress towards financial liberalisation, the number of cross-border mergers & acquisitions (M&A)
within the European Union has been low and pan-European banks
are rare[70].

The Second Banking Directive (89/647/EEC)[71] has been implemented to give way to M&As across Europe – however there
were and still are obstacles to cross-border transactions[72]. The consolidation process has so far been dominated by M&A within national borders - with the exception of the regionally integrated Nor-
dic and Benelux markets, the particular situation in the New Member States and single large acquisitions like Unicredit / HypoVereinsbank (including Austrian Bank Austria-Creditanstalt) and
Banco Santander Central Hispano / Abbey National. According to
PricewaterhouseCoopers[73], seven out of ten transactions were
within national borders (or more than half of the transaction volume

---

69   For empirical evidence on the integration of retail markets see *Hart-
     mann et al.* (2003), *Heinemann / Schüler* (2003), *Baele et al.* (2004),
     or European Commission (2004).

70   *Barros et al.* (2005).

71   EEC (1989).

72   *De Ávila* (2003).

73   PWC (2004).

was affected within borders) in the last decades. According to *Berger, DeYoung, Genay et al.*[74], the reason for the typically low market shares of foreign banks in Europe is the low profitability of the latter in developed economies. Alternatively, one could assume that stronger competition within European countries lead to lower profit rates. In less competitive markets with oligopolistic structure profit rates are possibly higher.

M&A activity[75] in the European financial market declined over the 1999 to 2005 period[76]. In 1999, of the 200 M&As reported in the European banking sector, less than 100 were national. From 2001 to 2004, the total number of annual M&As in EU-25 declined from 142 to 86 and only 30 in the first half of 2005, but cross-border M&A declined faster than national M&A. In 2000 in EU-25, total M&A value peaked at EUR 127.5 billion, of which EUR 76.4 billion were domestic[77].

Especially the cooperative and savings banks sectors consolidated largely on a domestic basis[78]. In countries with a low degree of market concentration, national consolidation was fierce[79] and competition was reduced. Instead of creating cross-border banks within a given sector – which was the role model for US bank consolidation[80] – domestic cross-sectoral transactions were preferred in order to create national champions in Europe[81]. Cross-border M&A activity predominantly happened in order to create regional clusters – especially in the Benelux, the Baltics, and in CEE. High profile cross-border deals such as the acquisition of British Abbey National by Banco Santander Central Hispano of Spain in 2004 or Italian Unicredit's acquisition of German HypoVereinsbank (including Bank Austria Creditanstalt) in 2005 remain exceptions.

---

74   *Berger et al.* (2000).

75   For a discussion on methodological issues concerning M&A data and foreign direct investment see e.g. *Borrmann* (2003).

76   ECB (2005).

77   ECB (2005).

78   *Pail* (1992).

79   *Angeloni / Ehrmann* (2003), *Pail* (1992).

80   See e.g. *Collender / Shaffer* (2003), *Nell-Breuning* (2005).

81   *Hahn* (2005a).

Regulatory changes at the European level had contributed to consolidation and increase in concentration[82]. The Second Banking Directive (Directive 89/646/EEC)[83] was introduced to (indirectly) promote competition, but led to increased concentration at the national level. On the one hand, banks saw the opportunity to become bigger and more efficient players at the national level to ward off possible foreign market entrants. On the other hand, this development is likely to hamper competition and, thus, may even negatively affect efficiency of financial intermediation.

Tab. 2: Number of credit institutions[84]

	1997	1998	1999	2000	2001	2002	2003	2004
Belgium	131	123	117	118	112	111	108	104
Czech Rep					172	83	77	68
Denmark	213	212	210	210	203	178	203	202
Germany	3,420	3,238	2,992	2,742	2,526	2,363	2,225	2,148
Estonia					7	7	7	9
Greece	55	59	57	57	61	61	59	62
Spain	416	402	387	368	366	359	348	346
France	1,258	1,226	1,159	1,099	1,050	989	939	897
Ireland	71	78	81	81	88	85	80	80
Italy	909	934	890	861	843	821	801	787

---

82   Other, more traditional arguments in favour of M&A include the creation of synergies and risk diversification (ECB, 2005).

83   EEC (1989).

84   Note: All credit institutions under the law of the given country, including subsidiaries and branches of foreign banks. Groups of cooperative banks may be counted separately. For Slovenia, credit institutions include banks, savings banks and savings and loan undertakings (cooperative banks). Before 2004, the savings and loan undertakings did not have the Bank of Slovenia authorisation and were not obliged to report the number of employees and local units (branches) and hence, the former figures are without the savings and loan undertakings. For Latvia, the figure for CIs includes small credit cooperatives (61 in 2004) and the number of branches includes small non-registered local units (since 2003). For Cyprus, data refer to domestic banks and international banking units but exclude cooperative credit institutions. For Czech Republic, credit unions are excluded.

	1997	1998	1999	2000	2001	2002	2003	2004
Latvia					23	23	23	23
Lithuania					54	68	71	74
Luxembourg	215	212	211	202	194	177	169	162
Hungary					230	223	219	213
Netherlands	648	634	616	586	561	539	481	461
Austria	928	898	875	848	836	823	814	796
Poland					711	664	658	653
Portugal	238	227	224	218	212	202	200	197
Slovenia					69	50	33	24
Slovakia					20	20	21	21
Finland	348	348	346	341	369	369	366	363
Sweden	237	223	212	211	211	216	222	212
UK	537	521	496	491	452	451	426	413
EU-15	9,624	9,335	8,873	8,433	8,084	7,744	7,441	7,230
NMS-10					1,346	1,198	1,172	1,144
EU-25					9,430	8,942	8,613	8,374

Source: ECB EU Banking Structures, October 2005

According to De Ávila[85], from 1990 to 1997, the consolidation process had led to a decrease in the number of banks in the EU by 26%. From 1997 to 2004, the number of monetary financial institutions in the EU-15 (including credit institutions and money market funds) declined by another 25% (from 9,624 to 7,230)[86] (Table 2). A large number of savings and co-operative banks, which mostly operate at the local level, and specialised credit institutions account for the majority of banks[87]. Only a few European banks are in the "big league of global investment banking". The mix of bank models differs by country causing different competitive conditions in national markets and the respective banking sub-markets.

During the same period, the overall number of branch offices declined in the EU member states (Table 3). Trends in specific countries were different. The number of bank branches in the Neth-

---

85   De Ávila (2003).

86   ECB (2005), Baele et al. (2004).

87   Llewellyn (2006).

erlands dropped by 46% (Belgium: -34%, Germany -28%), while in Greece the number of bank branches increased by 36% (in Italy and Finland by 22%). Several factors influence these changes: regulation, cultural differences, the degree of technological change in bank transactions, and the structure of the financial system, i.e. the relative strength of the cooperative and savings banks sector compared to commercial banks and the concentration in the market.

The Second Banking Directive (Directive 89/646/EEC)[88] with the "single banking license" aimed at facilitating the set-up of branches in different European countries. *Claessens* and *Laeven*[89] assume that greater foreign bank presence and fewer *restrictions* in the banking sector are indeed suitable for the creation of more competitive banking systems. Reduction of entry restrictions and new entrants can spur competition. The Second Banking Directive had led to an 58% increase in cross-border branching in the three years following the introduction of the single banking license[90].

But, subsidiaries still were the preferred form of market entry, e.g. due to the fact that subsidiaries can be managed more flexibly, debt holders are better protected against risk taking, national corporate taxes may make subsidiaries more attractive, and transfer price manipulations can be used by companies to reduce their host-country tax burdens[91].

Tab. 3: Number of branches

	1997	1998	1999	2000	2001	2002	2003	2004
AT	4,691	4,587	4,589	4,570	4,561	4,466	4,395	4,360
BE	7,358	7,129	6,975	6,610	6,168	5,550	4,989	4,837
CY					528	521	506	500
CZ					1,751	1,722	1,670	1,785
DE	63,186	59,929	58,546	56,939	53,931	50,868	47,351	45,505
DK	2,283	2,291	2,294	2,365	2,376	2,128	2,118	2,021
EE					210	198	197	203
ES	38,039	39,039	39,376	39,311	39,024	39,021	39,762	40,621
FI	1,294	1,254	1,188	1,194	1,571	1,572	1,564	1,585

---

88   EEC (1989).

89   *Claessens / Laeven* (2004).

90   *De Ávila* (2003).

91   *Gaspar et al.* (2002).

	1997	1998	1999	2000	2001	2002	2003	2004
FR	25,464	25,428	25,501	25,657	26,049	26,162	25,789	26,370
GR	2,510	2,687	2,742	2,862	2,968	3,263	3,300	3,403
HU					2,950	2,992	3,003	2,987
IE	1,180	1,076	1,083	1,007	970	926	924	909
IT	25,265	26,283	27,154	28,189	29,226	29,948	30,501	30,946
LT					156	119	723	758
LU	314	289	310	300	274	271	269	253
LV					590	567	581	583
MT					58	55	58	63
NL	6,800	6,787	6,258	5,983	4,720	4,269	3,883	3,649
PL					4,080	4,302	4,394	5,006
PT	4,746	4,947	5,401	5,662	5,534	5,390	5,440	5,408
SE	2,521	2,197	2,140	2,059	2,040	2,040	2,046	2,034
SI					717	721	720	706
SK					1,052	1,020	1,057	1,113
UK	16,340	15,873	15,470	14,225	14,554	14,392	14,186	14,001
EU15	201,991	199,796	199,027	196,933	193,966	190,266	186,517	185,902
NMS10					12,092	12,217	12,909	13,704
EU25					206,058	202,483	199,426	199,606

Source: ECB EU Banking Structures, October 2005

Note: A local unit or branch is an unincorporated entity (without independent legal status) wholly owned by the parent.

This rather complex structure makes monitoring more difficult and, thus, has important policy implications on supervision. From 1997 to 2004, the unweighted EU-15 average of five-firm concentration grew from 47% to 53%[92]. At the current stage of the European financial integration process, many countries, especially smaller EU member states, exhibit high concentration ratios in their domestic banking sectors, which were caused by massive domestic M&A transactions. Leaving aside Estonia, which is a particular case, in 2004 the CR-5 ratios, measuring in a given country the share of the five largest banking institutions in total sector assets, with 84% are highest in Belgium (which during 1997 and 2004 also experienced the sharpest increase in concentration) and the Nether-

---

92   *Carbó-Valverde et al.* (2005)

lands[93]. In Estonia, the five biggest banks according to assets have a market share of 99%; all five are foreign. Concentration remained relatively low in Germany, the United Kingdom, Italy, and Luxembourg reflecting different banking structures (see Table 4).

According to the European Central Bank, the concentration ratios in banking in the EU member states reflect a tendency towards monopolistic competition[94]. Nevertheless, *Bikker* and *Haaf*[95] and *Claessens* and *Laeven*[96] indicate the theoretical possibility that high concentration could be a consequence of economies of scale and scope and may be an outcome of rising efficiency and competitiveness of banks because e.g. banks aim at warding off foreign entrants. But, competition is to be encouraged and *Freixas, Hartmann* and *Mayer*[97] call for "an extension of the scope of competition policy in financial services".

Tab. 4: Concentration ratios (CR5) - share of 5 largest credit institutions in total assets[98]

	1997	1998	1999	2000	2001	2002	2003	2004
AT	48	42	41	43	45	46	44	44
BE	54	63	76	75	78	82	84	84
CY					72	69	70	69
CZ					68	66	66	64
DE	17	19	19	20	20	21	22	22
DK	70	71	71	60	68	68	67	67
EE					99	99	99	99
ES	32	35	41	46	45	44	44	42
FI	88	86	86	87	80	79	81	83

93 ECB (2005)

94 ECB (2005).

95 *Bikker / Haaf* (2002).

96 *Claessen / Laeven* (2004).

97 *Freixas et al.r* (2004).

98 Note: [w. ...weighted; unw. ...unweighted] The CR5 of a given country is the percentage share of the five largest credit institutions according to assets, in the sum of the assets of all credit institutions of the country. The list follows a host country residence approach and a non-consolidated basis. Banking subsidiaries and foreign branches are considered to be separate credit institutions resident in another country.

	1997	1998	1999	2000	2001	2002	2003	2004
FR	40	41	43	47	47	45	47	45
GR	56	63	67	65	67	67	67	65
HU					56	55	52	53
IE	41	40	41	41	43	46	44	44
IT	31	26	26	23	29	31	27	26
LT					88	84	81	79
LU	23	25	26	26	28	30	32	30
LV					63	65	63	62
MT					80	82	79	79
NL	79	82	82	81	83	83	84	84
PL					55	53	52	50
PT	46	45	44	59	60	61	63	67
SE	58	56	56	57	55	56	54	54
SI					68	68	66	64
SK					66	66	68	67
UK	24	25	28	28	29	30	33	35
EU15 unw. ø	47.1	47.9	49.8	50.5	51.8	52.6	52.9	52.8
NMS10 unw. ø					71.5	70.7	69.6	68.6
EU25 w. ø					37.8	38.3	39.8	40.2
EU25 unw. ø					59.5	59.8	59.5	59.0

Source: ECB EU Banking Structures, October 2005

Competition is very important for the financial sector, as it can matter for the performance of the providers of financial services, the quality of products and the degree of innovation[99]. The Structure-Conduct-Performance (SCP) hypothesis assumes that changes in firm performance are influenced by firm behavior, which is in turn affected by the market structure. Under the SCP paradigm, higher prices result from a more concentrated market with fewer competitors[100] where collusive behavior is more likely and oligop-

---

99   *Vives* (2001), *Claessens / Laeven* (2004).

100   *Carbó-Valverde et al.* (2005).

oly rents increase bank performance[101]. Based on the principles of
the SCP paradigm not only studies focusing on CR-5 ratios, but
also those operating with other indicators such as the Lerner Index[102] suggest increases in market power and reduced banking sector competition in Europe in the 1990s[103]. Not impressed by the
evidence, the ECB and the European Commission stick to the perception that competition has at least partially increased in
Europe[104].

A possible explanation for these different perceptions may be
that different measures of competition – *Lerner* Index, net interest
margins / total assets, return on assets, H-Statistic, *Hirschmann-
Herfindahl*-Index[105] – in the banking sector may lead to different
results. While certain indicators in certain markets for banking services may point to rising competition, more aggregate measures of
overall competition such as the return on assets may show opposing
results[106].

By aggregation of the results of different market competition
indicators and their assessment over time (1995–2001), *Carbó-
Valverde et al.*[107] found that net interest margins declined in all EU-
15 countries, but the Netherlands. A possible explanation for this
result may be that on the European scale in international deposit
and loan markets competition rose thus reducing net interest margins especially for large commercial customers in a period of slow
growth in Europe, while in regional and local banking, competition
decreased and regional and national champions with more pricing
power were created[108] – a perception that is consistent with M&A

---

101 *Bikker / Bos* (2004).

102 The *Lerner* Index calculates the difference between price and mar-
     ginal cost weigthed by price and is defined as (PTA - MCTA) / PTA.
     The higher the index, the greater the realised market power (*Carbó-
     Valverde et al.* 2005).

103 *Carbó-Valverde et al.* (2003), *Fernández de Guevara / Maudos*
     (2004).

104 *Barros et al.* (2005), ECB (2005), *Trichet* (2005).

105 For detailed data see e.g. *Hartman et al.* (2006).

106 *Carbó-Valverde et al.* (2005).

107 *Carbó-Valverde et al.* (2005).

108 *Bikker / Bos* (2004), *Carbó-Valverde et al.* (2005).

activity and sector consolidation in Europe. Therefore, little correlation can be found between different competition indicators[109].

2) Integration in other market segments: Changes in banking market competition in the European Union may also lead to shifts in market structures. In the past decade, market-based finance has gained in importance fuelled by institutional investors, technological innovation, and the implementation of a wider range of financing techniques. Despite the increasing number of market-based financial instruments during 1981 to 2001 in the three largest European economies, no general shift from a bank-based towards a more market-based financial system could be identified[110]. Bank lending still is the predominant source of external financing[111], though the degree of importance of various sources of finance (credit, securities, bonds) varies across the Member States.

3) European payments systems: The Single European Payments Area (SEPA) is a large-scale project, which will exhibit significant influence on competition and market structures in the European banking market. SEPA is intended to harmonise the European payments systems, which is deemed necessary after the introduction of the Euro, and is supposed to lead to increased cost efficiency and economies of scale[112]. SEPA is expected to lead to a substantial consolidation in the payments markets, because of higher competition, easier market entry for non-bank payments institutions, and economies of scale. Consumers will be offered some of the new products by 2008, while the implementation of SEPA should be completed by the end of 2010[113], when a majority of customers have migrated to the new system. After SEPA is successfully implemented within the European Union there will be no differentiation between national and cross-border payments and financial transactions.

Smaller banks may find it difficult to develop the necessary products and will have to cooperate with others while bigger finan-

---

109 *Bikker / Haaf* (2002), *Claessens / Laeven* (2004), *Carbó-Valverde et al.* (2005).

110 *Gaspar et al.* (2002), *Hartmann et al.* (2003).

111 European Commission (2004).

112 EC (2005d), *De Ploe / Denecker* (2006).

113 ECB (2006).

cial institutions fear that they have to bear a large share of the initial costs of delivering SEPA products[114]. The effects of SEPA will also be unequally distributed between member states, as banks in countries with higher price regimes will lose significant parts of their revenues if fees converge as a consequence of harmonisation[115]. While especially large European corporations and banks may enjoy major benefits from the proposed measures, banks' representative bodies fear a decrease in competition because of oligopolisation. These bodies rather expect higher prices and a smaller range of products offered to the customer as a consequence of the implementation costs of the new system[116].

4) Interbank money market: Since January 1999, the date of the introduction of the single currency, the money market has been the most integrated market. "The law of one price has established itself even without the emergence of a common cross-border trading platform"[117]. The Trans-European Automated Real-time Gross settlement Express Transfer (TARGET) system started its operations at the time the Euro was introduced and has contributed to the integration of the Euro money market. TARGET is a large-value payment system for the Euro and provides immediate intraday finality and settlement in central bank money, thus allowing banks to have more efficient and cheaper liquidity management, which might have in turn consequences for the local consumer loan offer[118]. Particularly large banks have greater incentives for cross-border arbitrage as they benefit from the greater pool of liquidity offered by the monetary union and the cross-country payment systems.

5) Bond markets: Since the introduction of the single currency, the integration of the Euro area government bond market made strong progress[119] Bond yields have been converging across the Member States. On national markets, domestic banks lost part of their comparative advantages in the field of underwriting and trad-

---

114 ECB (2006).
115 McKinsey estimates reported by *De Ploey / Denecker* (2006).
116 Zentraler Kreditausschuss (2006), WKÖ (2005).
117 *Hartmann et al.* (2003).
118 European Commission (2004).
119 European Commission (2004), *Hartmann et al.* (2003).

ing activities, what contributed to falling underwriting fees[120]. Although common news somewhat have gained in importance in determining government bond yields, local factors continue to play a role such as differences in perceived credit risks in different countries. The pricing of government bonds (with identical credit risk rating) has not fully converged. Fiscal constraints imposed by the Stability and Growth Pact "have led governments to reduce their budget deficits and debt exposures"[121].

Over the past years, corporate bond markets recorded considerable growth particularly induced by the introduction of the Euro and the sudden need to raise large sums for telecom licensing and privatisation. The reduction of government financing in connection with the budgetary constraints imposed by the Stability and Growth Pact had more non-financial companies seek bond financing and the share of European-wide bond funds has rapidly increased[122]. The home bias of bond portfolios in the Euro area became weaker hence more integration and competition led to a reduction of underwriting fees[123]. The country of issuance determines corporate bond yields to a lesser degree than credit ratings. To put it differently, over time the impact of country-specific factors on the corporate bond yields decreased. The Euro area corporate bond markets became "reasonably well integrated"[124].

6) Equity markets: According to Jean-Claude Trichet[125], there are still obstacles to cross-border activities within the Euro area equity markets. Nevertheless, a rising degree of integration is signaled by a decreasing cross-country dispersion of equity index returns. Common factors seem to gain: while in the 1980s only 20% of local return variance could be explained by aggregate European (and US) shocks, the proportion increased to 40% after the introduction of the Euro[126]. Especially the European Monetary Union led to a reduction in the influence of purely local shocks. The home

---

120 *Hartmann et al.* (2003); *Baele et al.* (2004), *Bikker / Bos* (2004).

121 *Hartmann et al.* (2003).

122 *Hristoforova* (2004).

123 *Baele et al.* (2004).

124 *Baele et al.* (2004).

125 *Trichet* (2005).

126 *Baele et al.* (2004), European Commission (2004).

bias in asset holdings (of insurance, investment corporations and pension funds) has been decreasing. Since the late 1990s, diversification by sectors seems to have become more advantageous than by geographical regions[127]. Still, the level of integration in the equity market remained below the expectations as shown in a review of 54 empirical studies on the integration of stock markets[128]. Differences among equity ownership of households indicate that there are still a number of barriers such as the fragmented securities settlement industry or differences in taxation of capital gains.

The overall assessment raised some concerns about an uneven distribution of the benefits across European regions due to diverging initial levels of development among market segments[129]. Southern European markets (Greece, Italy and Portugal) still lag behind with capital market infrastructure. France and Germany offer an intermediate picture. Despite adequate structural reforms, diversity will persist among regional financial market structures. For example, the importance of currency deposits and of loans has become even more heterogeneous among Euro area countries[130]. On the one hand, there are areas where the measures taken served the purpose of creating integrated markets (see box 2). In particular, the introduction of the European Monetary Union (EMU) lead to a strong one-time increase in the degree of integration. It eliminated exchange-rate risk, lowered information barriers and increased liquidity[131]. On the other hand, many areas of financial market integration demand further action (see box 2).

127 *Baele et al.* (2004).

128 *Inzinger / Haiss* (2006).

129 *Hartmann et al.* (2006).

130 *Hartmann et al.* (2003).

131 *Dvorak* (2006).

Box 2: Successful and problematic issues of financial market integration
Successful areas:
• The introduction of the Euro and the FSAP led to an integrated European wholesale market, which gives investors and intermediaries access to the markets of all member states from a single point of entry.
• The introduction of the Euro particularly fostered the integration of money markets and bond markets.
Areas of financial integration pending action:
• Retail markets remain largely disintegrated and will be subject to further EU Commission policy initiatives.
• Financial liberalisation led to national consolidation, the creation of national champions, and rising concentration ratios.
• Relatively few cross border mergers.
• Benefits mainly occurred to large banks and large corporate customers.
• Supervisory cooperation and convergence will be core subjects of the Financial Services Policy 2005–2010.
• Equity markets remained largely unintegrated although there appears to be a certain degree of rising convergence.

A. How has financial integration affected the sector's efficiency?

From the perspective of the Structure-Conduct-Performance (SCP) paradigm, higher prices and higher profits of the respective financial institutions result from more concentrated markets with fewer competitors. Alternatively, higher profits could be the result of greater efficiency[132]. Official EU sources[133] communicated the perception that the efforts to integrate the European financial markets have allowed the realisation of efficiency gains in the European banking sector and have brought European banks closer to the cost-efficiency-frontier. The empirical confirmation of this perception is still missing.

---

132 *Goldberg / Rai* (1996), *Bikker / Bos* (2004), *Carbó-Valverde et al.* (2003).

133 Economic Research (1997).

Economic efficiency[134] is the sum of technical and allocative efficiency. Technical efficiency assesses the firm's distance from the efficiency frontier (i.e. waste of inputs or underproduction of outputs). Allocative efficiency aims at production at minimal costs and measures whether the optimal proportions of inputs and outputs are used at given prices. X-efficiency is defined as economic efficiency minus misallocation, scale and scope effects[135]. It is also referred to as managerial or structural efficiency, because it depicts endogenous factors more than exogenous[136]. The cost to income ratio is not taken into account here because it is a biased measure. If monopoly profits are high, the cost to income ratio is low. In competitive markets, costs may be much lower (due to cost efficient banks), but income may be even less due to the competitive pressure. Thus, the cost to income ratio in the efficient market is higher than in the inefficient monopolistic market. In the context of our assessment, which follows the law-finance view, the question arises how regulation affects efficiency of the financial intermediaries and of banks in particular. Has (de)regulation lead to efficiency gains of financial intermediaries and have these gains be forwarded to the final customer?

The European financial sector integration process influences the market participants' cost and profit structures and also their ways to do business. Regulation and self-regulation of the market are mostly seen as opposite principles. It is usually argued that regulation leads to a decrease in market power of the regulatees and to an increase in transaction costs due to the burden of costs of regulation. In banking, both principles complement each other. Bank regulation sets minimum and maximum standards and general requirements for banks, which are needed and nevertheless reduce the degrees of freedom in business. In this way, the regulatory envi-

---

134 The difference between observed and optimal values of inputs, outputs and input-output-combinations is referred to as efficiency, while a suboptimal combination of inputs and outputs results in inefficiency (*Bikker / Bos* (2004)). For a detailed theoretical distinction between productivity and efficiency see *Coelli et al.* (1998). Further issues on measuring financial sector macro-efficiency can be found in *Fink et al.* (2004a) and *Berger / Humphrey* (1997).

135 *Berger et al.* (1993), *Nell-Breuning* (2005).

136 *Bikker / Bos* (2004), *Nell-Breuning* (2005).

ronment among other developments (e.g. technical progress) has an important impact on the organisational structures and thus indirectly on the efficiency of financial institutions (in terms of cost efficiency and organisational efficiency). In addition, regulation has a direct impact on banks via e.g. minimum capital requirements and certain requirements concerning risk-management[137]. With regard to European integration, (de)regulation had a direct impact on efficiency changes via e.g. the Solvency Directive (89/647/EEC)[138] and the Capital Adequacy Directive (93/6/EC)[139]. An indirect impact has been caused by changing competitive conditions via e.g. the Second Banking Directive (89/647/EEC)[140] or the Investment Services Directive (93/6/EC)[141]. These regulatory-induced changes in efficiency may directly lead to changing efficiency in the allocation of resources for (real) investment and thus affect economic growth. What does empirical evidence on European financial markets and efficiency changes tell?

Aggregate studies on bank efficiency in Europe in the 1990s[142] show that on average European banks with an efficiency rate of 70% lag behind their US counterparts with an average efficiency rate of 80%. These results turned out to be highly dependent on the respective market structure and the individual bank's position in the market. Especially small (mostly savings and cooperative) banks with strong regional market positions that are able to exercise a certain degree of pricing power tend to be relatively inefficient on the output side[143]. In turn, universal banks operating at a European scale tend to have more complex structures and thus show higher managerial inefficiency. In Europe, mid-sized banks with total assets of less than USD 150 billion were able to respond to regulatory changes more easily as far as their technical efficiency is con-

---

137 *Nell-Breuning* (2005).

138 EEC (1989).

139 EC (1993): Council Directive 93/6/EEC of 15 March 1993 on the capital adequacy of investments firms and credit institutions.

140 EEC (1989).

141 EC (1993).

142 *Bikker* (2002).

143 *Bikker / Bos* (2004).

cerned[144]. In all cases, market conditions as an important determinant of banking efficiency have to be included in these calculations as they bias the measurement of managerial efficiency particularly in the case of locally operating banks[145].

Wagenvoort and *Schure*[146] analyzed the impact of regulation on banking efficiency. They estimated an augmented Cobb-Douglas model with panel-data of 2000 European banks over 1993–1997. According to their results, liberalisation promoted the efficiency of European banks. Effects across countries were different due to a significant impact of environmental conditions[147]. *Iqbal Ali* and *Gstach*[148] showed in their time-series analysis that the liberalisation of the Austrian financial market led to a short-term reduction in efficiency with long-term efficiency gains in banking over 1990–1997. *Nell-Breuning*[149] analyzed the link between regulation and efficiency of banking and capital markets applying a Data Envelopment Analysis (DEA) for two European countries (D, UK) and the USA from 1990 to 2002. The results showed a dampening effect on economic efficiency of banks due to the regulation of capital requirements. In contrast efficiency gains in capital markets were achieved by deregulation aimed at promoting liberalisation in the European Union.

Bikker[150] estimated changes in European banks' cost efficiency during the 1990s on an aggregate level and suggests that consistent year-on-year rise in efficiency levels took place. The efficiency gap in comparison to US banking was reduced. These efficiency gains are not explicitly related to the regulatory changes in the European financial markets. However, direct links between certain regulatory steps and decreases in technical efficiency in the regulated banks could be established[151], particularly as the European financial markets face re-regulation at the supranational level rather than de-

---

144 *Nell-Breuning* (2005).

145 *Hahn* (2005a).

146 *Wagenvoort / Schure* (1999).

147 *Dietsch, Lozano Vivas* (2000).

148 *Iqbal Ali / Gstach* (2000).

149 *Nell-Breuning* (2005).

150 *Bikker* (2002).

151 *Nell-Breuning* (2005).

regulation[152]. In particular, re-regulation as highlighted by *Kane's* regulatory dialectic[153] has increased the costs of regulatory compliance.

As this section has shown, interest rate spreads in the European Union have decreased on average and economies of scale have led to rising technical efficiency. These advantages were generally not passed on to the customer. However, fees for banking services increased – helping financial institutions to build up substantial market power. All in all, a detailed analysis on the sector and country specific level is needed. The question whether bank intermediation in Europe works efficiently in the sense that it creates a level playing-field for all market participants and contributes to economic growth will be dealt with in the following sections.

B. European financial sector integration
a level playing-field for all market participants?

The bank landscape has changed significantly over the last decade. Besides the European Union's efforts towards financial integration and liberalisation, a number of international initiatives brought rising harmonisation[154] and banks are confronted with a huge number of regulations. Competition in cross-border wholesale markets on the European scale has increased and new competitors in the form of non-bank financial institutions have emerged[155]. In addition, banks have had to adapt to technological change. New products and new ways of distribution have been introduced.

As expected main benefits of integration, *Barros et al.*[156] identify the possibility to exploit economies of scale and scope, lower transaction costs, higher market liquidity, better risk diversification, and a more efficient valuation of securities. Expected fears include an increase in the risk exposure of the financial sector. In the light of the previous sections of this chapter, it remains open whether the measures taken to integrate and regulate the European financial

---

152 *Griller* (1992).

153 *Kane* (1981).

154 Active in this respect are among others the Basel Committee on Banking Supervision, the IMF, the OECD and the Committee of European Banking Supervisors (CEBS).

155 For a detailed analysis see *Pail / Petschnigg* (1992).

156 *Barros et al.* (2005).

sector were successful in providing a level-playing field for all
market participants or whether some institutions were given preferential treatment over others.

As far as competition in the European financial markets is concerned, the impression is that international competition especially in
the cross-border wholesale markets has intensified, but that at the
same time many banks were successful in building national or regional dominant market positions allowing them to exert a certain
degree of pricing power. Competition indicators provide an unclear
picture of the European banking market. While some competition
measures point to increasing competition in the European Union,
other indicators suggest less competition because of market consolidation and concentration. The increasing concentration in
banking at the national level raises the question whether the chosen
timing and sequencing of reforms led to the intended effects. For
example, sectoral liberalisation was introduced before cross-border
liberalisation, which has lead to the formation of large national
(domestic) banks operating in e.g. the savings and the cooperative
sector rather than large real "pan-European" banks in the various
sectors. Apparently, banks manage to mitigate increasing competitive pressures by oligopolistic behaviour or by raising product differentiation, which allows exercising stronger pricing power[157].

The effect of European financial integration on individual
banks depends largely on their position in the market, size and
competitive focus. The integration process favours large banks as
eased market access enables them to compete on a European scale.
For smaller banks the costly implementation of new regulatory
measures exerts a heavier burden than for their large competitors.
Many smaller banks were forced to consolidate and preferred domestic cross-sectoral transactions allowing them to create strong
regional and national market positions, leading to oligopolistic
competition in certain regions[158].

The Single European Payment Area (SEPA) is one example of
a large-scale harmonisation project, which is generally perceived as
unbalanced in its consequences on market participants[159]. While it

---

157 *Bikker / Bos* (2004).

158 *Collender / Shaffer* (2003); *Nell-Breuning* (2005).

159 *De Ploey / Denecker* (2006).

is broadly agreed that inefficiencies in the payment systems in the European Union need to be dealt with, the proposed measures are strongly contested. The costly introduction of new standards and products puts smaller banks at a disadvantage and results in higher output costs. While at the beginning of the migration phase from the current systems to the new ones demand will be shallow, banks will have to invest significant amounts of money for SEPA's implementation. The result will be a first-mover disadvantage and a possible slowdown of the process as a whole. Further regulation in this area would be a possible consequence[160]. As far as SEPA's consequences on competition in the financial sector are concerned, the European Commission[161] proposes to relieve non-bank payment institutions from supervisory control as their underlying risks are deemed substantially lower than the risks of banks. This view is strongly opposed by banks' representative bodies[162]. If payment institutions only needed to fulfil formal prerequisites, but would not be subject to supervisory control, systemic risks would be seriously underestimated and competition would be distorted. The Commission's intention to ease market entry could therefore easily lead to strong shifts in the market structure and negative effects for stability.

But SEPA is not only unbalanced between market participants, it also bears disadvantages for certain member states of the European Union. Drawing on a study conducted by McKinsey, *De Ploey* and *Denecker*[163] report that if harmonisation leads to a convergence of fees on the current European average, institutions in Italy and Spain – the countries with the highest transaction costs – would lose 29 respectively 12% of the revenues of their payments business. If prices would even fall to the level of the three countries with the lowest spreads, the industry would lose some EUR 14.3 billion of revenues, according to the McKinsey study. These losses would represent an enormous challenge for European banking institutions and will lead to more standardisation and a possible reduction of the service level especially for the more unprofitable sector of consumers.

---

160 ECB (2006).

161 EC (2005d).

162 WKÖ (2005).

163 *De Ploey / Denecker* (2006).

Summing up, European large-scale enterprises and pan-European banks will enjoy the major advantages of the new legal framework and will be among the winners of SEPA. Small and medium-sized enterprises will only be able to derive minor benefits from the system changes induced by SEPA. Small financial institutions will face increasing pressure from intensifying competition and costs in connection with the introduction of new products.

Regulatory measures such as SEPA and the development of European financial sector integration nourish the perception that the process exhibits unbalanced consequences on market participants and European Union member states and that European financial sector integration was so far not able to create a level-playing field for all market participants. Finally, it is most important that the final consumer and the economy as a whole gain from financial market integration. Concerning the real sector, changes and shocks in the financial environment particularly affect small and medium enterprises, which account for one half of total production and provide the bulk of employment in Europe as they are more vulnerable to changes[164]. Large firms have access to a larger pool of finance and they are often being preferred by financial intermediaries[165]. In this context, the following section will shed further light on the interdependency between financial market integration and economic growth.

V. European financial integration and economic growth

European financial integration is supposed to lead to macroeconomic benefits in terms of GDP growth and welfare gains[166]. Since the European Union lags far behind its goal defined in the Lisbon agenda, it would be adequate to consider a reassessment of the assumed positive impact of financial market integration on economic growth. What implication has the current design of financial integration on economic growth? Is the declining correlation between

---

164 *Guiso et al.* (2004).

165 Reasons for the unwillingness to lend to SMEs are among others the higher unit costs, limited information available, or the problem of default risk (*Fitzgerald* (2004)).

166 E.g. *Catinat et al.* (1988); EC (1988), *Breuss / Schebeck* (1989).

finance and growth as discussed by *Rousseau* and *Wachtel*[167] a consequence of the European integration process and have the efforts to exploit the nexus caused its disappearance? In the following we will draw attention to the complex link between financial market integration and economic growth and highlight problematic issues of assumed growth impacts[168].

Financial intermediaries play an essential role in the economy because they mobilise savings and allocate and redistribute capital for investment[169]. According to the paradigm of a supply-leading role of the financial sector, efficient capital allocation, overall cost of financial services, depth and breadth of financial intermediation have an impact on external investment[170] and thus on the structure of production, economic growth and employment[171]. In particular, industries which rely heavily on external sources of finance such as information technologies and pharmaceuticals grow faster in countries with more competitive and efficient financial systems[172]. However, it should not be forgotten that the mostly used source of corporate finance is the cash flow of successful firms[173].

Ex-ante studies showed that financial market integration is expected to boost economic growth by improving the efficiency of resource allocation induced by more competition, greater risk diversification and thus lower cost of finance for (real) investment[174]. *Giannetti, Guiso, Japelli et al.*[175] in an *ex-ante* analysis argue that increased competition is the main channel through which positive

---

167 *Rousseau / Wachtel* (2005).
168 For an in-depth analysis of the link between financial market liberalisation, integration and economic growth see e.g. *Thiel* (2001); *Carettoni et al.* (2001).
169 *King / Levine* (1993), *Levine* (1997).
170 For the impact of financial market changes on financial market stability see e.g. *Buch et al.* (2005), or *Buch et al.* (2005b).
171 For a detailed analysis on the link between investment and employment see *Fitzgerald* (2004).
172 OECD (2006); *Rajan / Zingales* (1998).
173 *Graff* (2000).
174 London Economics (2002).
175 *Giannetti et al.* (2002).

effects of financial market integration are expected to occur[176].
Contrary to these ex-ante expectations, changing financial market
structures in European banking led to increasing concentration at
the national level. On the one hand, this development could be det-
rimental to efficiency of financial intermediation and possibly hamper economic growth. On the other hand, the threat of new market
entrants could lead to more competitive financial intermediation.

Empirical studies tried to assess the growth potential of European financial integration and to forecast integration-related
changes in GDP growth in the European Union. In their ex-ante
analysis *Catinat, Donni* and *Italianer*[177] estimated the effects of the
liberalisation of capital and financial services by giving shocks
simultaneously to seven EU countries in the Interlink model of the
OECD. To learn about the macroeconomic impact of changes in
competition and of a reduction in interest rates that were estimated
to about 10%, a comparison of the simulation results with and
without the shocks was carried out. The results showed a considerable increase in real GDP of 1.5 % and in private consumption of
1% stimulated by lower consumer credit rates. In the short run,
negative effects on employment could be identified for the first
years of the simulation. *Breuss* and *Schebeck*[178] estimated the effects of EU accession for Austria following the "*Cecchini*-Report"
(EC, 1988)[179]. Their results showed that a decrease in interest
spreads and an acceleration of capital productivity should lead to a
7% increase in investment over the medium term. London Economics[180] focused on the elimination of the existing obstacles to full
integration of the equity and corporate bond markets. Using a multi-
country macroeconomic model, EU-wide real GDP was predicted
to rise by additional 1.1% per year on average in the long-run. The
average increase in total business investment was expected to be
0.6% and in private consumption 0.8%. The combination of a reduction in the cost of equity and bond finance together with an in-

---

176 See also *Claessens / Laeven* (2005); *Vives* (2001); *Cetorelli
      /Gambera* (2001).
177 *Catinat et al.* (1988).
178 *Breuss / Schebeck* (1989).
179 EC (1988).
180 London Economics (2002).

crease of the share of bond finance in total debt finance should result in these output gains.

In recent ex-post analysis, concerns have been raised about a potential market failure due to the changing nature of bank operations and access barriers to stock markets[181]. In terms of causality, the direction between real and financial integration remains an open issue and empirical evidence is mixed[182]. The question arises whether European financial integration has been successful so far. Were the measures taken to integrate and harmonise the markets really appropriate to boost economic growth throughout the European Union? What are the positive and negative effects on growth and are there differences between the short-term and the long-term perspective?

De Ávila[183], for example, covered 15 EU member states from 1960–2001 in a panel data regression framework. The results point to a positive long-run growth effect of at least 0.6% per year due to the liberalisation of capital controls and 1% per year due to harmonisation of banking regulations. These results are robust to the inclusion of other growth-promoting policy changes and provide ex-post empirical evidence for the expected positive view of the ECB on the impact of the integration process on economic growth. In this context, it seems necessary to refer to the fact that liberalisation and harmonisation via (de)regulation at the European level is time consuming due to the varying, lagged periods of implementation among countries and the expected competitive bias at least in the short run. Neimke, Eppendorfer and Beckmann[184] focus on integration in European banking and analyze macroeconomic effects on economic growth and the labour market over 1960–1999 analogous to the Cecchini Report (EC, 1988)[185] and its assessment of potential welfare gains of the Single Market Program. They identify ambiguous results showing that the degree of financial market integration proxied by cross-border activities of banks and insurance companies is far from reflecting a "Single Market for Financial Services".

181 Fitzgerald (2004).
182 Arteta et al. (2001); Edwards (2001); Rousseau / Wachtel (2005).
183 De Ávila (2003).
184 Neimke et al. (2003).
185 EC (1988).

First, foreign market penetration only has a weak impact on total factor productivity. Second, there are country-specific differences in the long-run growth effects due to differences in institutional characteristics. The ability to transform the weak impact on growth into a positive shift of total factor productivity differs according to remaining variances in the degree of national market regulations. Significant country-specific differences were also found in the ability to transform the so-called "growth bonus" into an "employment bonus". Variances in labour market conditions accounted for these differences. These ambiguous results are further supported by *Mariani* and *Padoan*[186] who show that financial integration is necessary but not sufficient to move towards the "Lisbon benchmark", which is defined by a favourable employment outlook and strong innovation. They analyzed the contribution of finance to innovation driven economic growth through technology accumulation. Their benchmark is not full financial integration, but a "EU knowledge driven economy as defined by the Lisbon Strategy". The authors also stress that the finance-growth nexus is far from homogeneous as the relative weight of credit and capital market finance varies across countries. In general, a substantial increase in financial market integration is needed to generate a "growth bonus" that can reduce unemployment.

Studies focusing on the short-term impact of financial development on growth have been unsuccessful in providing empirical evidence of a positive and significant correlation. According to *Rousseau* and *Wachtel*[187], the nexus between financial development and growth found on older data up to the 1990ies lost in significance over time. On more recent data, the relationship is not as strong any more as it has been shown by previous studies[188]. The empirical cross-country analysis included 84 countries over 1960–2003. They argue that the significance of the relationship between finance and growth depends on the stage of economic progress of a given country. The authors explain the disappearing nexus with the "Lucas[189] critique in action". Political efforts tend to eagerly exploit

---

186   *Padoan / Mariani* (2006).

187   *Rousseau / Wachtel* (2005).

188   E.g. *King, Levine* (1993); *Demirgüç-Kunt / Detragiache* (1998).

189   *Lucas* (1976).

the nexus with liberalisation but without the necessary sequencing of institutional reforms. In general, long-term studies on the finance-growth link find the positive exogenous growth effects of the financial sector to be considerably weaker (if they still exist at all) in already developed market economies than in newly industrialising countries. Short-term studies (1996–2000) are even more sceptical: in developed countries, the financial sectors do not play any significant role for growth, while the finance-growth-nexus remains important for economies in transition[190]. For the period from 1996 to 2000, Fink et al[191] conclude that the Supply Leading Hypothesis of the financial sector cannot be clearly confirmed for developed countries.

While the above discussed research focused on financial integration in general, research on the introduction of the Euro as a one-time increase in the degree of financial integration shows the following results: The ex-ante analysis conducted by *Breuss*[192] showed for nine Euro countries an uneven distribution of possible positive income effects among the groups of "hard-currency" and "soft-currency" countries. The application of the Oxford Economic Forecasting (OEF) model revealed on average an increase of 1.7% of real GDP in the medium run. As far as possible investment–stimulating effects due to increasing competition in the financial sector are concerned, total results depend on the assumptions about the exchange rate stability. The EMU (European Monetary Union) was also expected to lead to further convergence in the levels of interest rates, respectively an increase in interest rates in the "hard-currency group" by 0.3% and a decline by 2.8% in the soft-currency group" after five years. The ex-post analysis by Dvorak[193] investigates whether the introduction of the Euro has boosted physical investment growth for eleven Euro and six Non-Euro countries. The results indicate that physical investment increased by 3% to 5% within four years after the introduction of EMU. The effect disappeared in 2003. The application of industry level data showed that the growth impact of the EMU is not influenced by industry dependence on external finance.

---

190 *Fink et al.* (2004b).

191 *Ibidem.*

192 *Breuss* (1997).

193 *Dvorak* (2006).

Tab. 5: Change in financial intermediation in EU-15 and GDP

	1995	**2000**	**2004**
Stock market capitalisation (% of GDP)	49.8	110.2	91.0
Domestic debt securities (% of GDP)	135.3	92.3	146.0
Domestic credit to non-credit institutions (% of GDP)	88.1	181.6	146.1
Total domestic financial inter-mediation (% of GDP)	273.3	384.1	383.1
Total assets of credit institutions including foreign assets(% of GDP)	352.3	419.4	416.4
Nominal GDP at current prices (PPS trillion)	17.8	22.9	25.4

Sources: *Allen et al.* (2005); nominal GDP taken from AMECO

Contradictions and a high degree of instability among the empirical results trying to assess European financial integration's consequences on growth raise the question whether financial liberalisation in the European Union lead to instability within financial market segments or to "autonomous" growth of the financial sector with only few spillover effects to the real sectors (table 5). The above discussed results can be explained by the different developments in the European Union member states such as cross-border liberalisation, harmonisation, the introduction of the EMU and other developments, which differently affected the pace and the quality of the growth mechanism in Europe[194]. There co-exist different growth mechanisms at the (EU-wide) regional, national, and sectoral level. Different levels of financial market development, forms of financial structures, and differences in the composition of industries and firm size in the real sector account for the heterogeneity of the impact of financial market integration on growth[195] and for the different consequences of European financial integration on the various market segments.

---

194 *Carettoni et al.* (2001)

195 *Neimke et al.* (2003), *Gusio et al.* (2004)

**Box 3: Financial integration's and financial development's
long- and short term effects on growth**

Positive effects:

Long-term studies:

- Ex-ante analysis: possible positive growth impacts of full financial integration (e.g. London Economics (2002); *Catinat et al.* (1988); *Giannetti et al.* (2002); positive growth impact of EMU (e.g. *Breuss* (1997)).

- Ex-post analysis: long term gains in growth from 1960–2001 due to financial sector liberalisation and harmonisation of banking regulation in EU-15 (*De Ávila* (2003)); positive growth impact of EMU (e.g. *Dvorak* (2006)).

- Evidence on emerging markets: positive long-term influence of bond markets on growth (e.g. *Fink et al.* (2003)).

Short-term studies:

- no short term gains shown by analysis focusing on financial integration and liberlisation in general.

- positive impact of FSFDI on economic growth in the new member states (transition economies) depending on the level of human capital stock (e.g. *Eller et al.* (2006)).

Negative effects or no evidence of correlation:

Long-term Studies:

- Ex-post analysis: still long way to a Single Market and no homogenous finance-growth nexus among the member states (e.g. *Neimke et al.* (2003); *Mariani / Padoan* (2006)).

- General evidence: Correlation between financial development and growth is getting weaker over time (*Rousseau / Wachtel* (2005)); long-term positive exogenous growth effects of the financial sector are weaker for developed countries.

Short-term Studies:

- Differing transfer mechanisms for growth over the development cycle: no positive role of the financial sector for growth in developed countries, while importance of the finance-growth-nexus in transition economies (e.g. *Fink et al.* (2004b)).

Different growth impact of financial market integration among countries due to different financial market structures (e.g. capital market vs. bank based systems), economic environment (composition of industries, firm size, firm finance) and the competitive bias (differing times of implementation of EU-regulation at the national level).

Problematic issue due to the varying degree of integration and still existing obstacles among the market segments (banking vs. stock market). (questions: which industries and corporate investors profit?; do those sufficiently promote (real) investment, production and economic growth?).

Altogether, the comparison of ex-ante and ex-post analysis of expected versus observed growth effects of financial market integration (see Box 3) shows divergent results. While ex-ante research identified positive growth effects, ex-post empirical research shows ambiguous results. *De Ávila*[196] finds a positive growth impact only over a very long period including 30 years before financial market integration, whereas *Neimke et al.*[197] and *Padoan / Mariani*[198] identify deficiencies in the impact of financial market integration on economic growth. It cannot be excluded that the European financial market reform was more supportive for speculators than for investors in the real sector of the economy.

VI. Conclusion

It is the central aim of this chapter to identify problematic issues of regulation-induced financial market integration in order to draw lessons for the integration of the other services industries (Directive 2006/123/EC). We combine theoretical and empirical research results from two streams of literature – the law-finance view and the finance-growth nexus. Descriptive evidence allows analyzing changes in financial markets and financial intermediation and their impact on the real sector and economic growth. This is in contrast to definitions of financial market integration, which lead to the perception that regulation-induced integration per-se is the ultimate objective of the European Union's efforts. It is of utmost importance to ask whether the design of financial integration shaped by supranational re-regulation and selective liberalisation delivered the promised impact on efficient financial intermediation, investment and economic growth. This issue is important for the European population at large. It also deserves great attention in view of the pending integration of other services industries. Has the design of the financial market integration process stimulated efficiency and growth? Do the integration-induced changes in market structure create a level-playing field for all market participants? Has that contributed to income and wealth of the European people?

In financial market integration, regulation and integration measures affected market structures and competition in all market segments. Big players on the European level gained, whereas re-

---

196 *De Ávila* (2003).

197 *Neimke et al.* (2003).

198 *Padoan / Mariani* (2006).

regulation put pressure on small and medium-sized institutions. Consolidation led to higher market concentration and caused oligopolistic or collusive behaviour at the national level, which is harmful for the financial market as a whole. Fostering cross-border competition should have been given preference over concentration at the national level.

With regard to other services sectors, we learn that regulation-induced integration will be closely related to issues of consolidation and concentration, particularly at the national level. The market structures of various services industries will change considerably. It can be learned from financial market integration that it is necessary to ensure a level-playing field within the various market segments to avoid undue concentration and to ensure efficiency gains for the final consumer.

In the financial sector, although cross-border provision of financial services increased, foreign market entry via subsidiaries remained the preferred form of entry. After the implementation of the Services Directive (Directive 2006/123/EC), it will be of great interest to analyze how the changing strategies of providers of services in different markets will shape the competitive environment at the respective national and the European level.

European regulation, aiming at financial market integration in terms of liberalising cross-border business, was accompanied by international endeavours to implement and harmonise e.g. capital requirements. With the simultaneous impact of (de)regulation in terms of cross-border liberalisation on the one hand and stricter (re)regulation at the supranational level on the other hand, efficiency gains were offset by the latter. Measures linked to the introduction of the EMU might have superimposed the impact of other integration measures. To put it differently, the impact of regulation-induced integration needs to be clearly understood in the context of ongoing changes in the market structures. Timing and sequencing of reforms need to be coordinated with policy changes and the conditions, as the evidence of sectoral and cross-border liberalisation in the financial sector has shown. This equally applies to the implementation of the Services Directive.

With regard to the impact of financial market integration on economic growth, ex-ante analysis[199] of financial market integration

---

199 E.g. *Catinat et al.* (1988); *London Economics* (2002).

promised a positive growth impact. For EMU, these growth-stimu-
lating effects could be confirmed in ex-post analysis. By contrast,
ex-post assessments of financial market integration at best show
ambiguous results: only a weak and heterogeneous impact on total
factor productivity across countries could be identified. As financial
market integration and the adaptation to regulation are time-con-
suming, only weak, long-term effects might occur, if at all.

The industry-level approach by *Rajan* and *Zingales* (1998)
could provide fruitful directions for future research. For a larger
sample of countries, *Rousseau* and *Wachtel*[200] find a declining relationship between finance and economic growth in developed countries. Political efforts tend to eagerly exploit liberalisation, but
without the necessary sequencing of institutional reforms. The
questions arise, which industries and corporate or speculative investors profit from the observed rising level of financial market
integration, and whether those promote real investment, production,
economic growth and with it employment in order to bring the
European Union closer to its Lisbon targets. Future research will
need to thoroughly test the complex structure of the relationship
between financial market integration, external finance of real investment and output growth by different real sectors, firms of different size, and in different national markets.

Conclusions that can be drawn for the ongoing new regulation
and liberalisation initiatives of other services sectors are that integration per se will not suffice. Consequences on efficiency of large
and small firms and its contribution to economic growth and welfare need to be more carefully assessed. Any reform's effect for the
Lisbon process should be more carefully and thoroughly tested.
Based upon the experience from financial services, particular attention should be paid to whether planned integration measures in the
services sector might lead to rising market concentration at the national or regional level and whether they support growth and employment. A level playing-field needs to be guaranteed, small providers of services deserve special attention. Design and sequencing
of the reforms need to be coherent with the respective sector's
structure. Changes in the competitive environment must be eyed to
prevent oligopolistic structures from spreading into national markets. In the light of financial market development and its disap-

---

200 *Rousseau / Wachtel* (2005).

pointing effect on economic growth, new doubts arise whether powerful lobbying organisations are the appropriate advisors for future integration measures in the services sector at large.

References

Alberto Alesina / Vittorio Grilli / Gian-Maria Milesi-Ferretti (1994), The Political Economy of Capital Controls, in *Leonardo Leiderman / Assaf Razin* (eds.), Capital Mobility: The Impact on Consumption, Investment and Growth, Cambridge (Cambridge University Press) 1994, 289–328.

Franklin Allen / Laura Bartiloro / Oskar Kowalewski (2005), The Financial System of the EU 25 (Wharton University of Pennsylvania Working Paper 05/044), Philadelphia/PA 2005 (available at http://fic.wharton.upenn.edu/fic/papers/05/0544.pdf).

Hussein A. H. Al-Tamimi / Mouawia Al-Awad / Husni Charif (2001), Finance and growth: evidence from some Arab countries, in: Journal of Transnational Management Development Vol. 7 (2001) No. 2, 3–18.

AMECO (2007), Database, available at http://ec.europa.eu/economy_finance/indicators/annual_macro_economic_database/ameco_en.html, 7.3.2007.

Ignazio Angeloni / Michael Ehrmann (2003), Monetary policy transmission in the Euro area: any changes after EMU?, (= ECB Working Paper, No 240), Frankfurt 2003 (available at http://www. ecb.int/ pub/pdf/scpwps/ecbwp240.pdf).

Philip Arestis / Panicos O. Demetriades / Kul B. Luintel (2001), Financial development and economic growth: the role of stock markets, in: Journal of Money, Credit, and Banking Vol. 33 (2001), 16–41.

Carlos Arteta / Barry Eichengreen / Charles Wyplosz (2001), When Does Capital Account Liberalization Help More Than it Hurts? (= NBER Working Paper No. 8414), Washington/DC, August 2001.

Lieven Baele (2006), Real Interest Rates in an Integrating Europe, Tilburg University, January 2006 (available at http://www. finprop.de/Paper13_Baele.pdf).

Lieven Baele / Annalisa Ferrando / Peter Hördahl / Elizaveta Krylova / Cyril Monnet (2004), Measuring Financial Integration in the Euro Area, (= ECB Occasional Paper, No.12), Frankfurt 2004.

Pedro Luis Pita Barros / Erik Berglöf / Paolo Fulghieri / Jordi Gual / Xavier Vives (2005), Integration of European Banking: The Way Forward, (= Monitoring European Deregulation 3), London (CEPR) March 2005.

James R. Barth / Gerard Caprio Jr. / Ross Levine (2004), Bank regulation and supervision: what works best?, in: Journal of Financial Intermediation Vol. 13 (2004), 205–248.

Thorsten Beck / Asli Demirgüç-Kunt / Ross Levine (2001), Law, Politics, and Finance (= World Bank Working Paper, No. 2585), Washington/DC, April 2001.

Thorsten Beck / Asli Demirgüç-Kunt / Ross Levine (2003), Law, Endowments, and Finance, in: Journal of Financial Economics Vol. 70 (2003), 137–181.

Thorsten Beck / Ross Levine / Norman Loayza (1999), Financial Intermediation and Growth – Causality and Causes (= World Bank Working Paper, No. 2059), Washington/DC, February 1999.

Allen N. Berger (1995), The Profit-Structure Relationship in Banking – Tests of Market-Power and efficient-Structure Hypotheses, in: Journal of Money, Credit and Banking Vol. 27 (1995), 404–415.

Allen N. Berger / Rebecca S. Demsetz / Philip E. Strahan (1999), The Consolidation of the Financial Services Industry: Causes, Consequences, and Implications for the Future, in: Journal of Banking and Finance Vol. 23 (1999) No.2–4, 135–194.

Allen N. Berger / Robert DeYoung / Hesna Genay / Gregory F. Udell (2000), Globalization of Financial Institutions: evidence from cross-border banking performance, in: Brookings-Wharton Papers on Financial Services Vol. III, 23–158.

Allen N. Berger / David B. Humphrey (1997), Efficiency of Financial Institutions: International Survey and Directions for Future Research, in: European Journal of Operational Research Vol. 98 (1997) No. 2, 175–212.

Allen N. Berger / William Hunter / Stephen Timme (1993), Efficiency of Financial Institutions: a Review of Research Past, Present and Future, in: Journal of Banking and Finance Vol. 17 (1993), 221–49.

Nils Bernstein (2006), A View from Outside, in: Experiences with and preparations for the Euro, Linz, Austria, May 10–12, 2006, 57–63 (available at: http://www.oenb.at/de/img/conf-linz_18x24_tcm14-49917.pdf).

Jakob A. Bikker (2002), Efficiency and Cost Differences Across Countries in a Unified European Banking Market, in: Kredit und Kapital Vol. 35 (2002), 344–380.

Jakob A. Bikker / Katharina Haaf (2002), Competition, Concentration and their Relationship: An Empirical Analysis of the Banking Industry, in: Journal of Banking and Finance Vol. 26 (2002) No. 1, 2191–2214.

Jakob A. Bikker / Jaap W. Bos (2004), Trends in Competition and Profitability in the Banking Industry: A Basic Framework, (= DNB Working Papers 018), The Hague (De Nederlandsche Bank) 2004.

David Blum / Klaus Federmair / Gerhard Fink / Peter Haiss (2002), The Financial-Real Sector Nexus: Theory and Empirical Evidence (= EI Working Paper, No.43), Vienna, September 2002 (available at: http://www.wu-wien.ac.at/europainstitut/pub/workingpaper).

Arnoud W.A. Boot / Silva Dezõelan / Todd T. Milbourn (1999), Regulatory distortions in a competitive financial services industry, adopted paper presented at the Conference on financial modernization and regulation sponsored by the Federal Reserve Banks of Atlanta and San Francisco, September 1998.

Christine Borrmann (2003), Methodological Problems of FDI Statistics in Accession Countries and EU Countries (= HWWA Report, No. 231, Hamburg (Hamburg Institute of International Economics) 2003.

Fritz Breuss (1997), The Economic Consequences of a Large EMU – Results of Macroeconomic Model Simulations, in: European Integration online Papers (EIoP) Vol. 1, No. 10.

Fritz Breuss / Fritz Schebeck (1989), Die Vollendung des EG-Binnenmarktes: Gesamtwirtschaftliche Auswirkungen für Österreich. Makroökonomische Modellsimulationen, WIFO Studie, Februar 1989.

Claudia Buch / Kai Carstensen / Andrea Schertle (2005), Macro-economic Shocks and Foreign Assets of Banks (= Kiel Working Paper, No.1254), Kiel, July 2005.

Claudia Buch / Jörg Döpke / Christian Pierdzioch (2005b), Financial openness and business cycle volatility, in: Journal of International Money and Finance Vol. 24 (2005), 744–765.

Claudia Buch / Ralph P. Heinrich (2002), Financial Integration in Europe and banking sector performance, January 2002 (available at: ftp://ftp.zew.de/pub/zew-docs/div/buch.pdf).

Gerard Caprio Jr. / Lawrence H. Summers (1993), Finance and its Reform: Beyond Laissez-Faire Policy (= World Bank Working Paper, No. 1171), Washington/DC, August 1993.

Santiago Carbó-Valverde / David Humphrey / Joaquín Maudos-Villaroya / Philip Molyneux (2005), Cross-country Comparisons of Competition and Pricing in European Banking, in: Proceedings of the Federal Reserve Bank of Chicago 2006, Chicago/IL 2006, 176–189.

Santiago Carbó-Valverde / David Humphrey / Francisco Rodríguez-Fernández (2003), Deregulation, Bank Competition, and Regional Growth, in: Regional Studies Vol. 38 (2003), 227–237.

Alessandro Carettoni / Stefano Manzocchi / Pier Carlo Padoan, (2001), The growth-finance nexus and European integration, a review of the literature (= The United Nations University, Institute for New Technologies Working Paper, No. 01–5), Maastricht, December 2001 (available at: http://www.intech.unu.edu/publications/eifc-tf-papers/eifc01-5.pdf).

Michel Catinat / Eric Donni / Alexander Italianer (1988), The completion of the internal market: results of macroeconomic model simulations (= European Commission, DG for Economic and Financial Affairs, Economic Papers, No. 65), Brussels, September 1988.

Nicola Cetorelli / Michele Gambera (2001), Banking Market Structure, Financial Dependence and Growth: International Evidence from Industry Data, in: Journal of Finance Vol. 56 (2001), 617–648.

Stijn Claessens / Luc Laeven (2004), What Drives Bank Competition? Some Empirical Evidence, in: Journal of Money, Credit and Banking Vol. 36 (2004), 563–584.

216   Andreas Pichler, Katharina Steiner, Gerhard Fink, Peter Haiss

Stijn Claessens / Luc Laeven (2005), Financial Dependence, Banking Sector Competition, and Economic Growth (= World Bank Working Paper, No. 3481), Washington/DC, January 2005.

Tim Coelli / D.S. Prasado Rao / George Battese (1998), An Introduction to Efficiency and Productivity Analysis, Boston/MA (Kluwer Academic Publishers) 1998.

Robert Collender / Sherill Shaffer (2003), Local bank office ownership, deposit control, market structure, and economic growth, in: Journal of Banking and Finance Vol. 27 (2003), 27–57.

Dilip K. Das (2004), Emerging Market Economies: Liberalization and Performance Nexus, in: Kredit und Kapital Vol. 37 (2004) No.1, 117–141.

Diego Romero de Ávila (2003), Finance and Growth in the EU: New Evidence from the Liberalization and Harmonization of the Banking Industry (= ECB Working Paper, No.266), Frankfurt 2003 (available at http://www.ecb.int/pub/pdf/scpwps/ecbwp 266.pdf).

Wouter De Ploey / Olivier Denecker (2006), How Europe's Banks Should Prepare for Payments Reform, McKinsey Quarterly, February 2006.

Asli Demirgüç-Kunt / Enrica Detragiache (1998), Financial Liberalization and Financial Fragility (= IMF Working Paper, No. 98/83), Washington/DC, July 1998.

Asli Demirgüç-Kunt / Vojislav Maksimovic (2002), Funding growth in bank-based and market-based financial systems: evidence from firm-level data, in: Journal of Financial Economics Vol. 65 (2002), 337–363.

Michel Dietsch / Ana Lozano-Vivas (2000), How the environment determines banking efficiency: A comparison between French and Spanish industries, in: Journal of Banking and Finance Vol. 24 (2000), 985–1004.

Tomas Dvorak (2006), Does the euro lead to investment? Industry evidence, Working Paper of the Department of Economics, Union College, Schenectady/NY, September 2006 (available at: http://www.union.edu/PUBLIC/ECODEPT/dvorakt/research/inv estment_eer.pdf).

EC (1988), The cost of non-Europe in financial services, (= Research on the cost of non-Europe Vol. 9), Price Waterhouse, Brussels 1988.

EC (2005a), White Paper Financial Services Policy 2005–2010, COM(2005) 629 final, 1.12.2005.

EC (2005b), Single Payments Area: Pay Anywhere in the EU as You Would Do at Home (press release), Rapid IP/05/1514, 1.12.005.

EC (2005c), EU financial services policy for the next 5 years (press release) Rapid IP/05/1529, 5.12.2005.

EC (2005d), Directive of the European Parliament and of the Council on Payment Services in the Internal Market, Proposal, European Commission, COM(2005) 603 final, 1.12.2005.

ECB (2005), EU Banking Structures, October 2005 and preceding versions, European Central Bank, Frankfurt 2005.

ECB (2006), Towards a Single Euro Payments Area – Objectives and Deadlines, 4th Progress Report, European Central Bank, Frankfurt, 17 February 2006.

Economic Research Ltd. (1997), Single Market Integration and X-Inefficiency, in: European Commission (ed.), The Single Market Review – Subseries II: Impact on Services, Credit Institutions and Banking, Vol. 3. Luxembourg (Office for Official Publications of the European Communities) 1997.

Sebastian Edwards (2001), Capital Flows and Economic Performance: Are Emerging Economies Different? (= NBER Working Paper No. 8076), Washington/DC, January 2001.

EC (1993), Council Directive 93/6/EEC of 15 March 1993 on the capital adequacy of investments firms and credit institutions, OJ L 141, 11.6.1993, 1–26.

EC (2006), Directive 2006/123/EC of the European Parliament and of the Council of 12 December 2006 on services in the internal market, OJ L 376, 27.12.2006, 36–68.

EEC (1977), First Council Directive 77/780/EEC of 12 December 1977 on the coordination of the laws, regulations and administrative provisions relating to the taking up and pursuit of the business of credit institutions, OJ L 322, 17.12.1977, 30–37.

EEC (1989), Council Directive 89/647/EEC of 18 December 1989 on a solvency ratio for credit institutions, OJ L 386, 30.12.1989, 14–22.

European Commission (2004), Financial Integration Monitor, SEC(2004) 559.

Juan Fernández de Guevara / Joaquín Maudos-Villaroya (2004), Factors Explaining the Interest Margin in the Banking Sectors of the European Union, in: Journal of Banking and Finance Vol. 28 (2004) No.9, 2259–2281.

Gerhard Fink / Peter Haiss / Sirma Hristoforova (2003), Bond Markets and Economic Growth (= EI Working Paper, No. 49), Vienna, April 2003 (available at: http://www.wu-wien.ac.at/europainstitut/pub/workingpaper).

Gerhard Fink / Peter Haiss / Herwig Kirchner / Ulrike Thorwartl (2005), Financing through Bond Issues and the Nexus with Economic Growth (= EI Working Paper, No. 68), Vienna, September 2005 (available at: http://www.wu-wien.ac.at/europainstitut/pub/workingpaper).

Gerhard Fink / Peter Haiss / Hans-Christian Mantler (2004a), Financial sector macro-efficiency: concepts, measurement, theoretical and empirical evidence, in: *Morten Balling et al.* (eds.), Financial markets in Central and Eastern Europe, London (Routledge) 2004, 61–98.

Gerhard Fink / Peter Haiss / Goran Vuksic (2004b), Changing Importance of Financial Sectors for Growth from Transition to Cohesion and European Integration, (= EI Working Paper, No. 58), Vienna, July 2004 (available at: http://www.wu-wien.ac.at/europainstitut/pub/workingpaper).

Valpy Fitzgerald (2004), European financial market integration, private investment and employment creation, (= The United Nations University, Institute for New Technologies Working Paper, No. 04–40), Maastricht, June 2004 (available at: http://www.intech.unu.edu/publications/eifc-tf-papers/eifc04-40.pdf).

Edith Frauwallner (1992), Exkurs: Preiseffekte der europäischen Finanzintegration und Anpassungserfordernisse der Preispolitik der Banken – Darstellung und kritische Analyse der Price Waterhouse-Studie, in: *Stefan Griller* (ed.), Banken im Binnenmarkt (= Schriftenreihe des Forschungsinstituts für Europafragen Vol. 7), Vienna (Service Fachverlag) 1992, 1167–1188.

Xavier Freixas / Philipp Hartmann / Colin Mayer (2004), The assessment: European Financial Integration, in: Oxford Review of Economic Policy 20 (2004) No.4, 475–489.

Friedrich Fritzer (2006), Finanzsystem und institutionelles Umfeld als Determinanten der wirtschaftlichen Leistungsfähigkeit:

Österreich im Ländervergleich, in: Oesterreichische Nationalbank (ed.); Geldpolitik und Wirtschaft, Vol. 1 (2006) No. 6,
146–171.

Vítor Gaspar / Philipp Hartmann / Olaf Sleijpen (eds.) (2003), The
transformation of the European financial system. Second ECB
Central Banking Conference, Frankfurt, Germany, October
2002, Frankfurt (European Central Bank) 2003.

*Mariassunta Giannetti / Luigi Guiso / Tullio Jappelli / Mario
Padula / Marco Pagano* (2002), Financial Market Integration,
Corporate Financing and Economic Growth, Final Report (=
European Commission, DG for Economic and Financial Affairs,
Economic Papers, No. 179), Brussels, November 2002.

Ernest Gnan / Claudia Kwapil / Maria Teresa Valderrama (2005),
EU and EMU Entry: A Monetary Policy Regime Change for
Austria?, in: Oesterreichische Nationalbank, Monetary Policy &
The Economy. Quarterly Review of Economic Policy, Q2/05,
53–68.

John A. Goddard / Philip Molyneux / John O. S. Wilson (eds.)
(2001), European Banking: Efficiency, Technology and Growth.
London (Wiley) 2001.

Lawrence G. Goldberg / Anoop Rai (1996), The Structure-Perform-
ance Relationship for European Banking, in: Journal of Banking
& Finance Vol. 20 (1996) No. 4, 745–771.

Raymond W. Goldsmith (1966), The Determinants of Financial
Structure, Development Centre Studies, Paris (Development
Centre of the OECD) 1966.

Michael Graff (2000), Finanzielle Entwicklung und reales
Wirtschaftswachstum, Tübingen (Mohr Siebeck) 2000.

Stefan Griller (1992), Banken im Binnenmarkt, in: *Stefan Griller*
(ed.), Banken im Binnenmarkt (= Schriftenreihe des Forschungsinstituts für Europafragen Vol. 7), Vienna (Service
Fachverlag) 1992, 3–22.

Luigi Guiso / Tullio Jappelli / Mario Padula / Marco Pagano
(2004), Financial Market Integration and Economic Growth in
the EU (= CEPR Discussion Paper No. 4395), London (CEPR)
2004.

Franz Hahn (2004), Finance-Growth Nexus and the P-Bias, (=
Austrian Institute of Economic Research (WIFO) Working Paper 223/2004), Vienna (WIFO) 2004.

Franz Hahn (2005a), Environmental Determinants of Banking Efficiency in Austria (= Austrian Institute of Economic Research (WIFO) Working Paper 245/2005), Vienna (WIFO) 2005.

Franz Hahn (2005b), Determinants of Bank Profitability in Austria, A Micro-Macro Approach, Research Study by the Austrian Institute of Economic Research, Vienna (WIFO), July 2005.

Philipp Hartmann / Annalisa Ferrando / Friedrich Fritzer / Florian Heider / Bernadette Lauro / Marco lo Duca (2006), The Performance of the European Financial System, Presentation at the DG ECFIN Workshop on the future of corporate financing in an integration EU financial market, Brussels, 27th November 2006.

Philipp Hartmann / Angela Maddaloni / Simone Manganelli (2003), The Euro-area Financial System: Structure, Integration and Policy Initiatives, in: Oxford Review of Economic Policy, Vol. 19 (2003) No.1, 180–213.

Friedrich Heinemann / Martin Schüler (2002), Integration benefits on EU retail credit markets – evidence from interest rate pass-through (= ZEW Discussion Papers No.02-26), Bonn, April 2002.

Friedrich Heinemann / Martin Schüler (2003), How Integrated are the European Retail Financial Markets? A Cointegration Analysis, in: *Paolo Cecchini / Friedrich Heinemann / Mathias Jopp* (eds.), Incomplete European Market for Financial Services (= ZEW Economic Studies Vol. 19), Heidelberg / New York (Physica) 2003, 129–154.

Sirma Hristoforova (2004), The Causal Relationship Between the Bond Markets and Real Growth in Developed Economies, Dissertation, University of Economics and Business Administration, Vienna, July 2004.

Dagmar Inzinger / Peter Haiss (2006), Integration of European Stock Markets: A Review and Extension of Quantity-Based Measures (= EI Working Paper, No. 74), Vienna, November 2006 (available at: http://www.wu-wien.ac.at/europainstitut/pub/workingpaper).

Agha Iqbal Ali / Dieter Gstach (2000), The impact of deregulation during 1990–1997 on banking in Austria, in: Empirica Vol. 27 (2000) No. 3, 265–281.

Edward J. Kane (1981), Impact of Regulation on Economic Behaviour. Accelerating Inflation, Technological Innovation, and

Decreasing the Effectiveness of Banking Regulation, in: Journal of Finance Vol. XXXVI (1981) No.2, 355–367.

Robert G. King / Ross Levine (1993), Finance and Growth: Schumpeter might be right, in: The Quarterly Journal of Economics Vol. 108 (1993) No. 3, 717–737.

Michael W. Klein / Giovanni Olivei (2005), Capital Account Liberalization, Financial Depth, and Economic Growth (= NBER Working Paper No. 7384), Washington/DC, November 2005.

Rafael La Porta / Florencio Lopez-de-Silanes / Andrei Shleifer / Robert W. Vishny (1998), Law and Finance, in: Journal of Political Economy Vol. 106 (1998) No. 6, 1113–1155.

Ross Levine (1997), Financial Development and Economic Growth: Views and Agenda, in: Journal of Economic Literature Vol. 35 (1997) No. 2, 688–726.

David T. Llewellyn (2006), Whither European Banking: Convergence or Diversity?, in: *Michael, Christensen / Anders Grosen*, Den finansielle sektor Udvikling og perspektiver. Festskrift til professor Morten Balling, Copenhagen (DJØF Forlagene), 2006.

London Economics (2002), Quantification of the Macro-economic Impact of Integration of EU Financial Markets, final report by London Economics in association with PricewaterhouseCoopers and Oxford Economic Forecasting to the European Commission, London, November 2002 (available at http://ec.europa.eu/internal_market/securities/overview_en.htm).

Robert E. Lucas (1976), Econometric policy evaluation: a critique, in: Carnegie-Rochester Series on Public Policy No.1 (1976), 19–46.

Robert E. Lucas (1988), On the Mechanics of Economic Development, in: Journal of Monetary Economics Vol. 22 (1998) No. 1, 3–42.

Emmanuel Mamatzakis / Christos Staikouras / Natassa Koutsomanoli-Fillipaki (2005), Competition and concentration in the banking sector of the South Eastern European region, in: Emerging Markets Review Vol. 6 (2005) No. 2, 192–209.

Fabio Mariani / Pier Carlo Padoan (2006), Growth and Finance, European Integration and the Lisbon Strategy, in: Journal of Common Market Studies Vol. 44 (2006) No.1, 77–112.

Mark J. Manning. (2003), Finance causes growth: can we be so sure?, Contributions to Macroeconomics 3, in: The B.E. Journal of Macroeconomics Vol. 3 (2003) No. 1, Article 12 (available at: www.bepress.com/bejm/contributions/vol3/iss1/art12).

Ronald I McKinnon (1973), Money and Capital in Economic Development, Washington/DC (Brookings Institution Press) 1973.

Markus Neimke / Carsten Eppendorfer / Rainer Beckmann (2003), Deepening European Financial Integration: Theoretical Considerations and Empirical Evaluation of Growth and Employment Benefits, in: *Paolo Cecchini / Friedrich Heinemann / Mathias Jopp* (eds.), Incomplete European Market for Financial Services (= ZEW Economic Studies Vol. 19), Heidelberg / New York (Physica) 2003, 187–229.

Carmen von Nell-Breuning (2005), Die Veränderung der Effizienz im Banken- und Finanzmarkt als Folge von Regulierungen, Dissertation, University of Economics and Business Administration, Vienna 2005.

OECD (2006), Regulation of financial systems and economic growth, Economic Policy Reforms: Going for Growth. 2006 Edition, Paris (OECD Publishing) 2006, 115–128.

Marco Pagano (1993), Financial Markets and Growth: an Overview, in: European Economic Review Vol. 37 (1993), 613–622.

Astrid Pail (1992), Innerösterreichische Strukturreform, in: *Stefan Griller* (ed.), Banken im Binnenmarkt (= Schriftenreihe des Forschungsinstituts für Europafragen Vol. 7), Vienna (Service Fachverlag) 1992, 1167–1188.

Astrid Pail / Reinhard Petschnigg (1992), Wettbewerbstrends im Binnenmarkt, in: *Stefan Griller* (ed.), Banken im Binnenmarkt (= Schriftenreihe des Forschungsinstituts für Europafragen Vol. 7), Vienna (Service Fachverlag) 1992, 1043–1144.

Hugh T. Patrick (1966), Financial Development and Economic Growth in Underdeveloped Countries, in: Economic Development and Cultural Change Vol. 15 (1966) No. 2, 174–189.

PWC (2006), European Banking Consolidation, London (Price WaterhouseCoopers) April 2006.

Dennis P. Quinn (1997), The Correlates of Changes in International Financial Regulation, in: American Political Science Review Vol. 91 (1997) No. 3, 531–551.

Raghuram G. Rajan / Luigi Zingales (1998), Financial Dependence and Growth, in: American Economic Review Vol. 88 (1998) No. 3, 559–586.

Joan Robinson (1962), Essays in the theory of economic growth, London (Macmillan) 1962.

Dani Rodrik (1998), Who Needs Capital Account Convertibility?, in: *Peter Kenen* (ed.), Should the IMF Pursue Capital Account Convertibility? (= Essays in International Finance No. 207), Princeton/NJ (Princeton University Press) May 1998 55–65.

Peter L. Rousseau / Paul Wachtel (2005), Economic Growth and Financial Depth: Is the Relationship Extinct Already? (= UNU/WIDER Discussion Paper No. 2005/10), Helsinki, December 2005 (available at: http://www.wider.unu.edu/publications/dps/dps2005/dp2005-10.pdf).

Edward S. Shaw (1973), Financial Deepening in Economic Development, Oxford / New York (Oxford University Press) 1973.

Kevin J. Stiroh / Philip E. Strahan (2003), Competitive dynamics of deregulation: evidence from U.S. banking industry, in: Journal of Money, Credit and Banking Vol. 35 (2003) No. 5, 801–828.

Michael Thiel (2001), Finance and Economic Growth – A Review of Theory and the available Evidence (= European Commission, DG for Economic and Financial Affairs, Economic Papers, No. 158), Brussels, September 2001.

Jean-Claude Trichet (2005), Financial markets integration in Europe: the ECB's view, speech at the 9th European Financial Markets Convention Federation of European Securities Exchanges, Brussels 26th May 2005.

Xavier Vives. (2001), Competition in the Changing World of Banking, in: Oxford Review of Economic Policy Vol. 17 (2001) No. 4, 535–547.

Rien Wagenvoort / Paul Schure (1999), Who are Europe's efficient bankers?, in: European Investment Bank, European Banking after EMU (= EIB Papers Vol. 4 No.1), Luxembourg (European Investment Bank) 1999, 105–126.

WKÖ (2005), Richtlinie des Europäischen Parlaments und des Rates über Zahlungsdienste im Binnenmark – Stellungnahme, Wirtschaftskammer Österreich, Vienna, 23 December 2005.

Zentraler Kreditausschuss (2006), Anmerkungen des Zentralen Kreditausschusses zum Vorschlag der Europäischen Kommission für eine ‚Richtlinie des Europäischen Parlaments und des Rates über Zahlungsdienste im Binnenmarkt', Berlin, 6th February 2006.

Stefan Griller

The Services Directive:
Two Steps Forward, How Many Back?
Concluding Remarks

I. A Somewhat Surprising Initiative

Almost 50 years after the setting up of the Common Market, and more than 10 years after the "completion" of the Single Market, the European Commission presented a proposal for the Services Directive (SD),[1] which was adopted almost three years later and has to be transposed into the Member States' legal orders before the end of 2009. This is surprising insofar as the freedom to provide services has been forming a core part of the "Economic Constitution" of the European Communities from the very beginning. It could therefore be assumed that legal obstacles to the provision of services should

---

1   Directive 2006/123/EC of the European Parliament and of the Council of 12 December 2006 on services in the internal market, OJ L/2006 376/36.

and would have been removed long before the year 2004 when the Commission came up with that initiative.[2]

However, the preceding decades were, as far as services liberalisation was concerned, characterised by a double strategy which was partly far reaching but very specific and narrow in scope, and partly encompassing the entire field but fuzzy in its concrete consequences. The first part consists of numerous harmonisation directives regulating and at the same time liberalising specific services, e.g. financial services, television, or e-commerce. The second part was developed by the ECJ in its jurisprudence on the freedom to provide services. According to this case-law, "national measures liable to hinder or make less attractive the exercise of fundamental freedoms guaranteed by the Treaty must fulfil four conditions: they must be applied in a non-discriminatory manner; they must be justified by imperative requirements in the general interest; they must be suitable for securing the attainment of the objective which they pursue; and they must not go beyond what is necessary in order to attain it ..."[3] In other words: a broad array of national measures comes under the scrutiny of the Commission and, ultimately, the ECJ, and has to pass a proportionality test. The criteria for this test being considerably vague, this means that legal certainty often can only be obtained after burdensome and long-lasting litigation. Moreover, in cases passing the test, the obstacles persist and can only be removed by secondary legislation harmonising the Member States' standards.

The Services Directive appears to be based on the assumption that this approach is, and, especially under the conditions of EU-enlargement, will be inefficient. Relying on direct application of Articles 43 and 49 EC Treaty, it is being argued, would be "extremely complicated", and in many cases the lifting of barriers would require prior coordination of national legal schemes.[4] And it cannot be denied that such a stance is to a certain extent fuelled by the developments of the ECJ's jurisprudence, both in terms of num-

---

2   Draft Services Directive 2004 ("DSD 2004"): the proposal for a Directive of the European Parliament and of the Council on services in the internal market, COM(2004) 2final/3 of 5 March 2004. The original proposal was from February 2004.

3   Case C-55/94, *Gebhard*, ECR 1995, I-4165, para. 37.

4   Recital 6 SD.

bers and substance.[5] And this is even more so on the grounds of the plausible contention that only a small number of infringements can be "brought to justice" on a case-by-case-basis. This is the background to the initiative which indeed makes it less surprising.

II. The Novelties of the Services Directive[6]

A. Progress in Enhancing the Internal Market

At least two features of the new directive will substantially contribute to the removal of barriers to the provision of services in the internal market, even if they had little attention during the public debate on the directive. Both features are procedural in nature, which underpins the contention that the most remarkable progress is not the hotly debated reduction of the array of legally defendable national restrictions to trade in services, but rather procedural simplifications and enhanced surveillance. The first novelty is the "screening mechanism", the second are the rules on administrative simplification, specifically the establishment of "points of single contact". This is not to say that these are the only remarkable improvements. But it is submitted that these will be the most effective.

The "screening mechanism" – presented under the heading "Mutual evaluation"[7] – obliges the member states to present reports on measures restricting the right to establishment such as authorisation schemes and other restricting "requirements". In the same vain, also restrictions to the freedom to provide services will be subject to such a report which has to provide reasons for their conformity with the directive.

Being of a typical administrative nature, these requirements are far from being spectacular. However, they change, to a certain extent, the burden of proof: while, under the current system, the violation of the freedom of establishment or the freedom to provide services has to be shown by those questioning the legality, and the ECJ has to be convinced to that end, under the SD it will first be the Member States which have to give reasons for the conformity of existing restrictions. This puts the Commission in a more advanta-

---

5   Compare e.g. *Hatzopoulos* (2000), and *Hatzopoulos / Do* (2006).

6   For an in-depth analysis, and further references, compare the contributions of *Hatje* and *Maydell* in this volume.

7   Article 39 SD.

geous situation: it gets a better overview and can, on the grounds of the force of the arguments put forward, more easily identify the most problematic restrictions requiring legal scrutiny. It is even conceivable to argue that restrictions, which had not been notified according to the requirements of the directive, might be inapplicable. Consequently, this mechanism is indeed capable to reduce the "extremely complicated" way to remove barriers.

"Points of single contact"[8] shall ensure the possibility for service providers to complete all procedures and formalities needed for access to the envisaged activities, including applications for authorisation, through points of single contact. In practice, the multitude of requirements in combination with poor transparency of procedures and administrative competences is one of the most "effective" barriers to market access. Consequently, points of single contact will reduce these procedural obstacles, even if the requirement does not mean that all decisions have to be taken by one authority.

However, it should also be mentioned that the ambit of the two highlighted provisions will be very limited. For, they will not apply on those subject matters and activities which are exempted from the directive. And those exemptions are numerous, as will be shown.

B. Fresh Fragmentation and Frictions

1. The Country of origin principle

In the original Commission proposal,[9] the famous and most disputed Article 16 had the heading "Country of origin principle" obliging the Member States to "ensure that providers are subject only to the national provisions of their Member State of origin which fall within the coordinated field". This should apply to provisions relating to access to and the exercise of the service activity (including the behaviour of the provider, quality or content of the service, advertising, contracts, and liability), and it should be the responsibility of the state of origin to supervise the provider and the services.

Even if also in this original version, several exceptions and derogations had to be observed, this ambition triggered fierce opposition from the member states, and within European Parliament, and understandably so. For such a country of origin principle is

---

8   Article 6 SD.
9   DSD 2004.

categorically different from the mentioned proportionality test national restrictions have to pass under the "horizontal" EC primary law as it stands.[10] In those fields where, by contrast, the country of origin principle at least to a certain extent had been introduced by secondary legislation – e.g. with regard to financial services (credit institutions, insurances, etc) –, this was done hand-in-hand with a specific minimum harmonisation of Member States' provisions on market access, and partly also on the exercise of the service. Introducing a "horizontal" country of origin principle without such minimum harmonisation would have meant that in the EU-27 extremely different national standards would have been applicable side-by-side. Moreover, it was on the one hand side hardly imaginable that efficient enforcement abroad through home country control could have been achieved. On the other hand, it appeared even more unlikely that the authorities of the host State could have developed the ability to overlook 26 foreign legal orders in order to detect possible violations of the home country's provisions and introduce the necessary steps. In essence, this might have resulted in undermining the regulatory authority of the Member State's legal orders as such.

The opposition, however, was not only directed against the principle itself, but also against the scope of application of the directive, as well as the alleged insufficient number of exceptions to the principle. One might even argue that such multi-faceted opposition was to a certain extent precautionary in so far as it would have prevented "the worst" if no modification of the country of origin principle could have been achieved.

In the final version, the country of origin principle was discarded. Not only was the heading of Article 16 changed into "Freedom to provide services", but the cited passage was also changed to the more or less banal restatement of primary law that the Member States "shall respect the right of providers to provide services in a Member State other than that in which they are established". Consequently, what would have been the most spectacular and substan-

---

10   This is to a certain extent controversial especially with regard to the so-called Cassis-de-Dijon jurisprudence of the ECJ specifying the free movement of goods within the internal market. Compare for this discussion *Schroeder* (2007), esp. p. 135, who speaks of a "myth" that the country of origin principle would be enshrined in primary EC law.

tive – although highly problematic – regulatory change the original proposal had foreseen, was deleted from the final version and consequently will not take place. The remains of this effort, however, are limited and overly confusing. Regarding the freedom to provide services, it remains questionable whether the directive really entails a substantive reduction of the Member States' margin of discretion to impose restrictive "requirements in the general interest", as will be shown below. As far as the freedom of establishment of service providers is concerned, there is little controversy that the directive does not go substantially beyond the jurisprudence of the ECJ, and can consequently be addressed as sort of a clarifying codification of that jurisprudence.

Despite this far-reaching reduction of the original ambitions, the additional exceptions and restrictions achieved during the previous discussion process remained in place also in the final version. Against the background of the deletion of the country of origin principle, some of those exceptions are hard to understand, and are likely to produce fresh difficulties in opening up the services markets. What is even more questionable is the correspondingly reduced scope of the administrative and procedural provisions. It is not easy to understand why e.g. the screening mechanism should not be applicable to all service sectors.

2. Scope of Application

From the wording of the directive, it is certainly easier to determine what is exempted from its scope of application, than what is included. The directive shall not apply[11] to non-economic services of general interest; financial services; electronic communications services and networks; transport, including port services; temporary work agencies; healthcare services; audiovisual services; gambling activities; activities connected with the exercise of official authority; social services; private security services; notaries and bailiffs. There is also an express shield against the liberalisation of services of general economic interest, and the abolition of monopolies.[12]

An effort by the European Commission to list, by contrast, the activities covered produced the following result:[13] "most of the regulated professions (such as legal and fiscal advisers, architects,

---

11   Article 2 SD.

12   Article 1 paragraph 2 and 3 SD.

13   Commission (2007), 11.

engineers, accountants, surveyors), craftsmen, business-related services (such as office maintenance, management consultancy, the organisation of events, recovery of debts, advertising and recruitment services), distributive trades (including retail and wholesale of goods and services), services in the field of tourism (such as services of travel agencies), leisure services (such as services provided by sports centres and amusement parks), construction services, services in the area of installation and maintenance of equipment, information services (such as web portals, news agency activities, publishing, computer programming activities), accommodation and food services (such as hotels, restaurants, catering services), services in the area of training and education, rental (including car rental) and leasing services, real estate services, certification and testing services, household support services (such as cleaning services, private nannies or gardening services)."

More exceptions are framed not for specific activities but for entire regulatory areas and pre-existing legislation. Consequently, even activities covered are again exempted in this respect, albeit by differing wording. Such is the case for the whole "field of taxation",[14] for measures protecting or promoting cultural or linguistic diversity or media pluralism,[15] criminal law,[16] labour law and social security legislation,[17] the exercise of fundamental rights, collective agreements and industrial action,[18] and private international law, including the rules governing consumer protection.[19]

An explicit prevalence is established with regard to specific provisions governing the access to or the exercise of a service activity.[20] Among those provisions figures the directive on the recognition of professional qualifications, itself including a "horizontal" regime on the "free provision of services".[21] Thus, one of the most

---

14   Article 2 paragraph 3 SD (the directive "shall not apply").

15   Article 1 paragraph 4 SC ("does not affect").

16   Article 1 paragraph 5 SD ("does not affect").

17   Article 1 paragraph 6 SD ("does not affect").

18   Article 1 paragraph 7 SD ("does not affect").

19   Article 3 paragraph 2 SD ("does not concern").

20   Article 3 SD.

21   Articles 5-9 Directive 2005/36/EC of the European Parliament and of the Council on the recognition of professional qualifications, OJ 2005/L 255/22.

relevant mechanisms restricting the access of service providers to a market, the rules on professional qualifications, will remain untouched by the SD, even for service activities coming under the SD. A similar consequence flows from the prevalence of the posting of workers directive:[22] the regulation of the crucial issue of comparative advantages resulting from wage differentials between the Member States, and thus one of the most important levers regarding the fostering of competition in providing services is left outside the scope of the SD.

It is submitted that the resulting patchwork scope of application of the SD lacks homogeneity, and also comprehensible justification. Some of the mentioned exemptions of activities could be explained against the background of the country of origin principle as envisaged in the DSD 2004. However, such explanation appears not to be available after having discarded this principle in the final version.

Moreover, it is obvious that the activities captured by the directive, despite the many exceptions, still are inhomogeneous regarding their regulatory needs. This is due to the remains of the "horizontal approach" taken. Such regulatory impetus might be inadequate for activities as different as say construction services, distributive trade or consultancies. Exceptions of regulatory areas or provisions which might be justifiable for some activities might not be for others; the prevalence for the posting of workers directive might be one example. Thus, the flipside of this combination of horizontality and non-homogeneity probably results in a low liberalisation level as the available common denominator, while sector specific regulation might have allowed for more ambitious solutions.

In this regard, the financial services sector provides for an example how harmonisation and far reaching liberalisation – single license and home State control – could go together and arrive close to a country of origin principle. This is not to say that the results reached would be entirely uncontroversial; the contrary is true.[23]

---

22   Article 3 paragraph 1 (a) SD; compare also recital 86 SD. For details see Directive 96/71/EC of the European Parliament and of the Council of 16 December 1996 concerning the posting of workers in the framework of the provision of services, OJ 1997/L 18/1.

23   Compare for a critical appraisal *Pichler/Steiner/Fink/Haiss*, in this volume.

However, also this controversy might lead to the conclusion that even specifically tailored rules cannot avoid tensions and frictions. How should this be achievable under a "catch all directive" covering largely differing activities? Instead, it remains an open question – given the comparably small progress in removing substantive barriers to the establishment of service providers and to the provision of cross-border services – whether decoupling those provisions from the ones on administrative simplification and corporation, as well as on the convergence program, might have resulted in a more promising regulatory pattern for future reforms. Administrative provisions could have been horizontal without that many exceptions, substantive provisions could have been sector specific and combined with minimum harmonisation. Admittedly, this goes to the heart of the regulatory "philosophy" of the SD. However, against the background of dropping the country of origin principle this question appears to be unavoidable.

3. Progress Concerning the Elimination of Substantive Barriers?

The core purpose of the Services Directive is "to remove barriers to the freedom of establishment for providers in Member States and barriers to the free movement of services as between Member States and to guarantee recipients and providers the legal certainty necessary"[24]. Allegedly, this cannot be done solely by relying on direct application of primary law, namely articles 43 and 49 ECT.[25] Can this goal be achieved through implementing the directive, as far as substantive law is concerned, i.e. apart from the procedural innovations mentioned above?

Obviously, if direct application of primary law is considered to be insufficient, the aim must be to create added value in order to enhance the removal of barriers. It is hardly conceivable that a mere codification of primary law obligations in a directive could achieve this, or was intended. In this case, the Member States could avoid taking action by claiming that their legal order had already been in conformity with primary law, as is the usual reaction.[26] Thus translating primary law into secondary legislation would not necessarily

---

24   Recital 5 SD.

25   Recital 6 SD.

26   This is of course different for the newly introduced procedural obligations (like the establishment of single points of contact and the screening mechanism), which are not addressed in the above text.

trigger any innovative steps on the side of the Member States. Against this background, the purpose of the directive much more likely is to concretise primary law. And indeed, it cannot be denied that the directive includes an effort to that end. However, it is controversial whether this effort was successful.

With regard to the freedom of establishment for providers (Chapter III) the SD codifies the ECJ's jurisprudence insofar as it explicitly calls for non-discriminatory and proportionate authorisation schemes which have to be justified by an overriding reason relating to the public interest. The conditions for granting authorisation shall not duplicate requirements and controls of another Member State or in the same Member State.[27] A certain concretisation into the direction of tightening this jurisprudence is the setting up of blacklisted requirements which are per se prohibited without a chance defending them before the ECJ.[28] Other requirements are to be evaluated.[29]

Regarding the free movement of services (Chapter IV), the goal of imposing further limits to possible restrictions by the Member States is even more apparent. Article 16 seeks to replace the open-ended list of justifications as developed by the ECJ by only four requirements in the general interest: public policy, public security, public health, or the protection of the environment.[30] The same Article also includes a blacklist of restrictions.[31]

But was this effort of enhancing the two freedoms successful? First, it has to be said that further justifications for restrictions are made available by the general provisions of the directive, including extremely problematic notions like cultural diversity or consumer

---

27 Articles 9 and 10 SD.

28 Article 14 SD. It is true that the listed requirements were not accepted in previous cases before the ECJ. However, the ECJ always drew this conclusion on a case-by-case scrutiny while the directive generalises the respective outcomes.

29 Article 15 SD.

30 Article 16 paragraph 1 (b), and paragraph 3 SD. The latter in addition mentions employment conditions, including collective agreements. However, this might not go beyond Article 1 paragraph 6 and 7 and Article 4 Nr 7 SD.

31 Article 16 paragraph 2 SD. However, the categorical character of this blacklisting is less clear then that regarding the freedom of establishment.

protection.[32] It could even be argued that these additional justifications might not be subject to a proportionality test, given that the directive immunises the entire regulatory field ("does not affect", "does not concern"). Is this a successful effort to get rid of the ECJ's detailed scrutiny of such restrictions? Second, what is the significance of Article 3 paragraph 3 SD in this respect, requiring the Member States to apply the directive's provisions "in compliance with the rules of the Treaty on the right of establishment and the free movement of services"? According to the ECJ's jurisprudence, these provisions of the Treaty include an open-ended list of requirements in the general interest. Especially in combination with the contention that curtailing the variety of possible justifications might result in a violation of primary law (as interpreted by the ECJ) the conclusion would be that the directive's attempt to reduce the number of available justifications for restrictions has failed: the Court's jurisprudence would remain untouched.[33]

The wording of the directive does not entirely exclude such interpretation. However, it is submitted that taking the purpose of the directive into account, or to put it differently: teleological interpretation provides a strong argument against such attempts. Discarding the proportionality test would increase the potential barriers to trade in services, upholding the open-ended list of possible justifications would render the substantive provisions of the directive almost devoid of any legal significance. It is hard to impute such understanding given the clear goal to reduce barriers to trade in services.

Furthermore, the contention that secondary legislation may not reduce the Member States margin of manoeuvre in imposing restrictions would endanger the entire concept of creating and developing further the single market by secondary legislation, despite the fact that this concept is clearly spelt out in the Treaty. Nowhere the Treaty requires full harmonisation as a precondition for abolishing

---

32   Compare above in the text near n 14 to n 19. More details can be found in *Maydell* in this volume.

33   Obviously this is the stance taken by *Hatzopoulos* (2007), 20: A reduction of available justifications to the four reasons would, according to him, only be a valid interpretation, "if we admitted that the Directive fully harmonises the free provision of services – a claim which is certainly not true".

barriers.[34] Mutual recognition is not excluded,[35] and reducing the available justifications for restrictions entails mutual recognition in so far as the Member States have, with regard to additional reasons in the public interest, to accept and to trust in the measures taken by the home state.[36]

As a consequence, the better arguments strike for the solution that first, the attempt to reduce the justifying reasons for restrictions to public policy, public security, public health, and the protection of the environment, was not successful, and that instead additional justifications can be found among the general provisions. Second, all restricting national measures have to pass a proportionality test, and more reasons in the general interest than those mentioned in the directive are no longer available.

---

34   It is, however, true that the ECJ denies a "general power" of the legislature to "regulate the internal market". According to the ECJ, a measure adopted on the basis of article 95 TEC "must genuinely have as its object the improvement of the conditions for the establishment and functioning of the internal market": Case C-376/98, *Germany v. European Parliament (advertising of tobacco products)*, ECR I-8419, paras. 83 and 84.

35   Article 47 paragraph 1 explicitly allows for "directives for the mutual recognition of diplomas, certificates and other evidence of formal qualifications".

     Former Article 100b TEC which had been inserted by the Single European Act and deleted by the Amsterdam Treaty had empowered the Council to decide on provisions which had to be mutually recognised by the Member States (without any harmonisation). Article 100b never was effectively used. However, its deletion by the Amsterdam Treaty was accompanied by the conviction that such decisions on mutual recognition of foreign law might be taken by virtue of Article 95 TEC (the former Article 100a). Moreover, it can be argued that regarding the freedom of establishment and the freedom to provide services Articles 47 and 55 serve as *leges speciales*.

36   And this is, by the way, what the ECJ, harmonisation measures being absent, to a certain extent (levels of protection being equal) requires the Member States to do when it limits the option to invoke imperative reasons to cases where "that interest is not protected by the rules to which the person providing the services is subject in the Member State in which he is established": Case C-76/90, *Säger*, ECR 1991, I-4221, para. 44.

Even if this, comparably moderate, reading of the directive is accepted, it means that the reduction of barriers is much more limited than the first impression might suggest – because of the numerous additional justifications flowing from the general provisions –, and it reveals that legal certainty could not be created due to the poorly drafted text.

Similar concerns as those addressed above arise with regard to Articles 17 of the SD, but shall only be mentioned without deepening the discussion.[37] What is the significance of excluding certain services of general economic interest from the scope of Article 16? It is submitted that this cannot, at the same time, derogate from Article 86 paragraph 2 TEC which calls for the observation of the Treaty as long as such application "does not obstruct the performance, in law or in fact, of the particular tasks assigned" to such undertakings. Consequently, also the rules on the freedom to provide services have to be respected in principle. The Services Directive not being applicable means that we are referred back to primary law in its interpretation by the ECJ, including the jurisprudence on restrictive measures for services. Also this result cannot be characterized as far-reaching progress, but rather as stagnation.

III. Macroeconomic Effects[38]

Secondary legislation targeted at enhancing the internal market always serves an economic purpose.[39] The Services Directive is no exception in this respect. Its economic rationale is clearly spelt out in recital 4 to the directive: "Since services constitute the engine of economic growth and account for 70 % of GDP and employment in most Member States, this fragmentation of the internal market has a negative impact on the entire European economy, in particular on the competitiveness of SMEs and the movement of workers, and prevents consumers from gaining access to a greater variety of

---

37   Also Article 18 SD is not easy to understand, given that the country of origin principle disappeared from the directive. Why should it be necessary or advantageous to rely on a case-by-case-scrutiny on the safety of services, if it is possible to generally invoke public policy, public security, and public health?

38   For an in-depth analysis, and further references, compare the contribution of *Badinger/Breuss/Schuster/Sellner* in this volume.

39   Compare only Articles 2, 3 paragraph 1 (c), 14, 47, and 55 TEC.

competitively priced services." It is pointed out that the establishment of a genuine internal market is a matter of priority for
achieving the goal of the so-called Lisbon-agenda[40] "of improving
employment and social cohesion and achieving sustainable economic growth so as to make the European Union the most competitive and dynamic knowledge-based economy in the world by 2010,
with more and better jobs."

Regarding the timeframe, the contribution of the Services Directive to achieve that goal can at best be marginal given that the
directive is to be transposed into national law only by the end of
2009, more ambitious implementation programs not being visible.[41]
Nevertheless, it is certainly primarily the effects on growth and
employment which are the yardstick for success.

According to the study of *Badinger/Breuss/Schuster/Sellner* in
this volume, using a partial econometric framework, there will be
effects via the "trade channel" and via the "FDI channel". More
trade would lead to more competition, and consequently to higher
productivity, employment, investment and output. Results are sug-
gesting that productivity in the service industries covered would, in
the medium and long run, increase by 0.80%, employment by
0.85% – or 612.000 persons in the EU-25 –, and the investment
ratio by 0.55%. The aggregate GDP effect would be 0.7%. All these
results were reached on the grounds of the DSD 2004 including the
country of origin principle. The readjustment after the elimination
of this principle and its replacement by the modified general prohibition on restrictions is estimated: all those effects will be reduced
by 1/3.

Similar results are reached by the impact of FDI-effects,
namely from increased productivity. Taken both, trade channel and
FDI-channel, together, the overall macroeconomic effect for the
final version of the Services Directive for the EU-25 is an increase
of employment by around 400.000 persons, and an increase of GDP
by around 1% in the medium and long run. These results come
close to those of previous studies using different methods.

---

40   European Council, Presidency Conclusions, 23/24 March 2000 (Lis-
     bon), SN 100/00.

41   However, it is to be noted that the first round of the screening mecha-
     nism on the side of the Member States on existing barriers has to be
     completed before the end of 2009 (Article 44 SD). It is to be hoped
     that already this step could produce liberalizing effects.

Apparently, economists face nearly insurmountable difficulties flowing from institutional settings and – often poorly drafted – legal texts. They are expected to forecast effects on growth and employment at a point of time where determining factors like the scope of application and the substance of liberalisation (country of origin principle versus general prohibition on restrictive measures) are still under discussion. In the case of the SD these essential elements changed after the completion of the first studies. And even under the final text of the directive, it remains disputed to what extent the available reasons for restrictions were abolished, and what effects will result from the numerous and inhomogeneous exceptions. To give one example only: while recital 4 points to the fact that services account for 70% of GDP and employment in most Member States, it would be entirely flawed to assume that the Services Directive addresses this entire segment of the economy. It is even questionable whether, in terms of GDP-share, the majority of services fall within the ambit of the directive.

While the tension between the available factual (statistical, legal etc) basis and the needs for sound econometric modelling and forecasting is well-known in general, it appears to be specifically difficult in the case of the Services Directive. Not only were the changes during the legislative procedures numerous and substantial, but also is the outcome highly unclear. Moreover, it might well be that at least for some, but not all, services sectors, and especially for the mode of active service provision (e.g. and especially construction services), the economic potential (increased competition) would mostly flow from increased transborder mobility of workers; however, this is not regulated by the Services Directive, but by the posting of workers directive which remains unchanged. It is difficult to estimate such intricate but important details.

Against this background, interpreting the outcome of the various studies has to be done cautiously. However, all of them arrive at positive effects of the directive on growth and employment. Even if those effects are modest, the unisonous result that they would be positive appears to be reassuring.

Transdisciplinary discussion often reveals needs and chances for further investigation. In the case of the Services Directive among those surely is the more economic based notion of "services". It will help to overcome the "subsidiary concept" of services in Article 50 TEC, indispensable for a proper understanding of the SD given that it also covers the freedom of establishment for ser-

vice providers. Another aspect is the congruency or difference between the available statistical classification of industries and legal
delimitations. The bigger the differences and gaps, the less precise
forecasts and estimations will be, with inevitable consequences on
the reliability of steering effects of legal measures.

IV. Prospects

The ambitious approach of the original proposal of the Services
Directive, including the country of origin principle for the provision
of services, had been highly problematic from the outset. By many
this was apprehended and criticised as a threat to the protection of
non-economic concerns, and undermining the regulatory capacity
of law in general. However, the debate about the draft directive not
only lead to the elimination of the principle, but also to a messy list
of exceptions as well as highly unclear wording regarding substantial obligations such as the freedom to provide services. It has to be
concluded that both in terms of legal clarity and substantive progress, the directive is severely deficient.

What could be a revolutionary step forward, namely the newly
introduced procedural obligations to establish "single points of
contact" for service providers, and to introduce the "screening
mechanism" accelerating the elimination of remaining barriers, also
suffers from the numerous exceptions to the directive. Nevertheless,
in this respect the directive still is a remarkable step in removing
administrative barriers to the provision of services in the internal
market.

The retreat from the country of origin principle, the long list of
exceptions, and the yet remaining lack of homogeneity of the service industries covered, call for an appraisal of the regulatory approach itself. In a theoretical perspective, it is easily understandable
that a legislator would prefer a "horizontal" text applying to all
services. However, facing the fact that this could not be achieved
means raising the question whether the remains of "horizontality"
are worthwhile the compromises and frictions which had to be accepted. This author is not convinced that separating a truly horizontal administrative simplification and cooperation from sector
specific substantive liberalisation, or groups of sectors, would be
second to the "system" of the directive as it stands today. The crucial element in such an evaluation certainly is the weight of sector
specific regulatory needs. Addressing those needs – as happened in

sectors like financial services – could reduce the opposition against liberalisation, an opposition which is easier sustainable in a combined effort of many against an allegedly inappropriate catch all clause.

The Services Directive contains a review clause.[42] By the end of 2011 and every three years thereafter, the Commission has to present a comprehensive report on the application of the directive. This report shall also consider the need for additional measures for matters excluded from the scope of application, and can be accompanied by proposals for the amendment of the directive "with a view to completing the Internal Market for services". These reviews will provide for the opportunity to eliminate some of the deficiencies of the directive. As the review clause implicitly acknowledges: the Services Directive is far from completing the internal market for services. It is a small step into that direction.

References

Commission of the EC (2007), Handbook on Implementation of the Services Directive, Brussels 2007

Vassilis Hatzopoulos (2000), Recent Developments of the Case Law of the ECJ in the Field of Services, in: CMLRev 37 (2006), 43-82.

Vassilis Hatzopoulos (2007), Legal Aspects in Establishing the Internal Market for services (= Collège d'Europe, Research papers in law 6/2007), Bruges 2007 (available at http:// www.coleurop. be/default.asp?language=fr&switchlang=yes).

Vassilis Hatzopoulos / Thien Uyen Do (2006), The Case Law of the ECJ Concerning the Free Provision of Services: 2000-2005, in: CMLRev 43 (2006), 923-991.

Werner Schroeder (2007), Der Binnenmarkt für Dienstleistungen – zwischen Herkunftslandprinzip und sozialpolitischer Gestaltungsfreiheit, in: *Stefan Griller* (ed.), Die europäische Wirtschaftsverfassung *de lege lata et ferenda*, Vienna (Springer) 2007, 115-140.

---

42   Article 41 SD.

The Authors of this Volume

Harald Badinger, Economist, Assistant Professor at the Europainstitut of *Wirtschaftsuniversität*, Vienna.

Fritz Breuss, Economist, is *Jean Monnet*-Professor for the economy of European integration at the Europainstitut of *Wirtschaftsuniversität*, Vienna, and collaborator of the Austrian Institute of Economic Research – WiFo. Since 2002 he is President of ECSA Austria.

Gerhard Fink, Economist, is professor for Business Administration with reference to European Integration at Europainstitut of *Wirtschaftsuniversität*, Vienna. Since its foundation in 1996, he is serves as the treasurer of ECSA Austria.

Stefan Griller, Lawyer, is *Jean Monnet*-Professor for Public Law with special regard to European Law at the Europainstitut of *Wirtschaftsuniversität*, Vienna. He was the founding President of ECSA Austria in 1996 and since 2002 serves as the organization's Secretary General.

Peter Haiss, Economist, works in a major Austrian bank and is lecturer at the Europainstitut of *Wirtschaftsuniversität*, Vienna.

Armin Hatje, Lawyer, is Professor for European Community Law at the University of Hamburg, Germany.

Niklas Maydell, Lawyer, at the time of writing his article worked as a Research Assistant at the Europainstitut of *Wirtschaftsuniversität*, Vienna.

Andreas Pichler, Economist, at the time of writing his article worked as a Research Assistant at the Europainstitut of *Wirtschaftsuniversität*, Vienna.

Philip Schuster, Economist, worked in the afore-mentioned *Wirtschaftsuniversität* research-project on services liberalisation as a student researcher. At present, he is economist at the Vienna-based Institute for Advanced Studies.

Richard Sellner, Economist, worked in the afore-mentioned *Wirtschaftsuniversität* research-project on services liberalisation as a student researcher. At present, he is economist at the Vienna-based Institute for Advanced Studies.

Katharina Steiner, Economist, Research Assistant at the Europainstitut of *Wirtschaftsuniversität*, Vienna.